Lochsa Lodge, June, 2005

CLEARWATER COUNTRY!

CLEARWATER COUNTRY!

The Traveler's Historical and Recreational Guide

Lewiston, Idaho — Missoula, Montana

by

Borg Hendrickson and Linwood Laughy

Mountain Meadow Press

Clearwater Country!

The Traveler's Historical and Recreational Guide
Lewiston, Idaho – Missoula, Montana
by Borg Hendrickson and Linwood Laughy

Cover photography by Linwood Laughy.
Cover design by Jackie Holmes-Courtney.

Hendrickson, Borg
    Clearwater country! the traveler's
historical and recreational guide : Lewiston,
Idaho -- Missoula, Montana / by Borg Hendrickson
and Linwood Laughy. -- Rev. ed.
    p. cm.
    Includes bibliographical references.
    LCCN: 89-91006
    ISBN: 0-945519-22-2

    1. Idaho--Guidebooks. 2. Montana--
Guidebooks. I. Laughy, Linwood. II. Title.

F744.3.H46 1999   917.96'0433
                    QB199-103

Table of Contents

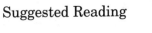

U.S. Highway 12
MILEAGE CHART

↓ Number of Miles
From Lewiston

Number of Miles
From Missoula ↑

From Lewiston		From Missoula
0	Lewiston (west city boundary)	218
3	Highway 95 North; Side Trip #1	215
11	Highway 95 South; Side Trip #2	207
27	Big Eddy Rest Stop & River Access	189
28	Lenore	190
39	Pink House Hole Recreation Area	179
40	Canoe Camp of Lewis & Clark	178
44	Orofino; Side Trip #3	174
52	Greer; Side Trip #4	166
65	Kamiah Valley; Long Camp of Lewis & Clark	151
66	Kamiah	152
74	Kooskia; Side Trips #5 & #6	144
76	Tukatesp'e Picnic Area	142
90	Syringa	128
94	Three Devils Picnic Area & Beach	124
95	Wild Goose Campground	123
97	Lowell; Side Trip #7	121
104	Apgar Campground	114
105	Glade Creek Campground	113
108	Knife Edge River Access	110
120	River Access	98
123	Wilderness Gateway Campground	95
130	Nine Mile River Access	88
148	Colgate Campground	70
150	Jerry Johnson Campground	68
151	Jerry Johnson Hot Springs	67
158	Wendover Campground	60
159	Whitehouse Campground	59
162	Powell; Powell Campground	56
163	White Sand Campground	55
165	Bernard DeVoto Memorial Grove	53
174	Lolo Pass; USFS Information Center	44
180	Lee Creek Campground	38
181	Lolo Hot Springs	37
188	Howard Creek Picnic Area & Trail Access	30
191	Lewis & Clark Campground	27
200	Fort Fizzle Interpretive Rest Stop	18
207	Lolo	11
218	Missoula (south city boundary)	0

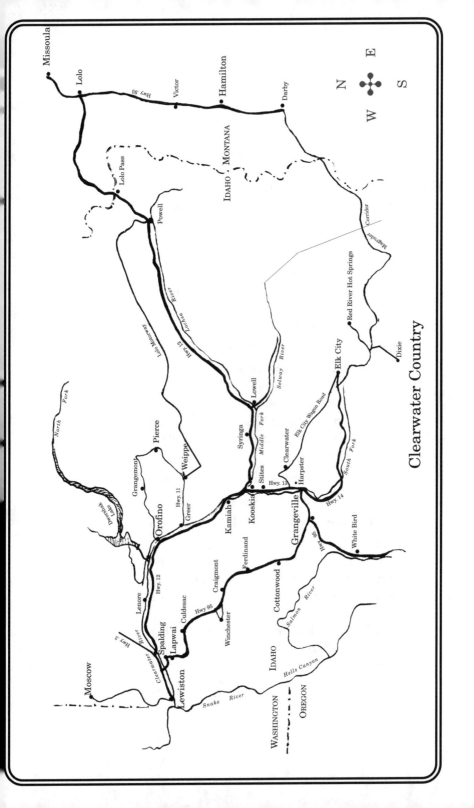

Clearwater Country

Credits

Hand-drawn Maps: Mary Lou Pethel
Artwork : Valeria Yost, Borg Hendrickson
Photographs:

Courtesy of Washington State University Libraries

> Rev. Henry Harmon Spalding
> Nez Perce Treaty Negotiations, 1863
> General O. O. Howard
> Chief Joseph

Courtesy of the Nez Perce County Historical Society

> 1890s Sternwheeler
> A Nez Perce woman
> Capt. Meriwether Lewis
> The Spalding Mission Printing Press
> Kate McBeth and her ladies' class
> Hill Beachy

Courtesy of The Smithsonian Institution

> Chief Looking Glass

Courtesy of the Idaho State Historical Society

Lewiston Main Street	Stuart
The Luna House Hotel	Boller Ferry
1800s Stagecoach	Gathering Camas
Spalding Mission Site	Capt. William Clark
Wanigan	Sue McBeth
Orofino Fourth of July	Early Day Elk City
The Greer Ferry	E.D. Pierce
McBeth Cabin	

Welcome

Should you awaken at dawn on the banks of the Lochsa River to watch the sun creeping up the backsides of the Bitterroots, you will have found your welcome to Clearwater Country. Or perhaps you'll watch an osprey searching for rainbows in a riffle of the Middle Fork of the Clearwater River, or leave warm footprints to cool in shadows of evening drifting across a white sand beach, or suck deeply the wafting scent of syringa blossoms that greet you along the roadside. With each experience you will find your welcome to Clearwater Country.

An unforgotten past also beckons — memories and imaginings of a land, people and passage of time rich in history. Along your route you may smell the smoke of an ancient Nez Perce village; squint at a September sun glistening off the faces of the Lewis and Clark expeditionists as they knee their horses, belly deep, across the river; point to General Howard's cavalry on the crest of a ridge while watching Nez Perce families paddle their hastily constructed buffalo hide bulboats to the gravel shoreline at your feet. You may hear the whistle of a nineteenth century sternwheeler or the distant gunshots of bandits relieving another miner of his hard-won gold dust. Throughout Clearwater Country you will travel midst the ghosts of a true Western saga — Indians and explorers, missionaries and miners, outlaws and vigilantes, settlers and soldiers...and the many conflicts and triumphs of a young and growing America.

And yes, we too welcome you and invite you to let us be your guides through the sun and shadows, the space and time of Clearwater Country.

Borg Hendrickson and Linwood Laughy

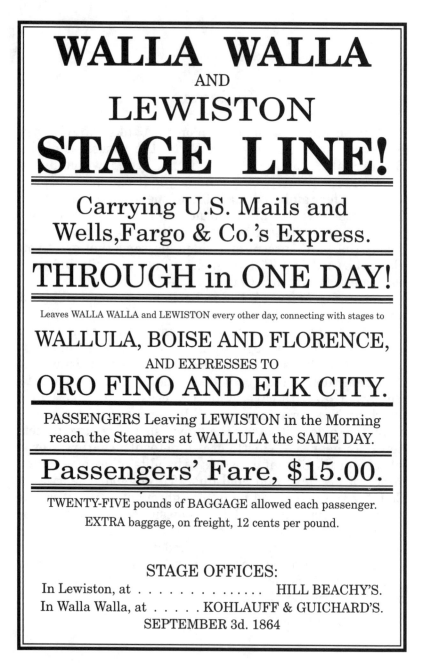

Cloth Poster Printed in Lewiston, 1864

Clearwater Country
Mile-by-Mile Historical Tour

You are about to begin one of Clearwater Country's most fascinating recreational opportunities: a journey through its diverse and colorful history. What follows here is a self-tour guide which will lead you mile-by-mile through the country and through the years — a voyage through space and time.

Whether traveling east or west, you can begin your tour at any point along the Clearwater Country route between Lewiston, Idaho, and Missoula, Montana. Simply find a mile number on one of the small green and white mileposts alongside the highway that matches an entry number in the guide below. If you are traveling east, read forward from that number; if traveling west, read in reverse order.

On Highway 12 and in this book, the mile numbers between Lewiston and Missoula appear in three numerical west-to-east sequences.

1. From North Lewiston eastward along merged Highways 95 and 12, the numbers run from 312 to 305. At 305 the two highways separate.

2. From that separation point eastward all the way to the Montana border at Lolo Pass, the Highway 12 numbers run from 11 to 174.

3. From Lolo Pass to Highway 12's junction with Highway 93 at Lolo, Montana, the numbers run from 0 to 32. *If traveling east*, at Lolo you'll turn north along merged Highways 93 and 12 to make the 11-mile trip to Missoula.

The milepost numbers in the self-tour below follow these three numerical sequences, but do remember: if traveling west, you simply read them in reverse.

The U.S. 12 route through Idaho follows four separately named, but continuous waterways: the Clearwater River, which joins the Snake River at Lewiston, the Middle Fork of the Clearwater, the Lochsa River, and its Crooked Fork. Along the route, the South Fork and North Fork of the Clearwater, as well as the Selway River and numerous smaller streams, branch off into the hills. The Crooked Fork and Lochsa flow west out of the Bitterroot Mountains, which form a natural boundary between Idaho and Montana. On the Montana side of the mountains, the highway follows Lolo Creek and then the Bitterroot River. All of these waterways are historically significant to the region and are integral to events covered in your Clearwater Country self-tour. Also important to the area's history are the Snake and Salmon Rivers to the west and south.

Between Lewiston and the Montana border, Highway 12 is designated Idaho's Northwest Passage Scenic Byway because it parallels much of Lewis and Clark's 1805-1806 Corps of Discovery round-trip routes through central Idaho and because of the river corridor's exceptional scenic beauty. A twenty-five mile extension of this byway branches south and west from Kooskia to Grangeville via Highway 13 and is included in the Side Trips chapter of this book.

Because Lewis and Clark were, for the most part, traversing the long used Northern Nez Perce Trail, the trail is also referred to as the Lewis and Clark Trail. In the nineteenth century the trail also colloquially acquired the name Lolo Trail. The highway parallels all three above-named trails, for the three are largely the same one trail. Thus generally, in this book, reference to one of the trail names implies all three, and usually, the original trail name is used: Nez Perce Trail.

Campgrounds, picnic areas, Lewis and Clark sites and Nez Perce National Historical Park sites are noted in the Mile-by-Mile section, and most also on the Mileage Chart at the beginning of this book. You will find several boat access sites along the main Clearwater and raft and kayak access sites along the Lochsa. There are numerous vehicle pullouts, some of which afford access to trails. Trailheads are noted in the Mile-by-Mile section but also, you may wish to refer to Trails in the Recreation chapter. In addition, you'll spot several fine beaches for sunbathing and swimming, especially upriver from Mile 51.6 on the Clearwater and along the Middle Fork, Selway and Lochsa Rivers.

Please realize that while the locations of picnic sites, trails, historical interpretive signs, side roads, and so on were accurately described at the time of the writing of this book, the Highway 12 corridor is a *living* place; i.e., a continually changing place. A once good trail, for example, may become obliterated by natural forces or an obscure trail may be made accessible by a U.S. Forest Service crew. In other words, don't be surprised if you find a few variances on the road from what you read here.

Occasionally, you may also find differences and even contradictions with some information in this book and that which you see recorded on roadside, interpretive historical signs along the route. Since historical research is an ongoing process, the information on these signs can be superseded by new findings and facts that reveal inaccuracies in the information on some signs. Some signs are also mislocated, albeit usually for the sake of safety and driver convenience. The information in this book is, at the time of its writing and to the best of our knowledge, accurate.

During the years 1999-2003, in preparation for the 2003-2006 nationwide Lewis and Clark Bicentennial commemoration, many area communities will be carrying out projects and creating attractions that will provide travelers with historical information. Of course, these yet-to-be-built sites are not included in this 1999 edition of CLEARWATER COUNTRY.

Below, a simplified diagram shows you the general layout of U.S. Highway 12 and the highways that join it.

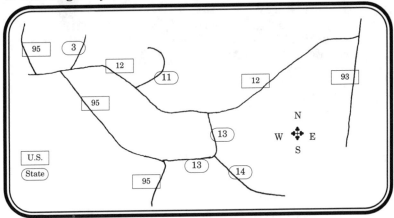

Skeletal Highway Map

A word of caution: while covering a wonderfully scenic route, the entire stretch of Highway 12 is narrow and curvy. Because of the curves, forward and rear visibility is often of limited distance. Stopping mid-highway for any reason is dangerous. To stop, wait until you reach a roadside vehicle pullout and then pull well off the highway.

When you do stop, you'll discover that taking your time as you drive Highway 12 is well worthwhile. You'll find many lovely picnicking spots, beaches, walking paths and places to just sit. Indeed, nearly every stop will bring you in touch with the sounds, textures, fragrances and sights of a wondrous natural world.

During those stops, you may wish to turn to the Recreation, Side Trips, and the six historical background chapters at the back of this book. There you'll find fuller information regarding Clearwater Country recreational opportunities and historical events that are woven throughout the Mile-by-Mile section.

Now come join hands with history for your Clearwater Country journey. You may begin at Lewiston, Idaho, reading immediately below; or in Missoula, Montana, reading in reverse starting on page 108; or at the milepost number of your choice.

ALL ABOARD
FOR THE
CLEARWATER COUNTRY
HISTORICAL AND RECREATIONAL TOUR

LEWISTON, IDAHO [Population: 38,000. All services available.]

In May of 1861, as a passion for gold drove hundreds of miners into the Clearwater River region, the Oregon Steam Navigation Company established its inland head of navigation here at the confluence of the Snake and Clearwater Rivers. Almost as quick as the flick of a rattler's tongue, a tent city and miners' supply station sprouted on the southeastern flat where Lewiston now lies. Although first called Ragtown because most of its structures were made of canvas, the town soon was named Lewiston in honor of explorer Meriwether Lewis. As gold rush boom towns emerged and flourished in the region during the 1860s, Lewiston linked the miners and a growing cluster of settlers and merchants to towns and cities along the Columbia River, the Oregon Trail and the Pacific Coast. Stagecoaches, sternwheelers, horses, wagons and mules brought foodstuffs, mining and farming equipment, building supplies and people to bustling Lewiston. From there packtrains of horses and mules and men, loaded with such items, snaked their way into the mountains. Thus, while Lewiston itself was not the site of a mine, it began in a sense as a mining town. And it became in 1866 the first incorporated town in what would become the State of Idaho.

At first Lewiston had no right to exist. It was nudged into being by gold-hungry folk at a time when permanent settlement by whites was disallowed in Clearwater Country. The land belonged to the Nez Perces, and the Treaty of 1855 supposedly secured Indian ownership. Nevertheless, before long the ragtag, *temporary* tent city of Lewiston was laid out with streets and log shack houses, twenty-five saloons, numerous gambling establishments, twenty some houses of ill-repute, and a few hotels, general stores and blacksmith shops.

In 1863, the same year the Territory of Idaho was established, one band of Nez Perces signed a renegotiated treaty with the United States through which Lewiston was ceded to the government. Lewiston was soon selected by the first governor, William Wallace, as the territorial capitol. Between the time of the first gold rush into Clearwater Country in 1861 and the establishment of Idaho Territory, Lewiston's population had crested in the thousands but then shrank in the afterglow of the rush to 375. The miners who left Clearwater

5

> *The number of drinking and gambling saloons was greatly in excess of stores and private dwellings, and to nearly all of these was attached that most important attraction of a mining town, the hurdy-gurdy. The sound of the violin which struck the ear on entering the street, was never lost while passing through it. ...The voices of auctioneers on the street corners, the shouts of frequent horsemen ...the rattle of vehicles arriving and departing ...troops of miners, Indians, gamblers, the unmeaning babble of numerous drunken men, the tawdrily appareled dancing women of the hurdy-gurdies, altogether present a scene of life in an entirely new aspect to the person who for the first time entered a mining town.*
>
> Thomas Langford
> VIGILANTE DAYS AND WAYS

Country followed new trails of adventure and greed to gold discoveries in southern Idaho, where the population then swelled. Southern Idaho legislators, who outnumbered those from the north, were hellbent on having the capitol moved to Boise, but a bill to accomplish this during the first territorial legislative session was met with a filibuster by north Idaho legislators. When a similar bill did pass the second territorial legislature, Lewiston citizens placed then Governor Caleb Lyon under house arrest, along with the territorial records and seal. It wasn't until 1865 that the irate residents of Lewiston saw the state seal, records, and treasury stolen from under their protective noses and actually moved to Boise by the newly appointed secretary of the territory, C. Dewitt Smith, with the help of U.S. troops from Fort Lapwai. Despite a legal scuffle which followed, Lewiston had permanently lost its status as Idaho's capitol.

Bolstered by increasing agricultural development in the region throughout the 1870s and 1880s, Lewiston's population gradually began a resurgence. Brick buildings, fancy homes, schools, and churches materialized on the dusty flat, and the business district once again thrived. Much of the Nez Perce Reservation was opened to white settlement in 1895. The railroad came to town in September of 1898; a toll bridge replaced a ferry across the Snake in 1899; and boats and coaches continued to supply Lewiston from locations farther west. In time, regional agriculture and timber processing became mainstays of Lewiston's increasingly stabilizing economy.

Lewiston's Main Street about 1890

Throughout these early years steamboats hauled freight — mining, logging and farming equipment up the river, and fruits, grain and lumber down — and in both directions, travelers with their own goods and bags and trunks. In 1940, the last sternwheeler, the *Lewiston*, pushed up the waters of the Columbia and Snake Rivers to reach the town of Lewiston. Not until 1970, by which time a series of four dams and locks had been completed along the lower Snake, would another vessel ply the Snake into Clearwater Country. On May 23rd that year, the motorized tug *Mary Gail* entered port, and Lewiston, four hundred seventy miles from the Pacific, became the farthest inland seaport in the western states.

During the 1880s and 1890s, the steamboats also functioned as pleasure boats. Sure signs of spring were fancy folks decorating the decks of sternwheelers cruising the river on festive excursions. These lavish occasions, replete with wine, food and music, were often connected to fund-raising efforts carried on by community-minded ladies' clubs. The huge paddlewheels churned against the current, past Nez Perce villages, pine groves and flowering meadows. After a leisurely picnic lunch ashore and perhaps a late afternoon dinner in the elegant dining quarters on board a 100- to 169-foot sternwheeler, the trip back to Lewiston was normally accomplished in about one-sixth the time of the upriver journey.

Aspects of Lewiston's history can be seen in several buildings which stand today — turn-of-the-century homes

Luna House Hotel

on Normal Hill, the old Camas Prairie Railroad Depot built in 1908-'09, the Lewis-Clark Plaza built in 1922 as a hotel. At the corner of Third and C Streets sits the Luna House Museum on the site of the former Luna House Hotel, which originated in 1862 as a tent structure and eventually was expanded into a rambling two-story log lodge. The museum documents much of the history of Lewiston and of Clearwater Country. Period costumes, domestic settings and implements, Nez Perce artifacts, mining history and the story of the early railroad can be viewed there.

At the Museum of Art and History on the corner of Main and Third Streets, a reconstructed Chinese Taoist temple can be toured. From 1890 to 1959, the original temple was a fixture of the town. The museum also hosts a wide range of gallery displays throughout the year varying from historical and contemporary paintings to artquilts, photographs and sculptures.

Lewiston and all of Clearwater Country stretching to Montana is historically perhaps most noted as an important link in the journey of the Corps of Discovery, better known as the Lewis and Clark Expedition. The Corps had been commissioned by President Thomas Jefferson, who viewed the expedition as an opportunity for the United States to lay claim to western lands and resources, and who challenged the expeditionists to discover and map the fabled Northwest Passage that would allow water transportation from east to west across the continent. Having struggled through the Bitterroot Mountains, which lie along the present-day border between Idaho and Montana, and been assisted by friendly Nez Perce Indians, the expedition first reached the mouth of the Clearwater as it enters the Snake here at today's Lewiston on October 10, 1805, in an atmosphere of increasing excitement. The explorers knew their destination, the Pacific Ocean, could now be readily reached via the Snake and Columbia Rivers.

On that date in 1805, following three days paddling westward on the Clearwater River in their dugout canoes, the historic expedition reached the juncture of what they called the Lewis River (Snake) and the Kooskooskee (Clearwater). Clark noted that "...the water of the South fork [Snake] is a greenish blue, the north [Clearwater] as clear as cristial." He also noted,

> The country at the junction of the two rivers is an open plain on all sides, broken toward the left by a distant ridge of high land, thinly covered with timber. This is the only body of timber which the country possesses; for at the forks there is not a tree to be seen, and during almost the whole descent ...down the Kooskooskee from its forks there are very few. ...The Indians inform us that [the Snake] is navigable for 60 miles [upstream]; that not far from its mouth it receives a branch [Grande Ronde River] from the south; and a second and larger branch [Salmon River] two days' march up... The [Snake] river has many rapids, near which are situated many fishing-camps...

Two hundred years after their coming, Lewis and Clark would likely be amazed to see the confluence of the Snake and Clearwater, for due to eight dams along the Snake and Columbia Rivers, the confluence is now a slackwater lake and the lone "Indian cabin" the explorers observed at "the forks" has been replaced by two towns that bear the explorers' names: Lewiston, Idaho, and Clarkston, Washington.

Today a paved walking, jogging, biking path spans the crest of a levee for about nine miles along the banks of the Clearwater and the Snake, from southwest to northeast Lewiston. (See Skeletal Map below.)

On Lewiston's western fringe, along the Snake River, Hells Gate State Park and Marina provide boat access and

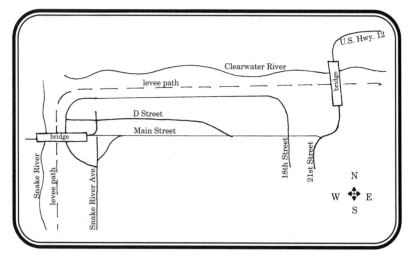

Skeletal Map of Downtown Lewiston and Levee

an overnight campground. The park and marina are located four miles south on Snake River Avenue. The campground has sixty-four RV hookup spaces, twenty-eight other spaces, and an RV dump site. The park also provides a swimming beach and day-use picnic area, restrooms, the Hells Gate State Park Visitor Information Center and a hiking trail.

You will find the city of Lewiston's visitor information center north of town on Highway 12. Just north of the Clearwater River bridge, the center is located in a white trailer on the northwest corner of the four-way, Highway 12 and Third Avenue North intersection. Turn west at the stoplight onto Third Avenue North, then immediately right onto West 22nd Street North. The center is open from 10 a.m. to 4 p.m. daily during spring, summer and autumn months.

Mile 312.0 From this point, Highway 95 winds north up the Lewiston Hill to peak near a viewpoint where one can observe the broad valley below — a spectacular sight for eye and camera lens. A century ago the vista from the hilltop was seen by those who rode with the finest reinsman in the territory, Felix Warren, as he and his stagecoach passengers came swooping over the crest of the hill and plunged down what was then a four-mile grade to Lewiston. It has been said that those who made that thunderous, rock-and-roll trip with Warren never forgot it. It was in 1875 that the six-foot three-inch, 250-pound, white-haired Warren established a Lewiston to Spokane coach line. He hired fifty employees — drivers, horseshoers, hostlers, agents, and blacksmiths — and set up an additional line to Grangeville, seventy miles southeast of Lewiston. He ran two types of stages: the deluxe, three-ton, sixteen-to-eighteen passenger Concords, and the mud wagons, which held six to eight folks and gave a rougher ride, but which were sturdier and could handle rugged roads.

To drive up the Lewiston Hill to the viewpoint overlooking the Clearwater Valley to the east, the Blue Mountains to the west, and the plateau region and Snake River Canyon to the south see Side Trip #1 in the Side Trips chapter.

Mile 309.8 On October 10, 1805, eight Nez Perce Indian lodges sat on the flat visible on the south side of the Clearwater. Perhaps a smoky fire near the riverbank kept an old woman warm as she sat bundled in a tanned elk hide on a woven reed mat. In buckskin leggings and shirts, her grandsons may have played battle games with small bows and arrows. Perhaps kneeling near the entrance to one large lodge, two young women, using mortars and pestles, ground roots into flour. At a little distance two more lodges also housed families, and near the riverbank a Nez Perce man may have been bathing in a hot bath made with heated stones thrown into a pool of water. The Corps of Discovery explorers approached from upstream and beached their dugout canoes so they could assess the difficulty of a rough looking rapid a short distance downstream. The travelers bartered for dried salmon for their lunch and dogs for their dinner, then sat on the riverbank to eat. Having just traveled through six rapids, "Several of them verry bad...," the party proceeded to run the downstream rapid, sustaining a small crack in one of their dugouts.

Mile 309.0 Five years after Lewis & Clark's 1806 eastward trip through Clearwater Country, fur trader Donald McKenzie led a starving and tattered group of fellow traders through parts of Hell's Canyon on the Snake River and across the mountains to the Clearwater River. They were part of the Wilson Price Hunt overland expedition to establish the Pacific Fur Company at Astoria, Oregon. The Nez Perces welcomed and assisted McKenzie, who promised the Indians that he would return to establish a trading post and enable them to barter for white man's goods, which was in keeping with the promises made by

1805-'06 visitors, Lewis and Clark. In August of 1812, McKenzie did return, and after exploring the Clearwater as far upstream as Kamiah, established a post here. Details were recorded in a journal kept by Alfred Seton, McKenzie's clerk. Seton noted that the group...

...removed down and chose upon a spot about 5 miles above the forks, on a Prairie where in the beginning of Septr. we commenced building with drift wood, as there was not a tree to be seen. In three weeks we had finished our buildings, which consisted of a store, a house for the men & one for Mr. McK. & myself.

After a trip to the Spokane River, where McKenzie learned of the outbreak of the War of 1812 between the United States and England, perpetual motion McKenzie, as he was known in the fur trade, hastened to Astoria with the news. Before his departure, however, he carefully cached all of his trade goods at the newly established Clearwater post. Seton wrote,

When it was decided...to carry the news of the war to the seacoast, deep holes were dug under the floor of one of the huts, there cannily and carefully our wares and merchandise were deposited, the clay with which the interstices of the roof were stopped was let in, and the buildings were burnt. We trusted that amidst the scene of desolation our treasures would remain unsuspected.

These goods were the next year to play an important part in another chapter of the history of the fur trade in Clearwater Country, as noted below at Mile 21.0.

Mile 309.0 The goose pasture between here and Mile 307 is part of the Lewiston Wildlife Reserve. The grasses and legumes planted in the field adjacent to the pullout provide a reliable food supply for the area's many birds, but especially for Canada geese.

Mile 307.9 Archaeological work near the mouth of Hatwai Creek, which flows from the north here, uncovered pit house floors dating back more than four thousand years and other evidence suggesting that this location was first occupied by humans more than ten thousand years ago.

Lewis and Clark stopped here during their eastward journey on May 5, 1806, in hopes of securing food from local villagers. Although unsuccessful in their attempts to barter for food, they smoked with the headman of the village and received from him "a very eligant grey mare" in exchange for a vial of eyewater. The previous autumn Clark had treated a number of wounds and ailments, including eye ailments, and his services as an amateur physician became a valuable trading commodity. The following morning, in fact, two payments of a horse each were made for medical services rendered by Clark. The younger of the horses was immediately butchered. It provided the expeditionists with a welcome and needed food supply.

Here also the Nez Perces presented Clark with his own horse that had been left with the Indians near the mouth of the North Fork (Mile 40.0) the previous autumn.

Mile 306.4 According to Nez Perce legend, this is the site of an event related to the Nez Perces' traditional trek to the plains east of the Bitterroots to hunt buffalo. As the story goes, one day many, many years ago Coyote fished, as he often did, with his huge net in the Clearwater River out from this location. Before long Black Bear appeared and asked Coyote why he was fishing rather than buffalo hunting with his people east of the mountains. Realizing he had simply forgotten to go buffalo hunting, Coyote became embarrassed. As Black Bear continued to hassle Coyote, Coyote became increasingly aggravated. Just when Black Bear was about to give up the tease and leave, Coyote hurled his fishnet across the river to the south hillside, then seized Black Bear and threw him high onto the north hillside. The fishnet and bear, permanent fixtures of Nez Perce legend, remain visible on the hillsides today.

To see the fishnet and bear from the pullout here, face the river and look at the hillside across the river. There you'll see the fishnet, a v-shaped bowl with a series of small gullies sloping into it. Now turn yourself around with your back to the river. On the highest hill above the highway, (at about 2 o'clock on a clockface) you'll see the bear, a squarish rocky patch on the hillside.

A wide variety of birds reside along the lower stretch of Clearwater River. As you can see on the island a short distance upstream and at other locations along the river, raised box nests have been placed for the Canada geese which nest in April and May. Two to three feet in total height, the Canada goose is grayish-brown with a black head and neck, lighter breast and white chin strap.

Mile 305.0 (Mile 11.2, if you are traveling west.)

> **Going east,** Highway 95 turns south off your self-tour route. Highway 12 continues east.
>
> **Going west,** Highways 12 and 95 merge at this point. Thus the numerical sequence on the roadside mileposts changes here.

Mile 11.0 Nez Perce legend tells of two mutually friendly colonies of ants and yellowjackets which inhabited the rocky hillside that rises abruptly on the north side of the river here. The headman of each colony jealously protected his own territory from encroachment by the other. One day, when the head ant approached the head yellowjacket sitting on a favorite rock eating dried salmon, a dispute arose. The yellowjacket declared the rock his by right of continued use. The ant argued such use did not constitute an exclusive claim to the rock, and the argument intensified. Soon that personified, heroic figure of many Nez Perce legends, Coyote, came along and told them both to hush and quit fighting or he himself would stop them. However, stop they did not. In fact, they became locked in vicious physical combat. At that point, Coyote drew upon his magical powers and turned them, arched in battle, into stone. Even today you can see them frozen forever in silent, motionless combat overlooking the north edge of the highway.

During their 1806 homeward trip, the Lewis and Clark explorers stopped on May 5th to dine near here at a large lodge housing ten Nez Perce families. (The approximate site has since been covered by highway construction.) The expeditionists traded for two dogs and some bread made from dried roots. The dogs were immediately butchered and a meal prepared. A Nez Perce man, who like most of the Nez Perces thought eating dogs was disgusting, derisively threw a puppy nearly onto Lewis' dinner plate. Lewis angrily threw the dog back, directly into the Indian's face, and threatened in sign language to tomahawk the man if the insolence continued. Fortunately for all concerned, the Indian withdrew.

A two-mile drive south on Highway 95 will take you to the Nez Perce National Historical Park Headquarters and Museum. The museum memorializes Nez Perce history and culture and houses a fine collection of traditional Nez Perce clothing and accouterments, utilitarian artifacts, a dugout canoe and a model of an ancient lodge. Also available are Nez Perce arts, crafts and books about the Nez Perces.

The Nez Perce National Historical Park is comprised of a string of thirty-eight sites stretching from the Wallowa region of eastern Oregon, through north central Idaho and southwestern Montana, and finally north to the Bear Paw Mountains. The park commemorates elements of Nez Perce history, particularly the 3 1/2-month long Nez Perce War of 1877, which occurred along a fifteen hundred mile route traveled by the non-treaty Nez Perces and the pursuing United States military.

Five miles south (Highway 95) sits the town of **LAPWAI**, a location interwoven into the historic past of the Nez Perces, including the Nez Perce War of 1877. Today Lapwai is a center of Nez Perce tribal affairs.

To drive to the Nez Perce Park Museum and Lapwai, described above, and the Spalding Mission site, written of below, refer to Side Trip #2 in the Side Trips chapter.

Mile 12.2 SPALDING Lapwai Creek stretches its flowing fingers into the Clearwater from the south opposite the highway here. One version of the meaning of *Lapwai* indicates that the creek's name stems from the Nez Perce "lap-lap" and "wai" meaning *butterfly* and *stream,* respectively. Evidently multitudes of butterflies at times flutter along the mud banks and pools of standing water in the area. A second interpretation cited in historical literature indicates that the word *Lapwai* refers to a boundary between two territories — perhaps between those Nez Perces who traditionally traveled to Montana to hunt buffalo and those who did not, or perhaps between the Clearwater River region and the Snake River region.

On the large flat south of the river, now thick with trees, lies the one-hundred acre site of the Spalding Mission. Replacing an earlier site established in 1836 up Lapwai Creek, the Spalding Mission was the first Christian mission set among the Nez Perces. The flat had long been a rendezvous point for the Indians, held an encampment of

Nov. 22, 1836
Fort Walla Walla

The Indians with our goods left yesterday for the Nez Perces country, and we ... leave today...They appear to be delighted with the idea of having us locate in their country, that they may be taught about God and the habits of civilized life.

Nov. 29, 1836
Nez Perces Mission

Yesterday reached this desirable spot where we expect to dwell the remainder of our earthly pilgrimage. ...our dwelling is an Indian lodge, which must serve us sometime... Blessed be God that we have been spared to accomplish a long...tedious journey...and are now...to enter upon the glorious, blessed, responsible work of laboring to introduce the blessings of that Gospel which brings life and immortality to light, among this benighted people...

Mrs. Eliza Spalding

July 18, 1836
Nez Perces Mission

What is done for the poor Indians of this western world must be done soon. The only thing that can save them from annihilation is the introduction of civilization. Their only means of support which is buffalo is fast diminishing. It is observed by those acquainted that in ten years there will probably not be a buffalo in the country.

April 21, 1838
Nez Perces Mission

...while we point them [the Indians] with one hand to the Lamb of God which taketh away the sins of the world, we believe it to be equally our duty to point with the other to the hoe, as the means of saving their famishing bodies from an untimely grave & furnishing the means of subsistence to future generations.

Henry Spalding

lodges when the Lewis and Clark expedition floated by in 1805, and, in 1838, was turned into a mission settlement by the Presbyterian missionary Henry Spalding and his wife Eliza. During their nine years at the mission, the Spaldings and their Nez Perce helpers built a home, school, church, gristmill, sawmill and a few other buildings, most of which were the first of their kind in what was to become the state of Idaho. The Spaldings also gardened and taught the Nez

Spalding Mission and Nez Perce Encampment

Perces agricultural skills, along with other more academic and religious lessons, and the couple gave birth to a daughter, Eliza, the first white child born in Clearwater Country.

The first few years of the Spaldings' effort were well rewarded, and the mission flourished. Despite some internal dissension among various members of the wider Oregon mission group, highlighted by strong criticism of Spalding's work by fellow missionary Asa Smith at Kamiah, Spalding remained steadfast in his pursuit of settling the Nez Perces through agricultural means. Even his dismissal by the American Board of Commissioners for Foreign Missions (later rescinded) did not deter him from his work. Yet gradually the Nez Perces began turning away from Christianity, and resentment of the Spaldings' presence among them took root. By 1847, the end of the Spalding Mission was at hand.

In November of that year, Spalding took his daughter west to Waiilatpu, the mission of Dr. Marcus and Narcissa Whitman, where Eliza was to attend school. Having left Eliza at Waiilatpu, Spalding made a side trip to nearby Fort Walla Walla. While he was there, the Whitmans and others were massacred at Waiilatpu by a group of Cayuse Indians. Spalding learned of this tragedy on his way back to Waiilatpu and believed that the Cayuses would kill him as well if they found him. Worried, too, about the rest of his family and his own mission, he began a desperate trek back to Lapwai Creek, traveling only at night. He was afoot the last ninety miles, most of which he traveled without shoes after his footgear fell apart. As he approached his mission site from the ridge to the west, he saw several Nez Perces ransacking the buildings. A group of friendly Nez Perces came to his aid and hurried him to the home of mountain man William Craig and Craig's Nez Perce wife, who lived up the Lapwai Valley and were already safely harboring Mrs. Spalding. There the Spaldings remained, unharassed but nevertheless housebound. A month later the missionaries were rescued by Peter Skene Ogden, the historically well-known Hudson's Bay Company trader, who had hastened from Fort Vancouver to negotiate the release of the survivors at Waiilatpu as well as that of the Spaldings. On January 1, 1848, at Fort Walla Walla, the Spaldings were reunited with their daughter Eliza, one of the survivors of the Whitman massacre. The first Christian mission period among the Nez Perces had ended.

From 1861 until 1902, the Spalding Mission site functioned as the Bureau of Indian Affairs' Nez Perce Agency. The agent's house is visible on the west side of Lapwai Creek. Still standing, too, are an early-1900s general store and the Spalding Presbyterian Church in which services were first held in 1886. The original Spalding homesite is marked with iron fencing, and interpretive signs pinpoint the locations of Spalding's gristmill and sawmill. The gravesites of Henry Spalding and his wife Eliza lie in the little cemetery on the flat. Picnic tables and fire grills invite visitors, who can drive into the site from the Nez Perce National Historical Park Museum entrance and parking lot.

To visit the Spalding Mission site, the museum and old Fort Lapwai, see Side Trip #2 in the Side Trips chapter.

Characters of a much less pious sort hung out along upper Lapwai Creek during the 1860s. Through the draw ran a main trail to the Pierce and Oro Fino gold fields. Gold passed by in the pockets, pouches and secreted caches of the miners, dispatchers and pony expressmen. Thus the upper Lapwai Creek hillsides were a logical site for the shebang, or hideout, of the scoundrelous Henry Plummer outlaw gang. Frequent ambushes and outright holdups made easy pickings in gold for the bandits. Hefty booty would generate mighty strong urges to celebrate, so that the shotgun-toting outlaws often rode a-whooping and a-hollering into Lewiston for a night full of gambling, carousing with the hurdy-gurdy gals, chug-a-lugging whiskey and now and then firing buckshot at the stars that shone above Main Street. Of course, once in awhile those shots were fired level with the dusty ground onto which some unsuspecting victim would fall.

Mile 13.9 Catholic Creek enters the Clearwater from the north here. The creek's name stems from the fact that it once ran alongside a Catholic mission building. In 1867, Father Joseph Cataldo and Brother Achilles Carfagno brought Catholicism to Clearwater Country as they built a clapboard Catholic chapel in Lewiston, a church which was attended mostly by whites. Then in 1868, hoping to work among the Nez Perces, Cataldo built a log mission cabin on the north bank of the Clearwater in this vicinity. In 1873, Cataldo moved his mission approximately ten miles south up the Lapwai Valley to a creek now known as Mission Creek.

Mile 14.6 Arrow Beach, which was earlier located a short distance below Arrow Bridge, is now gone — the result of development in the area. In 1967, however, when the beach still existed, it was the site of archeological diggings which unearthed artifacts dating to the 1500s. The excavation work revealed that a lodge had been occupied on the site at least from 1500 to 1850 A.D. Frequent findings of arrowheads in the vicinity resulted in the current name of the beach and bridge. You might imagine the original village scene: In a large permanent firepit, rocks heat on a bed of glowing coals — the hot rocks will later be dropped into water in tightly woven grass baskets in order to cook food. A hand-turned fire drill rests against a small kindling pile of broken brush and dry grass. An elkhorn wedge — used for splitting wood and hollowing out canoes — and a stone mallet lean against a partially completed dugout on the beach. A bone awl lies atop a pile of hemp waiting to be braided into rope. An oblong lodge ring, the rim of which rises about a foot above ground level, supports the pole frame of a grass mat lodge. Drying salmon hang from a crude pole scaffold standing beside the lodge. Near the water's edge a small mat-covered sweathouse emits white clouds of steam, and you can hear the quiet chatter of its occupants.

Mile 15.0 On October 8, 1805, during their westward journey, near disaster struck the Lewis and Clark party as they attempted to run their five heavily laden dugouts through rapids near the mouth of Colter Creek, now Potlatch Creek, which enters the Clearwater a half mile upstream from here. Sgt. Patrick Gass' canoe struck one boulder, spun and crashed into another causing a split in the canoe. Gass and his fellow passengers were tossed into the rapids but managed to cling to the canoe, which was wedged against the rocks and quickly filling with water. From a group of Nez Perces camped on a nearby island, a man hurried in a small dugout to Gass' rescue. Two of the explorers managed to assist from the smallest of their party's dugouts, until Gass and the other men, the water-filled canoe's contents and the canoe itself were brought to shore. The explorers spent the next day camped in this vicinity, quite likely at the Arrow Beach village site on the north riverbank, repairing the damaged canoe with driftwood and pitch and drying out the soaked trade goods and other supplies.

The expedition members, who had been escorted for weeks by a Shoshone man named Toby and his son, were surprised to find their guides missing that afternoon. The party heard later that the pair had been spotted running eastward toward the Bitterroots along an upriver trail. Apparently neither Lewis nor Clark made the connection between this event and their having taken on board earlier in the day two Nez Perce chiefs, Tetoharsky and Twisted Hair, who had agreed to serve as guides to the Columbia River.

Mile 15.3 Potlatch Creek, which flows down a northside draw (opposite the highway) and into the Clearwater, was once called Yaka Creek meaning *black bear creek*. It was dubbed Colter Creek by Lewis and Clark in honor of one of their men. Now the creek is named after the Native American potlatch, a traditional ceremony during which members of the community gave away goods. Unlike Euro-Americans who felt that a person derived status through accumulation of goods, the Indians felt that status was earned by giving away or sharing one's belongings. Such sharing was at one time essential, not only for honor, but for survival.

The downriver side of the mouth of Potlatch Creek served as the exploration party's campsite on May 5, 1806, during their return trip. Their campsite lay a short distance from two Nez Perce lodges, one of which was the largest the explorers had seen. "It is 156 feet long and about

15 wide," recorded Captain Lewis, "built of mats and straw in the form of the roof of a house. It has a number of small doors on each side, is closed at the ends, without divisions in the interior." Lewis observed that this lodge housed at least thirty families. The village headman, Nush-ne-pack-ke-ook, who became known as Cut Nose for a wound received in battle, accepted from Lewis a Jefferson Medallion embossed with the likeness of President Jefferson on one side and on the other a peace pipe, tomahawk and a pair of hands shaking in friendship. When the railbed was built through this area almost a hundred years later, such a medal was found in an Indian grave just upriver from the bridge which crosses Potlatch Creek. The medal had been well preserved by enclosure in several thicknesses of deer or buffalo hide. The embossed figures were clearly visible as well as the inscription "Peace and Friendship" — a message much more applicable to the Lewis and Clark exchanges with the Nez Perces than to the later interactions between the Indians and the missionaries, miners and United States military.

To view this Corps of Discovery camp location, drive to the north end of Arrow Bridge (Mile 14.8) and turn onto Highway 3. Drive three-tenths mile (northeast) and turn right into a large pullout. In all likelihood, the camp location lay on the small flat along the west side of the creek, just off the right side of the road.

Mile 16.2 Gibbs Eddy, the quietest segment of the river flowing here, is a frequented modern-day fishing hole (with boat access to the river).

Mile 19.0 Cottonwood Creek, flowing into the Clearwater from the south here, is named after the black cottonwood, a common deciduous tree in this area. Cottonwood shoots and leaves provide browse for deer and elk, while its flowers and seeds help sustain songbirds. This largest variety of American poplars also provides cover for birds such as pheasants, grouse and turkeys. Decades ago, the Nez Perces used the green wood of the black cottonwood, which hardens as it dries, to make packsaddles for their horses.

Mile 19.5 As you look out at the river here, imagine what a thoroughfare it was to the Indians prior to the mid-1700s when they acquired horses. Before then, in fifteen- to forty-foot, flat-bottomed, shovel-nosed canoes which had been burned and chipped out of drift logs, typically red fir, the Nez Perces paddled and poled from campsite to campsite and village to village along the river. Skins and lodge poles, bows and arrows, fishing spears, dried foods and cooking baskets, sundry other provisions and two to six passengers may have ridden in one canoe. The alternative to river travel? Foot travel, or in the winter at higher elevations, elkhide and vine maple snowshoe travel. Because of the basalt bluffs that frequently interrupt the river valley landscape, foot travel at times required the traveler to ascend to the high ridges running parallel to the river.

On October 8, 1805, the Lewis and Clark expeditionists were among the waterway's travelers. That day they pulled their one small and four large dugout canoes to shore on the south side of the river in this vicinity to trade for food with the Nez Perces. The explorers recorded seeing numerous Indian lodges and grazing horses along both sides of the river during their morning's paddle from their previous night's campsite at Lenore (nine miles upriver). The Nez Perces were busy harvesting and processing salmon. With blue and green beads and pieces of tin, the explorers traded for camas roots, fish and two dogs. Opinions between the two groups differed as to which of the three lunch entrees was preferable. After eating, the explorers again shoved their canoes into the current and continued west.

Mile 20.3-20.5 The private tree plantation which stretches along the south flat through here serves two purposes: experimentation with cultivated hybrid poplars as a future source of wood fiber for paper production to replace the rapidly dwindling supply of wood from national forests, and the development of white pine seeds and seedling stock that are blister rust resistant and usable for reforestation projects. Potlatch Corporation, which also owns half a million acres of forest land in Idaho, operates the plantation.

Mile 21.0 In the spring of 1813, upon returning to the site of their trading post and cache of the previous year (see Mile 309.0, page 11), fur trader Donald McKenzie and his fellow Astorians discovered that their carefully concealed trade goods and supplies had been plundered. From friendly Nez Perces the traders learned that responsibility rested with the Tashepas, described by the Nez Perces as their "turbulent and warlike neighbors" from the Snake

River. Upon learning that a group of Tashepas was camped along the river at this location, McKenzie and sixteen of his men paddled their canoes upstream and landed in front of the village. Three-hundred-pound, six-foot-three McKenzie proceeded to boldly walk among the armed warriors who greeted him and to empty their guns of all priming. As recorded by Alfred Seton, the trading party's clerk,

> This done, he told them we had come to their country to supply them with arms and ammunition, and thereby enable them to hunt successfully the buffalo, and be on an equal footing with their enemies the Blackfeet. That we did not wish to fight, but were prepared to do so to get back our goods..."

Detailing Seton to engage the warriors in a smoking ceremony, McKenzie proceeded to "ransack their lodges," recovering much of the stolen goods,

> with which we reembarked, and fired a salute, to show the natives, who were mostly young men without any prominent chief among them, that we were brimful of fight.

The traders then camped four or five hundred yards upstream, likely on what is now known as Hubbard Gulch, on the north side of the river a short distance above the Cherry Lane Bridge (between Miles 21.0 and 22.0). A few days later a friendly band of Cayuses camped near the McKenzie party and were visited the following day by a mounted war party of Tashepas. These warriors urged the Cayuses to join them in an attack upon the fur traders. The Cayuse chief refused and advised the Tashepas that he would not allow any harm to come to the whites while he was with them. The Tashepas "remained in their statue-like posture for four or five minutes, then suddenly wheeled and left our camp." A sure disaster for the Astorians was thus avoided, and the next day the McKenzie party, taking the Cayuse chieftain's advice, departed the area.

Mile 22.0 During the second half of the 1800s, steamboats stopped regularly at the northside flat above Fir Island, situated here. Early farmers from the benches above the river hauled grain downhill on wagons to place it on board the steamers at Fir Bluff Landing. The island itself was once

Vintage 1890s Sternwheeler on the Clearwater River

homesteaded, but became most well known for the mineral water bubbling from its only spring. Folks filled large bottles with the water and transported the bottles across the island on a specially built track and then across a ford at the island's upper end. The water was touted as a tonic and dispensed by a local early day physician at his *tumor* clinic.

Mile 23.0 On May 6, 1806, after traveling east along the north side of the river during the late afternoon and early evening, the Lewis and Clark expeditionists camped on a downriver flat near the mouth of Pine Creek, opposite here. A Nez Perce lodge of six families stood nearby. While the Nez Perces did not eat horses, Big Horn and Twisted Hair's brother, who were guiding the explorers at this time, evidently found this evening's meal of fresh colt to be acceptable fare during the lean days before the arrival of spring salmon.

Mile 26.0 On the north side opposite here, an Indian trail ran west along the river from Bedrock Creek. To travel eastward, travelers typically crossed the Clearwater at the mouth of Bedrock Creek. Thus, this is the location of a centuries-old river crossing.

At mid-morning on May 7, 1806, Captains Lewis and Clark, traveling east with their party on horseback, sought the assistance of a small group of Nez Perces camped just below the mouth of Bedrock Creek. Twisted Hair's brother, serving as guide, had suggested to the explorers that they would find a better trail, as well as more game, on the south side of the river. The horses were unloaded and the men spent the next four hours ferrying the party's gear across the swollen river in one available Indian canoe. Imperiled in crossings such as this were the group's essential survival equipment and supplies, trade goods and medicine, the leather bound diaries of several of the men, records of scientific data gathered all along the way and geographical records that would later be used to document America's claims to the entire Northwest. In retrospect, we today might feel aghast at the thought of such documents floating across this and other rivers midst a ragtag crew and heap of provisions in a dugout canoe! Also loaded into the canoe were two canisters of gunpowder which the party had buried the previous fall near their campsite at Lenore. The cache had been uncovered by a dog whose Nez Perce master retrieved the canisters and kept them safe in his lodge at his village. No doubt the explorers were extremely grateful for this act of helpfulness and honesty, a reminder of the decided friendliness of the Nez Perces.

Mile 26.7 In the late 1800s and early 1900s, the little hamlet of Agatha sat on the flat on the north side of the river opposite your location here — now merely a reminder of the white settler families that followed the miners into Clearwater Country. The Evans Ferry at this location forged a link between the end of the rail line at Kendrick to the northwest and the Camas Prairie to the southeast and was the only transportation crossing for a stretch along the river running from Spalding (Mile 12.2) to Greer (Mile 52.3). For awhile Agatha, therefore, served as a pivotal point in regional transportation and was touted as "the most important shipping point on the upper river" in an early report. Soon, however, transportation routes were altered to better facilitate growing numbers of visitors and residents, and Agatha joined dozens of other hamlets that blossomed and, in this case, relatively quickly faded into the ghost towns of regional history.

In the early 1900s, the Rothschilds of winery fame purchased land near Agatha and, because of the suitable soil conditions and climate, developed a vineyard on surrounding hillsides. In 1909, they reportedly shipped out six hundred tons of wine grapes on the railroad, which had first coursed its way up the Clearwater Valley a decade earlier. Plans for a winery were considered but squelched when the Rothschilds learned it was illegal to make alcohol on an Indian reservation.

Mile 27.0 The road that turns south at this point is called Peach Lane. Fruit growing is common in the Clearwater Valley and is not limited to peaches. Apples, plums, pears, cherries, blackberries, raspberries and strawberries are also grown here and, of course, as noted above, grapes.

Mile 27.5 Although the village of Lenore is upriver a mile, the lovely park located here is named Lenore Rest Stop. Locals, however, refer to the location as Big Eddy because of a large eddy (backwater swirl) in the river along the southwest fringe of the rest area.

Because the eddy is the central site of an Indian legend and an ancient homesite of the Nez Perces, this stop is also Site 19 of the Nez Perce National Historical Park. According to Nez Perce storytellers, magical coyote often dwells in a cave at the bottom of the eddy. Evidence that the area was traditionally long used by the Nez Perces was brought to light between 1967 and 1971, when an archeological site was excavated on the flat adjacent to Big Eddy (west fringe of the park). Unearthed was a village that included large oval pit houses occupied from 900 B.C. to 1300 A.D.

At high water in May of 1861, *The Colonel Wright*, a 110-foot sternwheeler whose decks were filled with tons of freight, strained to a standstill in the swift rapids above Big Eddy. Having loaded at Portland all the human and material ingredients of a gold rush town, the captain intended to pilot the craft upstream as far as he could in order to offer his passengers the closest point of debarkation to the rapidly emerging mining town of Pierce City some fifty miles northeast. In an attempt to lighten the sternwheeler's load, Captain White had earlier ordered the passengers ashore on the north side of the river downstream, opposite Mile 26.7 and near what would later become the small community of Agatha. The crew's first try at pulling the huge boat through the rapids by using a line tied to a pine tree and wrapped around the steam capstan ended when the line broke. Their second try also resulted in a broken line, but this break almost led to disaster when the sternwheeler was whipped into rocks along the shore and swirled about in the rapids. The pilot, Ephraim Baughman, managed, however, to back the boat out of the rapids and downstream to the passengers' landing site.

Among the passengers on the north shore was a merchant named S.S. Slater, who elected to promptly unpack his goods and create his own town which he figured would continue to be the farthest upstream point of departure for the mines. Before long, five canvas shacks masqueraded as the beginning of a city. Mining equipment and provisions filled two of the hastily constructed tents, while two were used to house the frequent passers-through. The fifth contained two bottles, three tumblers, a whiskey barrel and two stacked boxes that made up the bar. This first of Clearwater Country's many saloons measured eight feet square and was shielded from the elements by a roof of two red blankets and one blue. Thus the village of Slaterville was born.

However, the unsuccessful trip of the *Colonel Wright* stood as the last journey of the sternwheeler to Slaterville, and though the steamer *Okanagan* pushed its way to the fledgling burg on June 1st that same summer, the idea of regular steamboat travel to Slaterville was abandoned. After an existence of just twenty-seven days, so was the town .

Today at Big Eddy you'll find two restroom buildings, interpretive signs, picnic tables, drinking water and pop vending machines, a boat access ramp and parking area, a truck and trailer parking lot, grassy dog-walking areas, shady green trees and, typically, a nice breeze.

Mile 28.3 LENORE On October 7, 1805, after spending eleven days near Orofino, sixteen miles upstream, the Lewis and Clark Expedition set out towards the sea. Their first day's travel in newly constructed dugouts ended here at Lenore. They camped "on a starboard point opposite a run;" that is, on the north bank of the river opposite the mouth of Jack's Creek, which enters the Clearwater through the draw south of the Lenore bridge. Although riffles and rapids would give them a fright now and then, they were undoubtedly pleased to be traveling more swiftly and easily than they had during their recent arduous journey on foot and horseback over the Bitterroot Mountains. At the Lenore campsite they decided to lighten their load by burying two canisters of gunpowder "a Short distance from the river at 2 feet 4 Inches N. of a dead toped pine Tree..." (See related story at Mile 26.0.)

To walk in the footsteps of Lewis and Clark, drive across the Lenore Bridge and turn immediately to the right onto the dirt road running alongside the railroad tracks. Drive ahead one-tenth mile to a large open flat that fringes the river. There you'll be standing on the October 7th campsite of the Corps of Discovery. Today's travelers may camp at this undeveloped site for up to ten days. There is a toilet and a boat access ramp. Visible from the flat is the slope noted below which the explorers ascended during their return trip.

Seven months later, after crossing to the south (highway) side of the Clearwater near Bedrock Creek (Mile 26.0) on May 7, 1806, and traveling upstream "over a difficult and stony road," the Corps of Discovery left the river valley here and ascended the slope just east of Jack's Creek. Their climb took them to a small prairie from which they later descended to Big Canyon Creek in the vicinity of present-day Peck (Mile 34.8).

During the early 1900s, Lenore was the terminus of the largest grain tramway on the river. The tramway enabled the transportation of grain from the Camas Prairie on the south to the rail line running along the north bank of the river corridor. Sixty-five steel buckets traveled from the tiny and appropriately named town of Summit, which lay along the southern rim of the canyon. The grain buckets, which were connected to each other by moving cable, rode a stationary cable strung between more than a dozen wooden towers down the ridge. Each bucket could carry five forty-pound sacks of grain. The cable carried the buckets across the river to the railroad track.

Mile 29.0-30.0 The exposed vertical columns of gray rock visible on both sides of the river through stretches such as this are basalt, a volcanic rock resulting from the hardening of prehistoric lava flows. Millions of years ago, an ancient river ran through this region, likely following a route similar to that of today's Clearwater River. Then approximately sixteen million years ago, the region ranging from the Pacific Northwest Coast inland to the Bitterroot Mountains experienced an extended period of volcanic eruptions. During that period lava flows filled the area's valleys and canyons, and, in effect, leveled the region, creating what is today referred to as the Columbia Plateau. Since that period, natural erosion of the plateau has occurred, including that caused by the region's rivers. The Clearwater, for instance, has carved throughout the intervening years its present course. The fact that most of the Clearwater still flows over a bed of volcanic basalt tells us that the valley has not yet reached the depth of the original ancient riverbed lying beneath the basalt. This is true, despite the fact that the Clearwater began winding its way through the Highway 12 corridor over fifteen million years ago.

Mile 34.8 The side road which leaves Highway 12 at this point takes travelers up Big Canyon Creek to the little town of **PECK** (1 1/2 miles). The Peck area was first homesteaded in 1896 and officially became a town in 1899 when the rail line reached this point on the north side of the Clearwater River. Townsfolk named their community after railroad official George Peck, in hopes of influencing a possible decision to run a spur line up Big Canyon Creek, through Peck and on to the Camas Prairie to the south.

At the turn of the century, Peck was one of the larger towns along the Clearwater. Three hotels, a drug store, meat market, bank, church, post office, hardware store, pool hall, funeral parlor and newspaper office flanked her dusty Main Street. The land between Peck and the river was owned by Nez Perce families, so the town was farther from the river and the railroad than desired by the whites. But a daily stagecoach carried folks a mile to and from the ferry crossing to the railroad tracks on the north side. The ferry was later replaced by a bridge, the pillars for which still stand in the river.

On May 7, 1806, eastbound, the Lewis and Clark party descended from a high level prairie to the south of the present highway and reached Big Canyon Creek approximately a mile upstream from its mouth. The Indian trail they were traveling had left the river near Lenore (Mile 28.3) to avoid the bluffs between these two locations. The explorers then traveled up the creek through the location of the present community of Peck and camped just below the mouth of Little Canyon Creek as it joins Big Canyon Creek 2 3/10 miles south of the highway. This area, located along a major Nez Perce trail, was the site of a former Nez Perce village. Hunters from the Lewis and Clark party killed four deer the morning of May 8th and supplied the explorers with a breakfast of venison, a welcome change from many meals of horse meat. Their Nez Perce guides indicated that the previous winter had been so difficult that the Indians had resorted to eating pine seeds and boiled lichens from the many pine trees in this area. Lewis observed that several felled pines lay strewn about, apparently cut down for this purpose.

The afternoon of the 8th, the explorers climbed the ridge between the Clearwater River and Little Canyon Creek and traveled to Twisted Hair's root digging camp on the prairie a short distance south and west of present-day Orofino. Cut Nose and several other downriver Nez Perces accompanied them, and Twisted Hair and some of his men from upriver joined them along the route. On May 9th Twisted Hair took two young Nez Perce men and a member of the expedition a short distance north to the site of the party's canoe camp of the previous fall. They returned to the main party late in the evening with twenty-one of the explorers' horses, the cached gunpowder and balls, and about half of the saddles. The party's pace was leisurely now, for their guides had informed them that they would not be able to travel the trail back over the Bitterroots for some time, as heavy late spring snows in the mountains would make the trip impossible. The eight inches of fresh snow that fell on their camp that evening confirmed the accuracy of this prediction.

Mile 38.0 In fall and spring, travelers may see fishers riding the river in driftboats (similar to sea dories), jetboats or outboard skiffs, trying their luck at steelhead fishing. While the average number of hours it takes to catch a steelhead requires lots of sitting, the rewards are delicious.

Had you driven along this section of the river on July 26, 1997, you would have seen a motley band of inexperienced but fun-seeking history buffs paddling downriver in recently axe hewn dugout canoes. They had launched their canoes at Canoe Camp near Orofino (See Mile 40.0) and were participating in an event called The Lewis and Clark Experience by emulating the explorers' 1805 journey from Canoe Camp to Clarkston, Washington. Premiered at Clarkston during the Experience weekend was the now well known Ken Burns and Dayton Duncan television documentary "The Journey of Lewis and Clark." Burns, Duncan and Stephen Ambrose, author of UNDAUNTED COURAGE, spoke at the event as they presented the film to the public.

Mile 39.1 Pink House Hole Recreation Area is the location of a Clearwater River fishing hole on the banks of which once stood a pink house. Now on the Pink House flat there is a toilet, parking lot, two boat access ramps and a few undeveloped campsites along the river's edge.

Mile 39.6 You are now at the west end of the Riverside section of Orofino (main section of town at Mile 44.0). All services are available in Riverside, as well as in Orofino.

As you travel the Riverside section of Orofino, you will be passing by slabs of 82-90 million year old rocks called diorite. Their presence here serves as demarcation of a suture line that over ninety million years ago marked the western coastal fringe of the continent. Highway 12 here crosses that prehistoric suture line.

Mile 40.0 Directly across from the mouth of the Clearwater River's North Fork, this south-side flat was the Canoe Camp of Lewis and Clark. When they arrived here on September 26, 1805, most of the party were exceedingly ill due to a change in their diet from red meat to the Nez Perces' dried salmon and camas roots. The expeditionists spent the next eleven days here selecting and felling pines, burning out the centers in the manner of the Indians, and then chipping out the charred wood with their adzes. The work was particularly slow since three-fourths of the men were so terribly sick, including Meriwether Lewis himself, and also because several men had to be spared each day to hunt. On October 5th the explorers branded their thirty-eight horses and arranged for their care during the winter with the friendly and helpful Nez Perce headman Twisted Hair. The next night the party buried their saddles, a canister of gunpowder and bag of rifle balls in the sand "on the Side of a bend about 1/2 a mile below." On October 7, 1805, the Corps of Discovery launched their dugouts at this site. They were finally afloat and headed west again.

Here at the Canoe Camp site today, you'll find a dugout canoe, riverside viewing benches, a picnic table and a short interpretive walk with six informative panels focusing on the Nez Perces and the Corps of Discovery.

From the Journal of Captain Clark

September 26, 1805. ...we...camped on low ground on the south, opposite the forks of the river. but so weak were the men that several were taken sick...the weather being oppressively hot. Two chiefs and their families followed us and camped with a great number of horses near us; soon after our arrival we were joined by two Indians, who came down the north fork on a raft. We purchased some fresh salmon, and having distributed axes and portioned off the labor of the party, we began...

Friday, 27th. ...at an early hour, the preparations for making five canoes. But few of the men, however, were able to work... The hunters returned without any game and seriously indisposed, so that nearly the whole party was now ill. We procured some fresh salmon; and Colter, who now returned...brought half a deer, which was very nourishing...

September 28th. The men continue ill, though some of those first attacked are recovering. Their general complaint is a heaviness at the stomach and a lax which is rendered more painful by the heat of the weather and the diet... A number of Indians collect about us in the course of the day, to gaze at the strange appearance of everything belonging to us.

September 29th. ...The men continue ill, but all ...able to work are occupied at the canoes. The spirits of the party were much recruited by three deer brought in by the hunters.

September 30. The sick began to recruit their strength... The Indians pass in great numbers up and down the river...

October 1st, 1805. ...We were visited by several Indians from the tribes below and others from the main south fork. To two of the most distinguished men we made presents of a ring and broach, and to each of five others a piece of ribbon, a little tobacco, and the fifth part of a neckcloth. We now dried our clothes and other articles and selected some...in order to purchase...provisions, as we have nothing left except a little dried fish, which operates as a complete purgative.

October 2nd. ...Two men were sent to the village with a quantity of these articles to purchase food. We are now reduced to roots, which produce violent pains in the stomach. Our work continued as usual, and many of the party are convalescent.

At Canoe Camp, 1805

The hunters returned in the afternoon with nothing but a small prairie-wolf [coyote]; so that, our provisions being exhausted, we killed one of the horses to eat and provide soup for the sick.

October 3D. The fine cool morning and easterly wind had an agreeable effect upon the party, most of whom are now able to work. ...

October 4th. Again we had a cool east wind from the mountains. The men were now much better, and Captain Lewis himself was so far recovered as to walk about a little...

October 5th. ...The canoes being nearly finished, it became necessary to dispose of our horses. They were therefore collected to the number of 38, and being branded and marked were delivered to three Indians, the two brothers and the son of a chief, who promises to accompany us down the river. To each of these men we gave a knife and some small articles, and they agreed to take good care of the horses till our return. The hunters with all their diligence are unable to kill anything, the hills being high and rugged, and the woods too dry to hunt deer, which is the only game in the country. We therefore continue to eat dried fish and roots: Some of these roots seem to possess very active properties; for, after supping on them this evening, we were swelled to such a degree as to be scarcely able to breathe for several hours. Toward night we launched two canoes, which proved to be very good.

October 6th. ... We buried all our saddles in a cache near the river, about half a mile below [Canoe Camp], and deposited at the same time a canister of powder and a bag of balls. The time which could be spared from our labors on the canoes was devoted to some astronomical observations...

October 7th. This morning all the canoes were put in the water and loaded, the oars fixed, and every preparation made for setting out. But when we were all ready, the two chiefs who had promised to accompany us were not to be found, and at the same time we missed a pipe-tomahawk. We therefore proceeded without them...

In the year 1812, this site was also camp to a fur trading party headed by Donald McKenzie. The traders scouted the river upstream for beaver. Finding little sign, they returned downstream to establish a trading post near Lewiston. As recorded by McKenzie's clerk Alfred Seton...

We kept up the left hand fork on the [Clearwater] river that Lewis & Clark descended & in three or four days came to the Head of navigable water on this side of the mountains & the place where L & C had built their canoes. We encamped in their encampment. Here Mr. McK with 4 men went up the river...to determine if it had more the appearance of a beaver country above...When Mr. McKenzie returned...The country he had been through afforded no sign of Beaver, to which all our enquiries were directed, & as it was now found that we must lay aside hopes of getting beaver from this quarter, he thought it best to remove down to the Forks which is in the center of a numerous nation of Indians, from whom by chance we might now & then get a skin, & who abound in horses which we now perceive must be our only food.

About a quarter of a mile up the North Fork, a mammoth structure of much more modern interest now imposes itself on the scene — Dworshak Dam. Constructed from 1966 through 1973, the dam is composed of 6,700,000 cubic yards of concrete. Its construction created 19,824 acres of lake stretching fifty-three miles into the mountains. Dworshak Lake is surrounded by 47,000 acres of public-use land.

Before the dam, an estimated twenty thousand steelhead and from five to ten thousand chinook salmon annually returned from the Pacific to the North Fork to spawn. In fact, throughout centuries past most area streams teemed with these fish. However, in increasing degrees, as the Dworshak and a string of eight lower Snake River and Columbia River dams were built during the twentieth century, native fish populations have suffered. Indeed, some people suggest that the now submerged natural North Fork environment provided not only more permanently healthy fish populations, but also, thereby, a more permanently sustainable segment of the local economy.

The building complexes sitting directly east (upriver) and west (downriver) of the mouth of the North Fork are two fish hatcheries built to compensate for the loss of steelhead and salmon in the Clearwater and Snake Rivers. On the upriver side, the Dworshak National Fish Hatchery produces approximately four million steelhead and salmon smolts each year, making it one of the largest anadromous fish hatcheries in the world. The Clearwater Fish Hatchery, on the downriver side, adds an additional two million smolts to those that are released each year for their migration to the Pacific Ocean. After fifteen years of the Clearwater Hatchery's operation and over thirty years of the Dworshak Hatchery's operation and an expenditure on fisheries activities throughout the river system of three billion dollars, steelhead numbers are greatly diminished and the salmon are nearly gone. Several of the wild fish runs that migrate through the Clearwater, Snake and Columbia Rivers have now been listed as *threatened* or *endangered*.

Various sections of Dworshak Lake have retained locational names from pre-dam days. One section of water whose name identified a small backwater bay when the lower North Fork still ran as a river is Bruce's Eddy. The Indians for centuries fished salmon out of the eddy where the North Fork flowed through a large basin called *Te-mee-mup*. Using a structure of upright and horizontal poles wedged firmly into river rocks and extended across the river, the Indians constructed a framework for a makeshift weir. Shorter poles woven together with cedar bark into wicker-like panels allowed water to flow through but held fish back when the panels were set in place along the framework. Then the Nez Perce men fashioned scaffolds and fishing platforms which projected out over the river below their woven weir. Standing on the platforms, they fished with spears to which bone spearheads had been fastened.

Archealogical investigations within the North Fork Canyon have revealed human occupation of the area for over eleven thousand years. Prior to the building of the dam, fifty occupation sites dating back four thousand years were identified along the now submerged lower North Fork.

Dworshak Hatchery and Dam, the lakeside Big Eddy Recreation Area and the nearby Clearwater Fish Hatchery are open to visitors daily. See Side Trip #3 in the Side Trips chapter for directions to these sites.

Wanigan During a Log Drive

From 1930 until the spring of 1971, the North Fork was the scene of a yearly ninety-mile long log drive to the Potlatch Corporation mill pond at Lewiston. During this period, an estimated 1.8 billion board feet of logs came down the river. Each spring a *rearing* crew of more than thirty woolen-clad, spike-booted lumberjacks, skilled at log-birling and maneuvering jammed logs with long *idiot sticks*, packed gear and food onto a floating bunkhouse-cookhouse called a wanigan. At various upriver points, decks of logs, piled high during the preceding year, were released at high water for their downriver journey under the escort of the crew. The jacks knew well the dangers and challenges such a drive carried with it and the hard physical work it entailed. The river itself was the major threat during the high, gushing spring runoff when the water's temperature was in the icy mid-thirty degree range and the river raged so violently in places that it could toss a lumberjack around as easily as it might a fencepost.

Mile 40.8 The Clearwater National Forest headquarters sits south of the highway. Here you'll find books on regional history and wildlife, answers to your questions about the region, a wildlife display and a Clearwater National Forest three-dimensional map. On the walls you'll see two large historical paintings depicting an early Nez Perce village and a log drive on the North Fork of the Clearwater.

Mile 41-43 On September 25, 1805, explorer William Clark and his new Nez Perce friend, Twisted Hair, rode horses downstream along the north bank of the river to the mouth of the North Fork of the Clearwater in search of trees suitable for building dugout canoes. There they joined a Nez Perce family for a meal of roasted salmon and were transported across the river by dugout to inspect a cluster of ponderosa pines. Clark recalled a map that had been drawn for him with a campfire coal on a mat by an Indian on the Weippe Prairie two days before. The map had shown the Clearwater, Snake and Columbia Rivers, and now, noting the suitability of the stout pines beside the river for dugouts, Clark no doubt felt a surge of excitement at the nearness of the Pacific. As he returned to his party that afternoon, he walked the route of the present highway scouting a trail for the full party's travel the next day to what would become the Canoe Camp.

Mile 43.2 For RVers' convenience, a wide drive-through dump station is located here on the south side of the highway, along with a sign bearing a Clearwater Country map.

Mile 43.3 At about 9 a.m. on September 26th, a short distance downstream from the north end of the modern-day bridge that takes travelers into Orofino, the entire Lewis and Clark party entered the Clearwater on horseback along an angling ford that reached the south side of the river upstream from the eastern end of the present-day airport. They must have been a colorful and curious assemblage, buckskin fringes bobbing as the riders lightly kicked their horses' flanks until the horses were belly deep in the water. Many of the party were sick, slumping in their saddles, barely able to ride. The Shoshone woman Sacagawea, who rode with them, likely carried her infant Baptiste suspended in a cradleboard on her back. Goods and supplies teetered and creaked on the backs of pack horses forging into the sunlight reflecting off the rippling water. The party traveled downriver to a point directly across from the mouth of the North Fork of the Clearwater (Mile 40.0) and camped.

Mile 44.0 OROFINO [Population: 3700. All services available.]

Not to be confused with an 1860s mining town in the mountains to the northeast called Oro Fino, the present town of Orofino was founded in 1895. The Nez Perce Reservation had recently been opened for settlement, and a man named Clifford Fuller set up business in a trading post on the flat where Orofino now sits. Fuller also then established The Clearwater Improvement Company for the purpose of platting the town he foresaw at this location, and in 1896, he began a ferry crossing here.

In 1906, the town's main street was leveled by fire and thereafter rebuilt with brick. The town has been over the years a hub of the area's logging operations and county seat of Clearwater County.

Orofino Creek joins the Clearwater from the north here. Near the headwaters of this creek, gold was first discovered in Idaho in 1860, and, thus, this creek's name, Orofino, means *fine gold*. That first strike set in motion a stampede into Clearwater Country and, in turn, a progression of seemingly inevitable events which led to immense change in this land at that time belonging to the Nez Perces.

William Clark referred to Orofino Creek as Rock Dam Creek. The Lewis and Clark expeditionists had made camp a mile upstream from the creek on September 24, 1805.

Fourth of July Parade, Orofino, 1900

Clark and Chief Twisted Hair crossed the creek on the 25th in search of trees suitable for dugouts.

Just across the bridge, on the right, lies the city park, a pleasant picnic spot. While there, keep your eye on the riverbanks for sightings of usually solitary and always stately blue herons, or watch for them as you drive upstream or downstream from Orofino. Throughout the year in Orofino, area history is on view at the Clearwater County Museum on College Avenue. The museum is open afternoons. To reach the museum, cross the bridge onto Michigan Avenue, turn right onto Johnson Avenue and in one block, turn left onto College Avenue and drive 1 1/4 blocks.

Mile 45.1 On September 24, 1805, the Lewis and Clark party camped on an island which once lay in the river here but later became a railbed when fill for the railroad tracks was deposited at each end of the island. The perimeter of the island remains discernable today. Bedraggled and sick from a sudden change in diet, the explorers had stumbled along the river's north bank, following a day's rest at a Nez Perce root-gathering encampment on the Weippe Prairie several miles northeast of here. The island camp was not a comfortable one, for the majority suffered from dysentery and from the heat in the valley, particularly since they had just two days earlier left the cool, and in places freezing, mountains. It was just upstream from this location that Clark first met Chief Twisted Hair and smoked the pipe of friendship with him late on the evening of September 21, 1805. A party of five hunters, who remained in this vicinity while Clark returned to the Weippe Prairie the next day, camped on the island as well. The entire expedition stayed here the nights of September 24th and 25th before moving downriver to the Canoe Camp site at Mile 40.0.

47.3 On September 24, 1805, the Corps of Discovery passed along the hillside across the river from here. Captain Clark and five members of an advance party had traveled the route three days earlier. (See related entry at Mile 47.8.) The five remained in this area to hunt. Then on September 24th, the twenty-eight other members of the Corps and their Shoshone guide Toby and his son made their way along the hillside into a warm afternoon here and then headed downstream to camp. A few of the men were slowed along the trail by dysentery they'd acquired in response to their new diet of camas and salmon...and perhaps to Clark's dispensing of Rush's Pills, a laxative and mainstay of the party's medicine chest. Captain Lewis, for example, was "scercely able to ride on a jentle horse." Emotionally, however, the whole party was bouyed at sight of the Clearwater, for they knew that they had now reached a navigable river, one that would carry them to the sea.

Mile 47.8 Jim Ford's Creek enters the Clearwater from the north. Jim Ford was an early day logger who cut trees along the hills in this vicinity and floated logs to Lewiston.

During the evening of September 21, 1805, explorer William Clark, five of his party and a Nez Perce guide hiked down the ridge just east of the creek in search of the camp of Twisted Hair. Lewis and the rest of the exploration party had not yet reached the Weippe Prairie. Clark and his companions, according to Nez Perce oral history, had been spared being massacred the previous night by the intercession of Wat-ku-ese, a Nez Perce woman who had been befriended by whites while a captive of another tribe far to the east of Clearwater Country.

The Nez Perce guide located Twisted Hair's camp about midnight. Twisted Hair crossed the river, and in the wee hours of the night, he and Clark smoked the pipe in the tradition of friendship. This friendship was to serve the expeditionists well during the ensuing months and laid the foundation for harmony between whites and Nez Perces that would last more than sixty years. The next day, while his five men remained on the river to establish a camp and to hunt, Clark trekked back to the Weippe Prairie to rejoin Lewis and the rest of the party, who had that same day emerged from the mountains. On the 23rd, the explorers procured roots, bread and fish from the Indians and on the following day made their way to the river. (See related information at Mile 47.3.)

Mile 51.6 GREER

The hamlet of Greer unofficially began when mountain men William Craig and Jacob Schultz built a ferry three-tenths mile upstream during the gold rush of 1861 as a convenience to the miners traveling to Pierce City and Oro Fino (twenty-nine miles to the north and east). In 1877, the ferry was purchased by John Greer and his partner John Molloy.

When the railroad etched a rail route into Clearwater Country in 1899, John Greer and John Dunn platted a township, another small community linked to the bigger world by twin trails of steel. Whether determined by the toss of a gold piece or the cut of a card, what might have become Dunn continues today to dot a Clearwater Country map as Greer.

Should you drive across the Greer Bridge, you will find yourself at the base of the winding eight-mile long Greer Grade, which offers increasingly broad and beautiful vistas of the Clearwater Valley as you ascend. The grade roughly follows the route of the miners, settlers and outlaws of the 1860s and tops out on the wide Weippe Prairie, historic site of the Nez Perces' first meeting with the Lewis and Clark explorers. The highway continues across the prairie to the towns of Weippe and Pierce, Idaho's first gold rush town, and to a vast wild section of Clearwater Country. To drive to Weippe and Pierce, see Side Trip #4 in the Side Trips chapter.

Mile 52.2 A large beach across the river here and smaller beach on the highway side of the river are frequently used by sun-seekers during the summer months.

Mile 52.3 The Greer Ferry crossed the Clearwater just below this location. Here the trail from Lewiston to the gold fields at Pierce City and Oro Fino brought pack strings up to a hundred mules in length laden with tools, equipment, food and whiskey. Soon freighters, similarly loaded, careened down the steep descent from the prairie to the south, their wheels smoking from constant braking. At the bottom the wheels hissed as a boy from the waiting ferry poured water on their metal rims to avoid setting the ferry deck on fire when the travelers in their wagons boarded to cross to the north side. Traveling in the opposite direction were well guarded mule trains, heavy with nuggets and dust, headed to banks in Walla Walla. Wells Fargo pony express riders with mail for loved ones or news of the Civil War regularly crossed the Clearwater here. Some of Henry Plummer's outlaw gang rode the Greer Ferry on their way to murder outspoken, anti-outlaw Pat Ford in front of his Oro Fino saloon after he had earlier escaped ambush by them on the trail. Now and then agents of the government of China led mules downhill to the ferry — mules toting the skeletons of Chinese miners from Pierce City or Oro Fino on the first leg of a very long journey back to a proper burial in China.

Greer Ferry

In 1877, fearing General O.O. Howard and his troops might approach the Weippe Prairie from here after the Battle of the Clearwater, the warring factions of the Nez Perces cut the ferry loose and burned the ferry house.

In May of 1896, the *Lewiston*, a 513-ton steam-powered sternwheeler, forged her way up the river here — her captain hoping to pioneer a transportation route to Kamiah thirteen miles upstream. Just three years later the clink of driven steel proclaimed the coming of the railroad to Greer.

Mile 53.1 Through the steep, forested draw which stretches downward to the Clearwater's north bank flows the snow-fed waters of Lolo Creek. The Lewis and Clark Expedition forded upper stretches of this creek three times during the crossing and recrossing that was a part of their retreat from the deep snows of the Nez Perce Trail in June 1806.

The previous year, a September 21st camp on the banks of this creek (about twenty miles east of here) was for Lewis and the main party the last night spent on their difficult march across what explorer Patrick Gass called "these dismal and horrible mountains" — one night before the main party located both Clark and food in a Nez Perce village on the Weippe Prairie. Lewis recorded in his journal the evening's menu: a few grouse, the last of the horse meat, a handful of crawfish found crawling beneath Lolo Creek boulders and a coyote.

Mile 55.7 Tunnel Beach, one of the most popular beaches along the Clearwater for swimming and sunning, lies below the highway here.

Mile 58.7 In April of 1902, on the north slopes of the river here, an eastern entrepreneur named Alfred Day Pardee bought and developed a townsite which became known as Pardee. His plans included hardrock mining, which he thought would soon bring economic prosperity to the area. Because railroad construction had exposed numerous quartz ledges along the riverbank, eastern businessmen, like Pardee, were eager to make investments. However, no veins of gold ran through the quartz, and the financiers, including Pardee, soon departed.

Mile 60.0 Until the Northern Pacific Railroad punched its tracks through in 1899, folks who wanted to reach upriver locations had no recourse but to take the rugged overland wagon roads and foot trails up the hillsides to the prairies and then down again to the river. But with the coming of the railway, for the first time travelers could follow the easy water grade between Lewiston and Kooskia. Nevertheless, the problem of transporting rich grain harvests from the prairies above to the rail cars along the river remained. This problem was solved by a number of tramways which stretched the lengths of the hillsides at several locations between Kooskia and Lewiston.

One of those bucket-brigade tramways was situated just above this location, and at its base on the small flat on the north side of the river sat the tiny community of Tramway. The town's tram consisted of a series of buckets suspended from cables strung between a long row of timber uprights. Each descending bucket carried one sack of grain, and each fifth bucket could be reloaded for the upward trip with supplies for prairie farmers who waited in their wagons in lines sometimes as long as a mile. The tramway, built in 1902, was used until 1940. Tramway families once boasted a school population of seventeen children. In 1918, a flu epidemic permanently cut seven boys out of the class. Townsfolk were linked to Pardee (Mile 58.7) by a mile of track and from there could ascend the northern slopes by horse and wagon to the town of Woodland, first settled in 1890. Today the name Woodland is retained to identify an area of homes scattered across a stretch of alternating farmland and forest.

Mile 65.0 The Kamiah Valley, which extends generally from Mile 65.0 to Mile 69.0, is the birthplace of the Nee Mee Poo, or Nez Perces, and has for centuries played host to their villages and intertribal gatherings. Indeed, the very soil of the valley and surrounding country is deeply embedded with the rich history of the Nee Mee Poo.

Mainstream American culture did not arrive in this valley until 1806. On May 10th that year, during their eastward homeward journey, the Lewis and Clark Expedition arrived at one of the Nez Perce villages located alongside Lawyer's Creek, which flows across the valley and enters the Clearwater from the west at Mile 67.3. The village was situated about four miles up the creek. The explorers found an American flag flying in the village, the flag they had left for Chief Broken Arm near the North Fork (Mile 40.0) the previous autumn. The Lawyer's Creek village consisted of one longhouse of one hundred fifty feet, which contained twenty-four fires and about twice that many families.

After a stay of two and one-half days at Broken Arm's village, the expeditionists trekked down Lawyer's Creek and camped one night on the south side of the Clearwater directly north of Kamiah's current Main Street. The next day, May 14th, they drove their horses across the river and were themselves ferried across in Nez Perce dugouts. Moving then a mile downstream they set up what was to be their third longest camp (about forty paces north of the present railroad bridge visible here), historically now identified as Long Camp. As a base for their shelter, they used an existing three-foot high circle of stones which was thirty yards in diameter and surrounded a four-foot deep excavation of earth — the former location of an Indian lodge. Here they remained until June 10th while waiting for the snows to melt off the Nez Perce Trail, which traversed the Bitterroot Mountains and which the explorers knew would be the toughest segment of their journey home.

In the interim, they prepared themselves as best they could for the Bitterroot crossing. They traded for additional horses and stockpiled food supplies. As time allowed, they visited with their friends the Nez Perces in mutual learning exchanges, enjoyed occasional sweat baths, observed the Indians' methods of gelding horses "preferable to that practised by ourselves," and administered medical treatment to sick Indians. Charbonneau and Sacagawea's son Baptiste was taken "dangerously ill. his jaw and throat...much swelled." Clark, who served as unofficial doctor throughout the expedition, administered "a poltice of onions, after giveing him some creem of tarter..." As further poultices and potions were given and the child slowly recovered during the next several days, an abcess appeared on his neck, and Clark "applied a plaster of sarve made of the rozen of the long leafed pine, Beaswax and Bears oil mixed."

While the Indians seldom killed bears and, in fact, were "very much afraid of them and the killing of a White or Grizly bear is as great a feet as two of their enimey," the white men did kill black and grizzly bears and on one occasion shared the meat with the Indians. The Indian cooks threw a "parcel of small stones" on a brisk wood fire to heat, then

> laid on a parsel of pine boughs, on those they laid the flesh of the bear in flitches, placeing boughs between each course of meat and then covering it thickly with pine boughs; after this they poared on a small quantity of water, and covered the whole over with earth to the debth of 4 inches.

After three hours, all ate heartily of the roasted bear.

In their journals for this time period, Lewis and Clark both noted that the Nez Perce women were busy gathering and pounding wild roots. Sacagawea, too, gathered roots, in particular the yampa root, which the explorers had identified as fennel — the two plants being in the same plant family. On May 18th, Lewis noted that Sacagawea was engaged in storing up roots for the expeditionists' return journey across the Rocky Mountains. Yampa could be eaten raw, boiled, steamed or mashed and dried, thus was an easy root for Sacagawea to store and for the Corps to use.

The evening of June 8th, the explorers and several Nez Perces ran foot races till the former retired to their camp and "played at prisoners base until night. After dark the fiddle was played and the party amused themselves in danceing."

On June 10th, against the Indians' advice, the party departed their "long camp" at 11 a.m., "...each man being well mounted and a light load on a 2d horse, besides which we have several supernumary horses in case of accident or the want of provisions..." They ascended the steep hills, finding Collins' Creek [Lolo Creek] to be "deep and extremely difficult." Once on the prairie, they camped, shot two deer for supper and inspected the pale blue "quaw-mash," or camas, which the Nez Perces prized and had frequently shared with the explorers.

The party began the trip over the mountains on June 15th, but on the 16th they encountered snow which increased in depth and difficulty until by the 17th they found themselves "envelloped in snow from 8 to 12 feet deep..." The trail was obscured, travel terribly rugged, and no grass was exposed for horse feed. Feeling that they needed to secure an Indian guide in order to continue the journey, they cached all baggage for which they had no immediate use, their papers, roots and a few other food-stuffs and then started back. Two men with a rifle to offer as enticement were sent ahead to the Nez Perces to secure a guide. On the 20th the main party discontentedly decided to ride all the way back to the Weippe camas meadows where they felt they could engage in more successful hunting in order to restock their supply of food. Finally on June 23rd the two dispatched men rejoined the party with three guides for the price of two rifles, and on the 24th they all set out again to cross the mountains. The next evening Clark wrote in his journal,

> last evening the indians entertained us with set-
> ting the fir trees on fire. they have a great number
> of dry limbs near their bodies which when Set on
> fire create a very sudden and emmence blaize from

bottom to top of those tall trees. they are a boutifull object in this situation at night. ...the nativs told us that their object in Setting those trees on fire was to bring fair weather for our journey.

Indeed, this time the weather would allow their passage over the difficult mountains.

Thirty-three years later, in 1839, shortly after the first Presbyterian missions had been established in the Northwest, including the Spalding mission upriver from Lewiston, missionary Asa Smith and his wife Sarah moved to the Kamiah Valley. In August, Smith constructed a crude building as temporary quarters. In describing it, he wrote,

> Our house was made by grooving posts & setting them in the ground & filling up the sides with split cedar. The roof was made of dirt, our floor is the ground, our windows are cracks between the timbers, our door is made of cedar split out with an axe.

Later that year Smith constructed a more substantial home, approximately 14' x 28', that included two small windows and a wooden floor. Both buildings were located near what is now the southern end of the railroad bridge traversing the Clearwater here.

Smith devoted much time to the major task of developing a written form of the Nez Perce language. With regular tutoring by the headman known as Lawyer, Smith wrote the first Nez Perce dictionary and grammar. He was also a keen observer of Nez Perce ways and recorded much of what he saw in long letters to his superiors in Boston. In fact, during 1840, four of his letters totaled over thirty thousand words! Much attention was also given through his writing to what Smith considered the hopelessness of Christianizing the

> *I cannot say send ploughs & cattle for this people. I have no hope of converting them in this way. So far as I can see the tendency is not favorable. This is evidently what they want of us, & the more we do to encourage their selfish desires, the more difficult will it be to bring them under the influence of the gospel. My only hope is in giving them the pure unadulterated word of God & enabling them to understand it. This & this alone I believe will benefit them in this life & in the life to come.*
> Asa Smith
> Kamiah, August 1839

Indians and to what he believed were the foolhardy policies and actions of Henry Spalding. (See related story at Mile 12.2.) These same letters were instrumental in Spalding's temporary dismissal by the Mission Board in 1842.

Smith was not well received among the Nez Perces, and his wife was particularly displeased with the couple's situation. She, in fact, was ill and in tears much of the time during their two-year stay. Thus on April 19, 1841, the Smiths abandoned their site in the Kamiah Valley and traveled by canoe to the Columbia River and on to Vancouver.

The railroad bridge visible at this location, which was built in 1899, rests on a giant mid-river pivot, so that the central span could be rotated a quarter turn to provide free passage for sternwheelers. However, following the *Lewiston's* historic and far-reaching upriver trip on May 8, 1896, no sternwheeler ever ascended the river this far. In 1899, the bridge was opened once as a test of its usability, then swung back into place, where it has remained to this day.

If you wish to view the entire Kamiah Valley in order to gain a composite picture of the locations of the historical events described above and below from Mile 65.0 to 68.8, drive into Kamiah on Highway 12 and turn south onto Main Street. Drive two blocks and turn right (west) onto Fifth Street and proceed 4.2 miles along State Highway 64. This highway is curvy but, for that distance, paved and will take you uphill to a vantage point where there is a pullout. From here you may view the entire valley. (The pullout allows for turning around to make the drive back downhill, unless you are driving a lengthy motorhome. In that case, we don't recommend that you drive Highway 64.)

Mile 66.3 KAMIAH (*kam ee eye*) **[Population: 1400. All services available.]**

The town of Kamiah was first located on rented Nez Perce Reservation land near the river's edge due north of the present Main Street. In 1878, the first post office opened here. However, Kamiah did not gain much prominence until 1895, the year the reservation was opened for white settlement. In 1905, the original townsite was abandoned in favor of a purchased plot of ten acres around which the town eventually grew to its present size.

When the community of Woodland was settled atop the hills to the north, having to ford the river near the location of the current grain elevators was alleviated by a ferry built with logs floated down from Smith Creek on the Middle Fork of the Clearwater. This ferry, Kip-Kip's Ferry, ran from 1895 until the first bridge was built across the river in 1909. The uprights for this bridge can still be seen downriver from today's river crossing.

The town's name is derived from the Nez Perce word *kamo*, which referred to the dogbane plant (Indian hemp) from which the Indians made rope, *kamia*. Literally, *Kamiah* means *place of rope litter*, and refers to the litter left behind when the dogbane stem was split to expose the useful inner fibers.

A drive down Kamiah's Main Street is a trip backwards in time, for local merchants and artists have given the shop facades a colorful Western Victorian appearance — a glimpse into Kamiah's past.

Mile 66.9 Kamiah's Riverfront Park lies along the river off the west end of the bridge here. Tables, a children's playground and a lovely setting make this a nice stopover for a picnic lunch or evening stroll. Toilets are available and RV parking is allowed.

Mile 67.3 Across the river, Lawyer's Creek enters the Clearwater from the west. It is named after Chief Lawyer, prominent figure of nineteenth century Nez Perce history. Given the name Lawyer by the whites because of his fine skills as an orator, it was he who negotiated the treaty of 1863, which reduced the size of the Nez Perce Reservation to a tenth of the size provided for in the treaty of 1855. The newer treaty set the backdrop for both the splitting of the Nez Perce people and the Nez Perce War of 1877.

Mile 68.5 The Nez Perce National Historical Park site situated here commemorates the legendary creation of the *Nee Mee Poo*, The People, today known as the Nez Perces. Cunning Coyote, magical creature of Plateau Indian mythology, had been tearing down waterfalls along the Columbia River to the west to enable more salmon to travel upstream during their spawning migration from the Pacific Ocean when he heard of a monster that was devouring all the creatures of the Kamiah Valley. Coyote heeded the news, readied himself with five sharp stone knives and a fire drill and trekked to the valley. Clever Coyote then proceeded to trick the monster into inhaling him. Once inside,

49

Coyote lit the fat surrounding the monster's heart on fire, which enabled the previously ingested animals to escape in the smoke through openings in the monster's body. Coyote then severed the monster's heart and made his own exit. Once free, Coyote cut pieces from the dead monster's body and cast them to locations near and far throughout the known world to create all other Indian tribes. Then Coyote created from the enormous heart's blood the noble Nee Mee Poo to inhabit the beautiful Kamiah Valley and the surrounding mountains, plateaus and valleys. Gradually the monster's heart turned to stone and to this day remains visible protruding from the earth in the center of the park.

To view the heart, turn into the parking lot. A short walk from there will lead you to an overlook and two interpretive panels. You may also follow a paved pathway to an interpretive audio station located nearer the Heart of the Monster. In addition, there is a nature path running to a riverside slough and looping back to the parking lot along which you may spot wildflowers, grasses, birds and small mammals. Picnic tables and a restroom are available along the pathways.

Early the evening of July 13, 1877, over seven hundred Nez Perces, those known as the *non-treaties*, began winding their way down the slopes visible on the west side of the river. The Indians were in retreat from the Battle of the Clearwater, the second major battle of the Nez Perce War. In family groups, on horseback and on foot, leading hastily loaded pack animals carrying all their possessions, they descended to the valley and made camp across the river from *treaty* Nez Perces who lived near the Presbyterian church and government buildings just upriver from this location. Some of the young men of the treaty Nez Perces were scouting for Howard's military troops from whom the warring Nez Perces were retreating. Indeed, the river must have seemed as if it were the least of barriers between a divided people.

The following morning lodge skins were sewn onto willow frames to create bulboats, and the entire westside camp began ferrying across the river. A rear guard watched from the top of the ridges for signs of Howard's forces. Young boys swam across the two thousand-plus horses that traveled with the Indians. Women and children paddled the skin bulboats. Included in one boat was the one-month old daughter of Chief Joseph, that chief whose name would later become prominently and indelibly intertwined with the story of the war.

The last families crossed, as two blue columns snaked along the horizon, and the front of the military line began its descent down the long ridge toward the west bank of the river. Under orders to engage the Indians, Captains David Perry and Stephen Whipple led their columns into the valley, along the river's edge and around the bluff near the non-treaties' now abandoned camp. Panic ensued among the soldiers when the Nez Perces' rear guard opened fire from the east side of the river. Many of the soldiers dismounted to run for cover and others galloped back up the slope. By the time these soldiers had regained their command, more approaching blue figures appeared high on the ridgetop. Gatling guns and howitzers were brought into position as Howard's main force continued its march to the river. However, by this time the main Nez Perce group had crossed the flat which lies here and was setting up camp in the safety of the hills to the east, and the defensive flank of warriors faded into nearby timber.

For a fourth time in this war which had begun on the Salmon River twenty-seven days before, Howard was separated from his quarry by a river. Howard's main forces

...it was a lovely sight we beheld on arriving at the heights overlooking the Kamai [Kamiah] Valley. The fields belonging to the still loyal [treaty] bands of Nez Perces were green with grain not yet ripe, the hills beyond clad in spring attire, the beautiful river flowing between, and the Agency buildings shining white in the background. In fact, all nature appeared to bloom with loveliness, and to us...all this cultivation seemed most inviting, especially amid the scenes enacting around us and the warlike prospects ahead.

Joseph and his warriors, having nothing, passed through and among these possessions of their peaceful brothers. He crossed the river with his own means of transport and took his stand on the bluffs beyond. He also deployed a number of his men on the riverbank, either to dispute its passage or inflict some damage on the troops as they approached. This the cavalry did rather incautiously and receiving several volleys retired in some haste, if not confusion. After a slight skirmish the hostiles retired out of range.

Major J.G. Trimble
U.S. Army

did not cross the river until July 28th, two weeks later. In the interim, he aborted a plan to travel by another route to the Weippe Prairie where he presumed the Nez Perces were headed. At one point he was forced to accept the retreat of a group of cavalry in pursuit of the Nez Perces when the troops' treaty Nez Perce scouts were ambushed. Howard also took time for a trip to Lapwai for more supplies. On Sunday, July 29th, he attended services in the First Presbyterian Church (Mile 68.9) and heard a sermon delivered by a Nez Perce convert named Archie Lawyer, whose father, Chief Lawyer, had been instrumental in treaty negotiations with government officials.

At 5 a.m. on July 30th, the troops began climbing the hills to the east of the church in a column that included over seven hundred men and stretched out over two miles. The seven hundred men, women and children of the non-treaty Nez Perces had by this time completed their journey over the mountainous Nez Perce Trail and were beginning their travel through the Bitterroot Valley in southwestern Montana. Howard would not again engage the Indians for two and a half months and over a thousand miles.

Mile 68.8 This area is referred to by locals as **East Kamiah**. The large, old brick house which sits near the river about a tenth of a mile from this location is the oldest brick house in Idaho County and the former home of Lydia and Felix Corbett, who ran a ferry crossing here during the early 1900s when this area was heavily frequented by white travelers and Nez Perces who camped or lived in this vicinity.

In 1874, Susan McBeth arrived in the Kamiah Valley. A slight and frail but determined woman, she was driven by God's calling to minister to the Nez Perces. She moved into the tiny, fenced house which stands on the west side of the highway here in East Kamiah and is known today as the McBeth House. Lame and, therefore, unable to walk to the nearby church each day, she established in one of her home's two rooms a classroom, complete with benches for students and eventually a small organ. Here she prepared young Nez Perce men for the Presbyterian ministry. She also wrote a 15,000-word Nez Perce dictionary which she later submitted to the Smithsonian Institution. In 1879, she was joined by her sister Kate, who started a class for Nez Perce women. Lessons included religion and house-

McBeth House, East Kamiah

keeping skills. The McBeths' joint efforts in Kamiah came to an abrupt end in 1884, when Sue was ordered off the reservation by Indian Agent Monteith with whom she had been in conflict for several months. Kate was allowed to remain on the reservation, but was ordered to Lapwai. She continued to minister to members of the Nez Perce tribe for another thirty years. Sue moved to Mount Idaho, near present day Grangeville, and continued to receive Nez Perce visitors there until the time of her death in 1893.

On the east side of the highway sits the Nez Perces' first church with its adjacent cemetery. The original congregation was organized in 1871 under the leadership of Reverend H.T. Cowley. Construction of the church itself was begun soon thereafter with lumber sawed at a new government mill which had been established for the Nez Perces. In the spring of 1873, having thirty-five years earlier abandoned his mission at Lapwai following the massacre of missionaries Marcus and Narcissa Whitman at their post near Walla Walla in 1847, the Reverend Henry Spalding arrived in East Kamiah for a two-year stay. The church appears today much as it did in the 1800s, and headstones in the cemetery serve as reminders of the early missionary period among the Nez Perces. The church is today the oldest continuously used church in Idaho.

The stretch of land on which the Heart of the Monster, the McBeth House and the church are situated was the center of much community activity among the Nez Perces in the 1800s. The United States Indian Agency had erected buildings for government work in the area, and many Indian tipis were staked on these grounds for gatherings and special occasions. Sometime prior to 1877, a flour mill, blacksmith's workshop and sawmill were constructed here, and the U.S. Government built a ferry at a crossing a short distance from the Heart of the Monster site (Mile 68.5). Later the ferry was moved downriver to a location near the mouth of Lawyer's Creek.

Mile 72.0 Button Beach, just below the large turnout here, is popular for summertime swimming and innertube launching and for fishing in the spring and fall.

Mile 73.9 KOOSKIA (koos kee) [**Population 650. All services available.**]

The South Fork of the Clearwater joins the Middle Fork here near the town of Kooskia. Both of these branches of the Clearwater wind deep into Idaho County, which is comprised of millions of acres of wild, mountainous backcountry within 8539 square miles of land. Encompassing more area than Connecticut, Deleware and Rhode Island combined, the county is Idaho's largest. As the colorful sign at Highway 12's entrance to the town indicates, Kooskia is known to locals and visitors as north central Idaho's Gateway to the Wilderness. Each year thousands of people think of the town as a staging hub for relaxing and invigorating *wild* experiences made possible by Mother Nature.

Near the entrance sign stands the informative Kooskia Crossing Kiosk. Its illustrated panels describe regional salmon and steelhead trout migrations, the early Nez Perces, the Nez Perce War of 1877, and the Nez Perce National Historical Park. The panels also explain the role of fire in wildlife management, particularly with respect to elk, and introduce you to four other popular wild animals.

A half-mile drive on Highway 13 via the bridge takes you to downtown Kooskia, nestled between the steep hill faces that fringe the valley of the South Fork. During the summer of 1861, the valley ushered hundreds of miners and their clanking gear along the river's path to the newly discovered gold fields at Elk City, fifty miles to the southeast. In little time, the miners also discovered beyond Elk City a special backcountry bath used for centuries by the Nez Perces: Red

River Hot Springs. Before long, too, the community of Dixie came into being as a second homesite of the miners. A side jaunt to Elk City and nearby Red River Springs and Dixie makes for a fun drive through beautiful country. To make the trip, turn to Side Trip #6 in the Side Trips chapter.

RV parking sites and a lovely picnic area alongside the South Fork are available at the City of Kooskia Lion's Park — from Main Street turn west onto Third Street and drive one block ahead. If you plan to enjoy the nearby forests, you may wish to stop at the USFS Lochsa Ranger District office at 502 Lowary Street for information — immediately after crossing the bridge turn left onto Broadway, drive one block and turn left again onto Lowary.

A seventy-foot long mural depicting the Lewis and Clark expedition's meeting with a group of Nez Perces delights visitors entering the business district. During their May 10-June 10, 1806, encampment about nine miles downstream from Kooskia, members of the Lewis and Clark Expedition made numerous visits to this part of the upper valley to pursue game and trade with the Nez Perces for food and supplies. The expeditionists' journals refer to several of these forays, which included visits to the confluence of the South and Middle Forks. The journalists also recorded the first written English renditions of the Nez Perces' spoken name for the river: Kooskooskia, Kooskooskie and Kooskooskee. Later translated as *clear water*, the word became respelled in English as Kooskia and in Nez Perce eventually spelled as *Koos Kyk'h Kyk'h*.

However, the town itself, platted in 1895, shortly after the opening of the Nez Perce Reservation to white settlement, was first called Stuart for James Stuart, a Nez Perce surveyor. The town quickly sprouted a hotel and restaurant, a blacksmith shop, furniture store, a sawmill and several general stores. In 1899, when the Clearwater Short Line reached this point, the name Kooskia was chosen for the rail station. Thereafter the station name gradually became used to refer to the town, and in 1909, the name was officially changed.

As you drive Main Street today, you can imagine those early years in Kooskia by noting several vintage, high-front buildings which still stand and give the town a true Old West flavor. For a brief time Kooskia was the terminus of the rail line and the departure point for traffic headed to

Stuart, Later Renamed Kooskia

the gold fields at Buffalo Hump, Thunder Mountain, Dixie and Elk City. When the line was extended to Stites, however, Kooskia settled into much of its present-day role as a small trade center for the forest-related and agricultural activities that largely support the residents of the surrounding area. Today Kooskia is also important as a supply and outfitting axis for hunters, horseback riders, hikers, rafters, kayakers and others bound for Idaho County's backcountry areas adjacent to the South Fork, Middle Fork, Selway and Lochsa Rivers.

At the turn of the century, Kooskia was the base of Idaho County's only grain and freight tramway, which ran down the hillside west of town. Warehouses on both ends of the 1 1/4-mile long tramway had a combined capacity of 100,000 bushels of grain. Two long, stout rings of cable carrying thirty buckets were capable of handling 190,000 pounds of wheat and other grains daily. Railway service to the prairie in 1908-'09 brought about the gradual loss of patronage for the tram. However, it remained in use until 1939.

U.S. Highway 13 runs through Kooskia's Main Street and continues southward to follow the South Fork. Highway 13 to Grangeville is a spur of the Northwest Passage Scenic Byway and traces yet another segment of the history of Clearwater Country. To travel to Grangeville turn to Side Trip #5 in the Side Trips chapter.

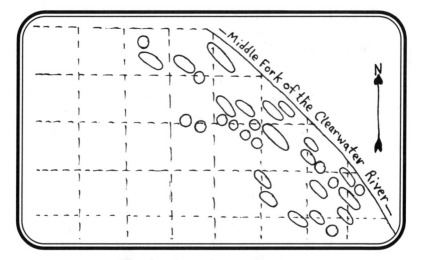

Ancient Village Site at Mile 74.7

Mile 74.7 Here along the Clearwater's Middle Fork, the large flat across the river was in earlier centuries a village site of the Nez Perce Indians. When anthropologist Herbert Spinden visited the site in 1907, he found trees up to eighteen inches in diameter growing inside lodge rings, which suggested the site had been unoccupied for many years. Lodge rings made of stones piled about one foot above ground were excavated two to three feet below ground. The circular rings were about twenty-five feet in diameter. Elongated rings were eighteen feet wide and sixty to eighty-five long. Firepits inside the latter were spaced about twelve feet apart. Spinden located twenty such longhouse rings and sixteen round rings. All longhouse rings were constructed parallel to the river's edge, and the circular lodges were scattered amongst them. The village site covered an area approximately eight hundred feet long and two hundred fifty feet wide on the flat opposite today's highway.

On several occasions in 1806, members of the Lewis and Clark Expedition came to the South Fork area to hunt, explore and trade with the Nez Perces for supplies in preparation for the explorers' upcoming eastward trek through the Bitterroots. On June 1st, two of the explorers, who had traveled eight miles upstream along the north side of the river, experienced a serious mishap, probably at this location. Captain Clark recorded the event:

Two of our men, who had been up the river to trade with the Indians, returned quite unsuccessful. Nearly opposite the village, their horse fell with his load down a steep cliff into the river, across which he swam. An Indian on the opposite side drove him back to them; but in crossing most of the articles were lost...Understanding their intentions, the Indians attempted to come over to them, but having no canoe, were obliged to use a raft, which struck on a rock, upset, and the whole store of roots and bread were destroyed...We therefore created a new fund, by cutting off the buttons from our clothes and preparing some eye-water and bascilicon, to which were added some phials and small tin boxes. With this cargo two men set out in the morning to trade, and brought home three bushels of roots and some bread, which, in our situation, was as important as the return of an East India ship.

Mile 75.2 In the early 1900s, the Boller Ferry offered a crossing point for settlers and Indians traveling to or from Kooskia. While the ferries of the day appeared small, they were large enough to carry horse-drawn wagons, some two at a time, horses and riders, and of course foot travelers. The ferry was guided across by cables which in some cases ran through a wheelhouse. Despite a modern perspective of the quaintness of such ferries, they were vital links in the travel and transportation routes of Clearwater Country.

Boller Ferry

Mile 75.9   On the south side of the Middle Fork, Clear Creek drains the draw that stretches into the hills. Shortly before the opening battle of the Nez Perce Indian War of 1877, Chief Looking Glass and his band moved to the flat along lower Clear Creek, which was within reservation boundaries and therefore in compliance with the Treaty of 1863. Looking Glass on two occasions sent his brother, Took-alix-see-ma, to the Nez Perce camp by Tolo Lake near present-day Grangeville to urge White Bird's and Joseph's people not to start a war with the whites.

After the war had begun, however, Gen. Howard became concerned that Looking Glass and his people might join the warring factions of the Nez Perces. Thus Howard ordered Captain Stephen Whipple with two cavalry companies to proceed to Looking Glass' camp and arrest him and his band and remove them to Mount Idaho on the edge of the Camas Prairie. Just after dawn on July 1, 1877, Whipple, his troops, and about twenty civilian volunteers from Grangeville began descending the hills visible on the west side of the creek. Befuddled by the soldiers' approach, Looking Glass twice sent an emissary under a white flag to explain to Whipple that this band was not involved in the war. Alas, however, the response was an edgy volunteer's rifle fire, followed by a spontaneous barrage of fire from the soldiers. Several Indians were wounded as they scattered into the foliage along the creekbed. Some swam the river here — a woman and her child-in-arms drowned in the attempt.

The soldiers destroyed the village, rounded up about seven hundred horses and a number of cattle and herded them all to Mount Idaho. Looking Glass and his band were left, no longer simply astonished, but enraged. Whipple had not only failed to carry out his assigned mission, he had also ensured the addition of Looking Glass' band to the numbers of warring Nez Perces. Three days later Looking Glass, Red Owl (from the lower South Fork), and approximately one hundred fifty men, women and children of their two bands joined the non-treaties at Cottonwood. The Nez Perces now had an embittered war leader, ready to fight to his death.

Today Kooskia National Fish Hatchery occupies the flat lying about a quarter mile up Clear Creek. The hatchery was established in 1969 as an adjunct to Dworshak National Fish Hatchery downriver near Orofino. The operations of both have played into regional efforts to mitigate chinook salmon and steelhead trout losses resulting from federal dams on the Clearwater and Snake Rivers in the Columbia River Basin. Salmon and also steelhead hatchlings are reared here in preparation for their journey to the ocean. Steelhead trout are spawned from February till May and chinook salmon in August and September. The hatchery is open daily for informal self-tours. Employees welcome questions. To reach the hatchery, cross the bridge at Mile 75.2 and turn immediately left onto Clear Creek Road; drive east about one mile.

Mile 76.3 Tukatesp'e, or *Skipping Stones*, picnic area lies here near a local swimming hole. There are tables and grills.

Your cooking a meal at this spot may be a more traditional activity than you imagine, for three to four thousand years ago, this was a kitchen and tool manufacturing area for the Natives living here then. An archaeological dig showed that, flanked with equipment and space for grinding grains and roots and butchering meat, a fire hearth was located here. A find of many stone tools indicated that this site was further used for scraping and tanning hides.

The facts that so much activity took place in such a small area as this and that archaelogists have been finding a plethora of evidence of ancient human habitation throughout Clearwater Country suggest that the population of humans in the river corridor three to four thousand years ago may have been much greater than was the Nez Perce population of the late 1700s. During the 1700s, the Nez Perces had interacted with European traders boating and trekking inland from the mouth of the Columbia River. The traders inadvertently brought diseases to which the Indians had not earlier been exposed. Anthropologists now feel certain that those diseases severely impacted the Natives during that century and caused their population to diminish.

From 1950 through 1975, this site was popular with some localites and most unpopular with others, for here was located Betty's Steam Bath. Those who frowned upon Betty's did so because the ladies who worked here offered more than a hot tub of water to visiting fellas. In the springtime, it's likely the ladies enjoyed this locale's wildflowers. Today's springtime visitors may enjoy them, too, by eyeing the north hillside. The first flowers to polka-dot emerging greens with yellow are buttercups and arrowleaf balsamroot. In years past, the Nez Perces ate the inner sections of young balsamroot flower stems and balsamroot seeds, roasted and ground.

Mile 76.8 Maggie Creek, which enters the Middle Fork here from the north, was named after a woman named Ip-Nah-My-Yah-Kin-My, who lived near here and had been given the English name Maggie.

On the hills across the river, grazing whitetail deer are often seen in the

Arrowleaf Balsamroot

early evening hours. Whitetails, in fact, may be spotted on either side of the river along the length of the Middle Fork.

The pale blue camas flower, whose roots have been so central to the Nez Perce diet, are noticeable, April through June, in the lower areas of the Middle Fork and the high prairies and meadows that lie above both sides of the valley. The narrow plant with grass-like leaves at its base grows from twelve to twenty inches tall when its six-petal blossoms open column-like along the upper half of its stem. After blossoming time, Nez Perce women for centuries past used fire-hardened, sharpened sticks about three feet long with antler crosspieces as handles to dig the bulb-shaped roots of the camas. The women then cooked the bulbs by placing them in a pit to bake for a couple of days. After being baked, the bulbs were eaten or dried or ground. The Nez Perces fed camas roots to the famished Lewis and Clark expeditionists when the latter first entered Clearwater Country on the Weippe Prairie in 1805.

Camas

Gathering Camas

Mile 77.1 Earlier in this century, Howard Wilson, known locally as the *white Indian*, lived here on the north side of the highway with his dogs in a semi-subterranean house on Indian land he had inherited from his Nez Perce foster mother, Sally Ann. She was wife of a white man, Billy Wilson, when Howard was traded to Sally Ann for a cow and calf by an Elk City woman who had reportedly found Howard in an orphanage in New York City. By unusual happenstance, Howard's natural mother, who then lived in California, later heard about him, came to see him and convinced him to move with her to California. However, after only a short stay there, Howard elected to return home to the Middle Fork where he remained the rest of his life.

Mile 78.7 In the 1950s, studies were conducted regarding the feasibility of a hydroelectric dam stretched across the valley at this location between the north and south bluffs. Were the plan carried out, Highway 12 and acres upon acres of its river valley surroundings upstream from this point would have been inundated with water.

The cliffs here are named Penny Cliffs after Ben Penny, a soldier who fought in the Nez Perce War of 1877 and then settled near here with his Nez Perce wife. An old wagon road which came up from Boller Ferry (Mile 75.2) swung around the south cliffs along the riverbed during low water.

Bald eagles frequent this section of the river autumn to spring. Because the early Nez Perces used eagle feathers as decorations for their hair and clothing, they sometimes took young eagles from nests and raised them in order to pluck the eagles' first and second sets of feathers. Then the birds were released.

Mile 79.5 In earlier centuries, Nez Perce foot travelers used a trail which routed them around the cliffs on the south side of the river. By driving poles into cracks in the rock and laying other poles across them, the Indians made crude walkways which bridged the most difficult sections.

Now and then beavers or trees felled by beavers are spotted along this stretch of the Middle Fork. Prior to the late eighteenth and early nineteenth centuries, beavers were widespread throughout much of North America. Then, great demand for beaver pelts began to increasingly lure trappers westward until, within a twenty year period, their success had decimated beaver populations. In Clearwater Country, however, the number of beavers had never been high, a fact which kept at bay trapping pressure along the Clearwater corridor. In retrospect, it was also a key reason the Nez Perces were one of the last of America's Native peoples to be encroached upon by Euro-Americans. Today, spotting these flat-tailed creatures in the corridor is a special treat.

Mile 80.4 Across the river from Red Pine Creek, once known as Penney Creek, which empties into the Middle Fork here from the north, a wagon road once plunged down the hillside, and crossed the river at the head of the island here. The wagon road offered a route to the Middle Fork and upriver points for folks living in Tahoe, a turn-of-the-century hilltop hamlet, now a rural residential area, as well as to residents of Kooskia (Mile 73.9). For a few years a post office named Lorena sat on the first bench above the river across from the creek. Supposedly the post office site was named in honor of the postmaster's lover who had jilted him and caused him much longing. Narcissus still bloom in right-angled rows where the post office once stood.

The large flat downriver from the post office site was once a favorite Nez Perce fishing campsite where in three days, according to an elderly Nez Perce woman, her band would catch "twenty-five horses" of salmon; that is, so many salmon that twenty-five pack horses would be needed to transport the fish. Traditionally the area was home to the Salwepu band of Nez Perces, who must have lived comfortably here, protected from rain or snow and hot summer sun by cedar bough umbrellas at the western corner of the flat where sunken circles of earth remain today as evidence of early inhabitants.

Later, the lower end of the flat was the site of a hand-hewn log hostel. Records show that "Although he [the hosteler] is a single man and the possibility exists that there will be female guests," the Idaho territorial governor granted a hosteler's license to the bachelor-owner "because he is a man of good repute."

Currently the acreage is home to Mountain Meadow Press, publisher of this book, CLEARWATER COUNTRY!, one of the publisher's Clearwater Collection books focused on the history of this region.

The cable car which carries the owners to and from the site was built in 1976 and is one of three private tramways which provide access to homes on the Middle Fork's south side. These trams are battery operated, suspended from 1 1/8-inch steel cables approximately five hundred feet long and have carrying capacities in excess of a thousand pounds. Years ago at various locations along the rivers, single-person trams hung on cables stretched from anchor points on each side of the river. A passenger would sit on a small platform or in a basket and hand-over-hand, or with a ratchet handle, pull himself across.

Mile 82.7 The availability of a stream or spring determined the locations of most towns, villages and homesites during the 1800s and early 1900s. Along the bank of Suttler Creek, a man named Charley Suttler settled in 1875. The creek quenched his need for water and irrigated his garden and orchard. The creek's source is high on Woodrat Mountain where an old log cabin once hosted a colony of woodrats. Locating alongside the creek no doubt also enabled Mr. Suttler to enjoy one of the most delicious and, at that time, plentiful foods of the region — salmon. According to an early twentieth century inhabitant of lower Suttler Creek, this stream literally teemed with salmon during the annual migration period.

Near the Charley Suttler homestead, a post office named Kooskia operated for a few years after the site was purchased by Mr. and Mrs. Frank P. Turner in 1889. The Turners eventually moved to the newly formed town of Stuart, now Kooskia, at the confluence of the rivers eight and one-half miles below. When they moved, the post office at Suttler Creek was left without a postmaster and was, therefore, also moved. Its new location was the bench across from Red Pine Creek, where it became the Lorena Post Office noted in the above Mile 80.4 entry.

Mile 87.5 You are here crossing the west boundary of the Clearwater National Forest, a U.S. Forest Service management area that includes 1.8 million acres of public land extending up the Lochsa River and including much of the watersheds of the North Fork of the Clearwater River and of the Palouse and Potlatch Rivers to the north. Elevations on the forest vary from sixteen hundred to nearly nine thousand feet. This variation creates what many call a *vertical climate*, indicating that the weather, flora and fauna at any one point in time can differ greatly from lower elevations to higher. A spring day in the valley, for example, may remain a winter day in the high country. Wildflower blossoming in the valley may be followed weeks later by blossoming near the mountaintops. Deer and elk meander downhill, to warm sunny slopes on spring days but uphill to cool high-elevation meadows in July.

Were we to combine the Clearwater National Forest with its neighboring Nez Perce National Forest to the south, we would realize that in this region over four million acres of forest and five thousand miles of trails are available for the enjoyment of outdoor recreationists. Taken together, these two forests include as much land mass as the two states of Rhode Island and Delaware combined, more than the state of Connecticut, almost as much as the state of New Jersey. These forests are, in turn, bordered by the St. Joe National Forest to the north, the Lolo National Forest to the east, and the Payette National Forest to the south. It is not difficult to conclude that Clearwater Country offers a vast wild wonderland of the non-commercial sort for visitors like you.

Mile 88.4 Ranger Station Number One was erected at this site in 1929. It became a busy stop for travelers who needed campfire permits and forest information. The cottonwoods and other deciduous trees on the small bench to the north of the highway provide clues to the old station's former location. Today the sand beach below the highway here is simply known as *Number One* by locals and has for years been a popular swimming and picnicking spot.

On the highway's north side, Smith Creek Road (Forest Road #101) winds up the mountainsides to the west entrance of the historic Lolo Motorway, which generally traces the route of the Nez Perce National Historic Trail, also recognized as the Lewis and Clark National Historic Trail and the Lolo Trail. However, before embarking on a Smith Creek Road side trip, stop at the USFS Station at Kooskia for information. Smith Creek Road is steep, narrow and curvy and is unsuited for motorhome or most pull-trailer traffic. Also, entrance to the west end of the Motorway may be restricted during the Lewis and Clark Bicentennial years.

Swan Creek flows into the Middle Fork here from the north above the beach. While swans are not often seen in the river corridor in large numbers, in the autumn, travelers may see a few tundra swans resting on the waters of the Middle Fork for a day or two during their annual north-to-south migration. To sleep on the water, the swans anchor themselves by standing on rocks in the shallows, then, turning their heads backwards, they lay their long necks and chins down across their backs which serve as convenient soft pillows. One swan will stay awake, standing guard and cooing quiet reassurances every few minutes to let the sleepers know that all is well. With heads down, the swans can be mistaken for flotillas of snow...or queen-size fluffs of meringue!

Mile 90.0 SYRINGA

From 1896 through 1908, the community of Syringa boasted its own post office. Local folk grew peaches, plums, pears, cherries, grapes and apples here, but the winter weather made orchards difficult to maintain. Some folks raised sheep, but struggled to keep the woolies out of the claws of cougars. In August 1910, resident Cora McLean, fed up with the loss of several sheep, set out to solve the problem. After one missed shot, with two bullets she felled one of the largest cougars ever seen in the area. While the hamlet's population of people and cougars has fluctuated since those years, Syringa remains a recreational hub.

From the north a little upstream from here, Big Smith Creek flows through the community on its way to the Middle Fork, along which you may find the syringa shrub, after which the community is named. The syringa is a native variety of mock orange that grows from six to twelve feet high and displays delicate white blossoms in May and June. The syringa is the Idaho State Flower. The Nez Perces used the syringa's leaves, softened into a pulp, for soap and its tough stems for bows.

In areas like this along the Middle Fork, ospreys may be seen perched in large nests of sticks atop dead tree snags which tower over the river, or the birds may be seen circling the clear stream to spot fish. With its whitish breast and head and brownish-black coloring elsewhere, an osprey can be mistaken for a bald eagle. Like the eagle, the osprey is a member of the hawk family, but is the only hawk that dives towards the water then plunges feet-first to catch a fish. It is also smaller than the eagle. The osprey typically emits sharp whistles, but when its nest is threatened, a shrill *cheereek*.

Syringa

Mile 91.5 All along the rivers that flow through Clearwater Country, such as the Middle Fork running here, one should not be surprised to spot a fat porcupine lumbering up a hillside, a family of raccoons retreating up a tree, a snowshoe rabbit hopping into roadside grasses, an otter slipping through the water as if he too were liquid, or a beaver slapping a wet warning when humans approach. Watchfulness often results in sightings of these and other wild creatures all along the Clearwater Country route.

During spring, summer and fall, wildflowers of many sorts blossom throughout the area. Particularly showy are cascades of ocean spray, a tall bush with clusters of white blossoms which look like the spray of ocean waves. Another splendid display of blossoms may be seen along the roadside in patches of purplish-pink fireweed. While these fiery-colored blossoms may resemble a field aflame, the plant actually was given its name because of its tendency to be one of the first plants to sprout in burned areas of the forest. In early spring, winter's brown hills flourish with white plum blossoms, and the blackberry bushes begin to bud. By mid-August, both plums and berries will be ripe. Enjoy!

Mile 93.2 During the early 1900s, in a little cabin near the mouth of Two Shadows Creek, a man named Miller lived. He was a loner, a woodsman, well known for his fine dewberry wine and for his pet skunk. The small meadow on which remnants of his cabin sit later served as a crew camp during the pick and shovel construction of the first wagon and auto road up the river.

Mile 94.3 Three Devils Picnic Area, situated here, is a local favorite and offers travelers a great place for a stop. Three Devils includes tables, grills, water, toilets and two hundred yards of leisure-enticing sand. Even a five minute stroll through the trees is worthwhile.

Early day loggers, skilled at cross-cut sawing and fast-footed log birling, floated poles and logs down the Middle Fork during spring high water. However, only the highest of spring runoffs would enable the timber to escape the clutches of the *three devils*, three large boulders blocking the center of the channel in the rapids that run past the upper portion of the beach. In about 1922, the *devils* were blasted away in order to remove this obstacle to the then growing lumber industry in the region.

A number of beaches, such as Three Devils Beach, lie along the Middle Fork and are enjoyed by travelers and locals June to October — for swimming, picnicking, quiet conversation or lone contemplation. Hoping to capture the ambiance of a season, now and then artists and photographers set up solitary workshops in the sands. Early summer or early autumn fly fishers leave ridged wader prints on the sand as they slosh into the river to lay a line across deep pools on the shadowy opposite side of the river. In the heat of the summer, you may see rafters hauled out for lunch on a south side beach.

Mile 95.3 Wild Goose Campground, situated here, is named after year-round residents of Clearwater Country — Canada geese. Flocks of these large, dark geese with black heads and

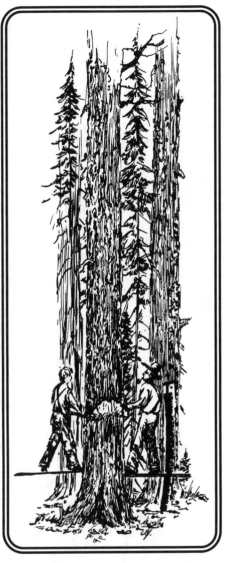

Cross-cut Sawing

white chin straps frequent the river and feed in nearby grain fields. Their loud, familiar honks often alert travelers to look overhead for a v-shaped flock in flight.

Although an uncommon visitor to Clearwater Country these days, flocks of sandhill cranes do also sometimes fly over, often so high they can barely be seen. A flock of cranes sounds similar to Canada geese but looks like a flock of blue herons wearing bustles and red caps. However, if the honks come from *high* overhead, the birds are likely to be cranes. If you spot a silent, lone grayish-blue bird standing stately and tall on the river's edge, it is likely to be a heron.

Year's past, sandhill cranes were more frequent in this area, as suggested by several local place names, such as Crane Meadows and Crane Hill. During their late spring 1806 stay in the Kamiah Valley (Miles 65.0-69.0), a member of the Lewis and Clark expedition brought in a few-day's-old sandhill crane specimen, and Lewis noted that "crains are abundant in this neighbourhood." Clark recorded that the cranes were usually seen in pairs and threes.

Wild Goose Campground includes seven campsites with picnic tables, fire pits and grills, water and toilets, midst large red cedars and grand firs. A picnic-only area and small beach further complement this beautiful setting.

Mile 96.6 Just upstream from the large vehicle pullout here, the Lochsa and Selway Rivers join to create the Middle Fork of the Clearwater River. An interpretive sign here details the Forest Service campgrounds on the Lochsa and Selway and notes area hiking trails. The sign also provides information about four of the river corridor's inhabitants: elk, geese, river otter and osprey.

Mile 97.0 LOWELL [All services available.]
One day in the late 1890s, lost and starved Henry Lowell literally stumbled into Clearwater Country and was rescued and nursed back to health by Billy Parry. Parry had earlier settled near here after searching for a new home that might match his New England physician's recommendations. While the community of Lowell was never platted, a post office was established here in 1903 for the twenty-one residents who lived in the vicinity. Then the place needed an address, and the name of the first postmaster, Henry Lowell, seemed to suffice.

The Lochsa River derived its name from the Flathead Indian word for *rough water*. Much of its sixty-five mile length is considered to be one of the nation's finest whitewater kayaking runs. The Selway, a stretch of over one hundred miles of virgin river — the longest such stretch in the contiguous United States — winds through a narrow, rugged, forested canyon. According to local historians, Selway is also a name derived from an Indian language and means *smooth water*. Eighteen miles up the road which follows the pristine Selway River, fifty-foot high Selway Falls roars over giant rocks, disputing the denotation of the river's name. The first six miles of the road are paved, and the road ends a short distance above the falls at the head of the Selway River Trail, a horseback and hiking trail which laces its way through the wilderness. USFS campsites await visitors along the way. To travel the Selway River Road, see Side Trip #7 in the Side Trips chapter.

Before the 1961 completion of Highway 12, Lowell was a welcomed stopping off point for folks who ventured to travel the potholed, dusty road that wound a little farther into the mountains. Today Lowell is every bit as pleasurable a place to stop — to take a leisurely drive up the Selway, to hike lightly or hike seriously, to fish, swim, raft or kayak, or pack a horse for a trip into the wilderness.

Mile 97.4 Lottie Creek enters the Lochsa from the south. This creek was named after Lottie Casady, daughter of Billy Parry's wife Maude, all of whom lived in Kooskia during the early 1900s and spent summers horseback riding and camping in the Lochsa and Selway River region. (See related entry at Mile 97.0.) Just upriver from this point, an old cable car hangs. Such cars once took folks, hand-over-hand, across area rivers.

Mile 99.0 In the 1880s, after pursuing many of the gold strikes made in the west, Pete King came into the country. As an eighteen-year-old, his first experiences in the California gold rush had apparently sealed his vocational destiny. The creek that enters the Lochsa here and bears his name became the terminus of his gold-bespeckled dreams. Here he built a cabin and proceeded to spend two thousand dollars in a vain attempt to divert the stream to a new, more productive channel as part of his mining operations. Productivity, however, was not the result.

Pete King was also the name given to a ranger station built in 1908-'09 at the present site of the Idaho highway maintenance station a short distance downstream. When a road reached this location in 1920, the station became a supply center for those who managed the surrounding forest. In time the station joined Pete King as part of Lochsa history.

In 1934, raging fires swept along the Lochsa and Selway Rivers after being given their first wind in an old burn on Pete King Creek. The fire jumped the Lochsa and blazed its tentacles up the Selway while another fiery appendage crawled up the Lochsa's south side. Another fire started at the same time on McLendon Butte, blackened a route up both sides of the Lochsa and burned into the Gold Creek and Boulder Creek drainages at higher elevations. Eight thousand men fought the Pete King fire, all the men the Forest Service at Missoula could possibly round up for the fire lines. By the time fall rains finally put out the fire, 275,000 acres lay burned. The devastation this fire wrought is still visible today, but as the forest will, it sprouted new growth the following spring and began the natural process of rejuvenation, and the low, tender brush provided needed forage for big game grazers.

Mile 100.0 Cat Creek enters the Lochsa from the south. The creek has likely been named after the regions' biggest cat, the tawny-colored cougar, or mountain lion. Cougars can grow to five or six feet in length...plus a three-foot tail! Often slinking unnoticed through grasses and brush, cougars are rarely seen by humans, notwithstanding the fact that they often inhabit draws adjacent to tributaries of the area's main rivers and hunt at times at low elevations. The latter is particularly the case in winter when deer and elk leave the increasingly deep snows of the high country to forage at lower elevations.

Mile 103.2 Hellgate Creek which enters the Lochsa on the south here is named for Hellgate Rapids which froths and boils below the creek's mouth.

Mile 103.9 In 1907, Canyon Creek, flowing into the Lochsa here, played a role in a war that was being waged by two national railroad giants, the Northern Pacific and a branch of the Union Pacific called the Oregon Railway and Navigation Company. The objective of the dispute was the linkage of major lines which approached Idaho from both east and west and the prized timber, mineral and agricultural resources of the Clearwater Country region. Survey crews pushed their way up the Clearwater. One railroad company selected the north side of the Lochsa and the other the south side, and the race began.

When the OR&N crews reached Canyon Creek, they built a pack bridge to enable mule trains to continue bringing in supplies. One of the OR&N crewmen, known only as

Johnnie Behind the Rock, was strategically positioned —
and we can presume well armed — to allow only OR&N
crew members to cross the bridge. The men of the Northern
Pacific were thus forced to construct their own bridge
across the creek, which they did. The same process was
then repeated at Deadman Creek farther upstream. During
this competition the two crews also pulled up each other's
survey stakes and cut loose one another's boats and pack
animals. The race came to an abrupt end when a truce was
declared between the two railroad giants and the decision
was finally made to abandon altogether the idea of a rail
line up the Lochsa. The river and its canyon had once again
earned its Indian name, Lochsa — *rough river.*

In 1935, Canyon Creek became the site of a federal
prison work camp housing up to one hundred seventy prisoners whose task was to build road. They labored eight hours a
day and in the first three years completed eight miles of
roadbed. In 1943, the camp's occupants were replaced by one
hundred thirty-five Japanese American internees, sent here
during WWII. They were detained here for two years, during
which time they too worked on the road.

Mile 104.3 Apgar Campground is named for an early day
fire crewman in the Lochsa Ranger District. This wooded
campground along the Lochsa provides picnic tables, fire
rings and grills, water, toilets and seven campsites nestled
among cedars. Access could be difficult for large
motorhomes or vehicles with long pull-trailers.

Here, in the camp area, the Carlin Hunting party, spoken of below (Mile 105.4), spent 2 1/2 days recovering from
a life-threatening ordeal after being rescued by military
personnel a mile upstream.

Mile 105.0 Lovely Glade Creek Campground, another of
the smaller USFS campgrounds along the Lochsa, includes
eight campsites, fire rings, toilets and a bit of beach. Glade
Creek enters the Lochsa here from the north.

Mile 105.4 On November 22, 1893, this site was the scene
of a dramatic rescue. A five-man hunting party known as
the Carlin party had become trapped in the canyon by deep
snows in the vicinity of Jerry Johnson Hot Springs (Mile
150.3). In desperation, they made a failed attempt to raft
the Lochsa's churning, icy waters to safety. When they
could see that this plan was doomed, four members of the

party abandoned George Colgate, their sick cook, and spent twenty days clawing their way along twenty-five miles of snow-covered bluffs and brush beside the river until they were finally rescued here.

Mile 106.7 In 1908, a man's skeleton was found in a cabin about three miles up the creek that enters the Lochsa here from the north and buried nearby. The man was never identified, and so a creek that might have been called by a proper name simply became known as Deadman Creek.

During the race between the Northern Pacific and Union Pacific Railroads to survey a rail line up the Lochsa each built a separate pack bridge across Deadman Creek. The distance between the two bridges? Less than ten feet! (See related story at Mile 103.9.)

Mile 108.4 Knife Edge River Access, located here, is one of a series of relatively new boat access sites along the Lochsa. These sites have been developed in response to increasing numbers of whitewater kayakers and rafters who flock to this river and to the Selway River during late spring high water time. Both of these rivers stir excitement and offer thrills to those seeking truly wild Clearwater Country experiences. The colorful names river runners have given some of the Lochsa's rapids testify to the river's rowdiness: Eye Opener, Triple Hole, Ten Pin Alley, Killer Fang Falls, Grim Reaper and Big Drop. If you are looking for a river run, guides are available at Lowell (Mile 97.0). If you're traveling along the Lochsa during highwater time but do not want to run the river yourself, keep your eye out for the wild ones wearing wetsuits riding the waves.

The name of the access site, Knife Edge, duplicates the name of the narrow, serrated-looking ridge which runs along the south side of and parallel to the river. Boat access sites such as this may be used for camping if, as is the case with Knife Edge, campsites are built into the area.

Mile 109.2 Coolwater Creek enters from the south, across the river here from an inviting beach.

Coolwater Creek drops down from Coolwater Ridge, where a number of years ago the Idaho Fish and Game Department live-trapped over one hundred black bears as part of a study on elk calf predation. The bears were tagged and transported to other national forests, some as distant as three hundred miles. The following spring, when department personnel conducted a similar but smaller trapping project, they discovered with surprise that many of the newly trapped bears wore ear tags — the earlier trapped bears had found their way home.

Mile 110.0 Bimerick Creek which enters the Lochsa from the north here drains Bimerick Meadows which lie high on 5562-foot McLendon Butte. In 1906, the creek and meadows were named Bimerick after a trapper and prospector who worked in the area. The meadows are popular elk grazing grounds and, of course, hunting grounds for people in the autumn. The State of Idaho distributes hunting licenses to about 200,000 Idahoans and almost 25,000 out-of-staters each year, as Idaho boasts one of the West's finest, most diversified big game populations.

Mile 110.6 Fire Creek, entering on the south side here, serves to remind us that in late summer, hot sun, low humidity and lightning storms can spark fire in the forest. Old cedar snags still standing sentinel along the river's edge here were once witness to the ravages of a forest fire.

Mile 111.9 The creek which flows into the Lochsa from the south here is called Split Creek due to the way in which it has divided itself near its mouth. The Split Creek Pack Bridge, four-tenths mile west, leads to Split Creek Trail which runs up the bank of the Lochsa and then climbs the face of the ridge on the east side of the creek's valley, affording a hiker or horseback rider access to the wilderness.

Each year as spring snows diminish throughout Clearwater Country, crossings such as this carry strings of riders leading pack horses and mules with pairs of large canvas packs slung from side to side over their backs. Saddles creak, a "giddi-up" is heard, and the line moves ahead on a slow, steady, and now and then perilous trek into the wilderness. In the early days, such trains of riders and pack animals were the only means of traveling from place to place, a functional necessity. Today they provide pleasure to a growing number of backcountry horse people. The trail access area here accommodates horses.

Split Creek Trail forms part of the Idaho Centennial Trail, which traverses the length of the state. The Centennial Trail merges here with the Lochsa River Historical Trail, running north of and paralleling Highway 12 upstream ten miles. (See Trails in the Recreation chapter.)

A few Pacific Dogwood trees grow to twenty feet tall above the trailhead parking pullout on the north side of the highway. In June, you may spot their large, showy white blossoms or later, their red berries. This area along the Lochsa and parts of the Lower Selway River valley constitute what botanists call a coastal disjunct, an ecosystem niche that contains several plant species rarely found east of the Cascade Mountains of western Washington.

At this point Highway 12 enters a fourteen thousand square mile region known to geologists as the Idaho batholith, under which lies a vast bed of granite created nearly eighty million years ago.

Mile 113.4 Old Man Creek finds its way to the Lochsa from its origin at Old Man Lake in the mountains to the south. According to local lore, Nez Perce hunters traveled to the lake in late summer and early fall, and the older men of the party would remain in camp at the lake while the younger Indians climbed still higher into the mountains.

Mile 114.9 On the south side of the river, Horsetail Falls Creek fans out across the face of a rock ledge before cascading like a wild white horsetail over the bluff. The fall's grandest season is, of course, springtime when its ice and snow-fed water is at its greatest volume.

While such springtime wetness usually quenches the forest's need for water, it can not prevent the scorching that may occur summer to late fall when forest fires burst out at sundry spots. Some years those fires are minimal in extent and duration and are natural and even healthy events that allow areas of the forest to be replenished by new growth. Now and then, however, the extent and duration of seasonal fires is exceptional, such as the more than thirty-one hundred fires of 1910. The first fire call came in May with more to follow in June, but the fires which raged during July and August throughout the Clearwater, St. Joe, Flathead, and Lolo National Forests drew more than ten thousand civilian fire fighters into action. In mid-August just as the thousands of fire fighters on the fire lines thought the blazes might be controlled, a wind of unusual velocity swept the blazes into an inferno. Miles upon miles of fire trenches were hastily abandoned as safety became the focus of both Forest Service personnel and civilians. One crew was forced to cling like frail spiders to the breast of an outcropping of granite while the flames and smoke swirled around them. Another crew under the leadership of Forest Ranger Ed Pulaski took shelter in a sweltering hot and smoky cave. At one point Pulaski dropped the wet blanket he held over the mouth of the cave in order to knock to the ground two of his men trying to flee. Although Pulaski suffered severe burns on his head and arms, he had ensured the safety of all but one of his fifty men. On the Clearwater itself, fire fighters dashed into the river, dunked themselves fully under water, and held bunches of wet clothes over their heads for protection when they surfaced for air. One among them shared his watery haven with a similarly frightened black bear. Within two days, three million acres, including thousands in the Lochsa region, had been blackened, destroying about eight billion feet of virgin timber. Eighty-five people, mostly fire fighters, had died. Fiery 1910 still holds the record for the most devastating fire season in the history of Idaho.

The area you are driving through here is known as the Black Canyon of the Lochsa. From Fish Creek at Mile 120.1 to Split Creek at Mile 111.9, the canyon walls are particularly close and steep and, hence, limit the amount of sunlight that can reach the river.

Mile 115.4 Shoestring Falls, opposite the highway here, looks like a foaming daredevil leaping from rock shelf to rock shelf in the spring, but for most of the year the falls flows narrowly through the rocks and deserves its name.

This area is the range of rocky mountain goats, which occasionally can be seen from the roadway on high, rocky outcrops near the top of either side of the canyon. The goats will first appear as small white figures, hardly noticeable until they move against a background of grays and greens. The Clearwater Mountains, which range north and south along the western side of the Bitterroot Mountains, have been home to goats for centuries. On their return trip through these mountains, Lewis and Clark's three Nez Perce guides advised the explorers that many goats inhabited an area north and east of here. The Nez Perces, who hunted these animals, referred to them as *white buffalo*. During Lewis and Clark's June 1806 stay among the Nez Perces in the Kamiah Valley, the explorers obtained from the Indians enough goat hair to restuff the pads of their saddles.

Mile 117.6 An interpretive sign located here provides information about the Selway Bitterroot Wilderness, along the northern edge of which you are driving. The capitalized word "Wilderness" is an official designation carrying particular meaning. Travel, for example, in designated wilderness areas is limited to hiking or horseback riding, and most forest management processes — including fire — are left to nature. The 1.2 million acre Selway Bitterroot is one of a precious series of crown jewels — that is, of remaining wildernesses in the United States. On the south, it is bordered by the 2.4 million acre Frank Church/River of No Return Wilderness, the single largest designated wilderness in the contiguous forty-eight states. Because these two central Idaho wildernesses are themselves surrounded by national forests, you are traveling through the vastest concentration of authentically wild country left in the United States, outside of Alaska.

The Selway Bitterroot gets its name from the Selway River which joins the Lochsa to create the Middle Fork of the Clearwater at Mile 97.0 and the Bitterroot Mountains which run north and south along the Idaho-Montana border. The mountain range's name derives from a plant that grows most commonly in the mountain regions of Montana and Oregon. The Nez Perce Indians used the roots of the bitterroot, dried or boiled, for food.

The Frank Church/River of No Return Wilderness gets its name, likewise, from two sources. The River of No Return is the famed Salmon River, which runs through the wilderness. Frank Church was from 1956 to 1980 a prominent United States senator from Idaho who favored environmental protection.

During their 1805 westward journey, the Lewis and Clark expeditionists traversed the Nez Perce Trail, which runs north of here in a direction roughly parallel to the river and Highway 12. Maps of the party's route have since been dotted with names given to the explorer's camps, in some cases originally by them, but eventually for permanent use by former forester and local historian Ralph Space, who had carefully studied the trail. The names include Portable Soup Camp, Jerusalem Artichoke Camp, and Horsesteak Meadow Camp — names which certainly depict the state of their food supply. At Jerusalem Artichoke Camp, for example, Sacagawea had introduced the explorers to an edible wild plant much like artichokes which became their evening's meal. Gradually the expedition descended to lower elevations and the names of the camps change in tone — Full Stomach Camp and Salmon Trout Camp. However, they would again find themselves hungry before their trail finally opened onto the Weippe Prairie, about forty-five miles west of this location.

Mile 119.2 Eel Creek flows in from the north here. Eel Creek receives its name from the Pacific lamprey eels that spend up to half of their life cycle in mountain streams and rivers such as those of the upper Lochsa canyon. For about five years, eels live here as blind, toothless creatures that feed on algae in the gravel. The eels then migrate like salmon to the sea where they attach themselves to ocean fish and live as parasites for two to three years, growing in length to two or more feet. Then, again like salmon, the urge to return to their home stream to spawn causes them to travel upstream hundreds of miles to the place of their birth. For centuries, the lampreys have been a part of the traditional diet of the Nez Perce Indians.

Eels are also believed to protect salmon smolts migrating to the sea by providing alternate prey for predators pursuing young salmon. However, no efforts were made in the construction of eight downriver dams to address passage of lamprey eels, and the numbers of eel adults migrating back to Clearwater Country during the past twenty years has declined by an estimated ninety-five percent.

Mile 120.1 A large pullout here serves as a boat access area, trailhead and general rest stop. From the highway's south fringe, steps lead down the riverbank to a small sandy beach. In summer, the cool waters of the Lochsa make for good swimming. In spring and early summer, whitewater adventurers launch kayaks and rafts from the beach.

Fish Creek flows into the Lochsa from the north. Fish Creek Trail, which begins a half mile up the dirt road running north of Highway 12 alongside the creek, gives hikers and horseback riders access to sixty thousand acres of roadless canyon country, a prime habitat for deer, elk, bear, cougar, many smaller animals and fish. If you're in the mood for a short, relatively easy hike and, perhaps, an opportunity to drop a fishing line into a cold stream, you may enjoy the first stretch of Fish Creek Trail. After leaving the creek at the trailhead, in about one hour's walking time, the trail returns to the creek at the base of a deep mountain valley. If you'd like to continue past this point, refer to the Trails section of the Recreation chapter in this book.

A few paces up the north side dirt road, you'll find access also to the Lochsa River Historical Trail, running east and west from this point. (See Mile 121.6 and the Trails section of the Recreation chapter for more information.)

On their 1805 westward journey, part of the Lewis and Clark expeditionist's route paralleled Fish Creek. The explorers camped beside a connecting stream, Hungery Creek, on September 18th. Hungery Creek flows into Fish Creek at a point roughly five miles up Fish Creek Trail.

Fish Creek earned its name by offering great rainbow and cutthroat trout fishing to locals, albeit greater in earlier years than now. One fish that has, in fact, become diminished in population to the point that it was in 1998 listed as *threatened* under the Endangered Species Act is the bull trout, often called the dolly varden. Catching this olive green fish with yellow spots on their backs and salmon or orange spots on their sides is illegal.

Fish Creek has also served as spawning grounds for steelhead and salmon. In the spring as sunshine melts mountain snows, four-to-six-inch steelhead and salmon smolts here begin their six hundred mile journey to the Pacific Ocean. Some of these are native fish; others are planted stock. Planted fish have been raised to the fingerling stage in hatcheries at Kooskia and Orofino, as part of the ongoing, but not highly successful, struggle to save the anadromous fish runs that once were so integral to the natural processes of Clearwater Country habitats.

Mile 121.6 The Lochsa Historical Ranger Station, located here, was built in 1920 as a Forest Service station and then converted in 1976 to a historical walking tour of an early day ranger station. Among the museum's volunteer staff are retired forest service employees and local folks who have lived and worked in national forests. The station is open to visitors seven days a week, 9 a.m. to 4 p.m., from Memorial Day through Labor Day weekend.

The Lochsa River Historical Trail is part of the original trail used by early Forest Service employees to bring supplies upriver to the ranger station. This trail parallels U.S. 12 between Sherman Creek (Mile 122.6) and Split Creek

(Mile 111.9), wending its way along the north side of the canyon and affording views of the Selway Bitterroot Wilderness to the south. This trail is also a part of the Idaho Centennial Trail, which traverses the full length of Idaho. The Centennial Trail leaves the Lochsa at Sherman Creek and begins an ascent to the historic Nez Perce Trail which follows the ridge that divides the Lochsa drainage from that of the North Fork of the Clearwater River.

Mile 122.6 With its eighty-nine sites, Wilderness Gateway Campground is the largest of the Lochsa campgrounds. Eleven of its sites include hitching racks and other accomodations for trail riders and stock. Available here, too, are a children's playground, covered picnic shelter, RV dump station, short walking trails, and an ampitheater for gatherings and performances. A camp host lives here during the summer months and is available for questions.

Boulder Creek Trail begins at the campground and leads backpackers and horse riders to Stanley Hot Springs (about five miles in) and further into the Wilderness. The trail shares its name with the creek flowing from the south.

Sherman Creek, which empties into the Lochsa from the north, rises on 6696-foot Sherman Peak, named in 1868 in honor of Gen. William T. Sherman by a U.S. Army officer, Major Truax, who led a crew trying to build a roadway across the Bitterroots. The peak is a remembered September 18, 1805, landmark of the Lewis and Clark Expedition because it was from high on this mountain that Clark first caught sight of the Camas Prairie to the southwest and felt a surge of excitement at knowing these

> ...cold morning. I proceeded on in advance with six hunters to...find deer or something to kill and send back to the party. The want of provisions, together with the difficulty of passing the mountains, dampened the spirits of the party, which induced us to resort to some plan of reviving their spirits... From the top of a high mountain [Sherman Peak] at twenty miles, I had a view of an immense plain and level country to the Sw and W. ...Made 32 miles and encamped on a bold running creek passing to the left, which I call Hungery Creek, as...we had nothing to eat.
>
> William Clark
> Sept. 18, 1805

rugged mountains eventually did level off. Viewing the prairie revived the explorers' spirits at least modestly as they trudged hungry and cold through this country.

Mile 124.8 Noseeum Creek's name commemorates an Idaho critter which may not deserve such recognition, for the noseeum (*no see um*) is a tiny black bug that in some parts of Clearwater Country can be particularly annoying to people. The bug is called the noseeum, because it is so difficult to see, although easy to feel — ouch!

Mile 128.5 Bald Mountain, believed to be so-named because of its barrenness, gives rise to Bald Mountain Creek, which empties into the Lochsa here.

On their homeward trip in 1806, the Lewis and Clark party were led to Bald Mountain by their three Nez Perce guides, who managed to bring the explorers to a suitable camp each evening despite the obliteration of much of the trail by snow. On June 26th, the day they arrived at Bald Mountain, they had traveled across a mountainous region where the snow "was 10 feet 10 inches deep on the top...," according to Clark's journal. Apparently snows were melting late that year, but the southerly exposed side of Bald Mountain had been, as Clark estimated, free of snow for about ten days. Fresh shoots of grass covered the hillside, and Clark remarked in his journal,

Bear Grass

...there is a great abundance of Species of beargrass which grows on every part of those Mountains, its growth is luxuriant and continues green all winter...

The bear grass plant, which is sometimes called Indian basket grass, is evident in Idaho's mountainous regions from June through August. Its bouquet-like cluster of long, sharp-edged blades of grass are thought to provide roughage for bears when they first emerge from their dens in the spring. In the summer a tall, tough stem, up to five feet, grows out of the center of the plant and blossoms at the top into a large, lightbulb-shaped white flower cluster. Besides baskets, the Nez Perces of the past wove bear grass and cedar bark together to make fez-style hats worn particularly by the women. Herbert J. Spinden, who conducted a 1907 study of the Nez Perce culture under the auspices of the Peabody Museum of Harvard University, noted in his report that bear grass was "used either in its natural cream color or stained dark brown or yellow." He also stated that at the top of the hat pendants were sometimes hung from a "double thong," and that hat decorations were typically "zigzags." Today, bear grass leaves are harvested by Northwesterners who dry them for use in commercial basket making — hopefully, with care for resource sustainability.

As the Lewis and Clark party surveyed the Bitterroots from Bald Mountain, they found the view frighteningly magnificent. Wrote Lewis in apparent growing appreciation for their guides,

> From this place we had an extencive view of these Stupendous Mountains, principally covered with snow like that on which we stood; we were entirely serounded by those mountains, from which, to one unacquainted with them, it would have Seemed impossible ever to have escaped, in short without the assistance of our guides, I doubt much whether we, who had once passed them could find our way to Travelers rest... those Indians are most admireable pilots.

While the horses enjoyed their much needed food, the explorers' hunting efforts had proved less rewarding. A journal entry informs us that on the next day the evening meal consisted of "a pint of bears oil to a man, which with their boiled roots, made an agreeable dish."

Mile 129.6 Nine Mile River Access is a popular access point for whitewater enthusiasts bearing kayaks and rafts.

Mile 131.3 Holly Creek enters from the north. A plant that grows in this area and bears leaves that look much like those of English holly is the Oregon Grape. Elk and deer enjoy eating these leaves, as much as local humans enjoy using the leaves for Christmas decorations. The Nez Perces of old used parts of these plants in the making of medicinals.

Mile 134.0 Skookum Creek descends from near the Nez Perce Trail, which lies five miles directly to the north of this location. Along the trail, beside a small pond, sits the September 17, 1805, Sinque Hole Camp of Lewis and Clark. A short distance west of the camp lies the Smoking Place, the site at which Lewis and Clark's Nez Perce guides suggested the party stop for a rest and a smoke on June 27, 1806.

On November 13, 1893, after crossing to the north side by raft, four members of the Carlin Hunting Party (see related Mile 148.0 entry) abandoned their sick companion George Colgate here and began trekking downstream. As one among them wrote, Colgate made "no motion or outcry as he saw us disappear, one by one around the bend."

Mile 135.4 From Eagle Mountain Pack Bridge a trail winds to 7414-foot Eagle Mountain and then connects to trails leading to Wilderness Gateway Campground (Mile 122.6) and to the Mocus Point Pack Bridge (Mile 143.0) On the south, three-tenths mile upriver from Eagle Mountain Pack Bridge, Eagle Mountain Creek enters the Lochsa.

Mile 139.7 Indian Grave Creek, flowing from the north side of the Lochsa, rises on Indian Grave Peak. Buried near the peak is the body of Albert Parsons Mullickan, a four-teen-year-old Nez Perce boy. In the summer of 1895, he and his family had camped along the Nez Perce Trail to pick huckleberries, fish and hunt when the entire group became ill, apparently from food poisoning, and Albert died.

Saddle Camp Road, which leaves Highway 12 at this point, joins the Lolo Motorway nine miles to the north. The Motorway parallels and in parts overlays the original Nez Perce Trail, which was created and used by Nez Perce Indians of centuries past to cross the mountains in order to reach the buffalo hunting plains to the east. While the Motorway does provide spectacular views of a wild expanse of Clearwater Country, the Motorway and Saddle Camp Road are mountain roads and, thus, are not suitable for luxury cars or large RVs, nor for drivers unaccustomed to narrow, curvy, steep dirt roads. If you wish to travel Saddle Camp Road to the Motorway, first check with USFS personnel at Kooskia or Powell regarding road conditions, the suitability of your vehicle, and possible restrictions to Motorway access, such as travel permits during the Lewis and Clark Bicentennial years of 2003-2006.

Saddle Camp Road is also the best route to Castle Butte Lookout, perched atop 6659-foot Castle Butte. The view from the lookout includes the Bitterroot Mountains, the Selway Crags, Seven Devils near Hell's Canyon on the Snake River, and other mountain peaks and ranges. This lookout is one of several in Clearwter Country that can be rented for up to seven nights from the U.S. Forest Service. The lookouts provide spectacular campsites for mountain meanderers. To find out rates and available lookouts, check with USFS personnel at Powell, Kooskia, Grangeville, Orofino, or at Fenn Ranger Station on the Selway River.

Mile 142.1 Weir Creek winds about thirty-five miles into the forest, past Weir Creek Hot Springs and on to its headwaters on Moon Saddle, across which runs the Nez Perce Trail. The name of the creek suggests, of course, that the Indians once used weirs here to catch fish.

Keep your eye out along the route for the nearly robin-size mountain bluebird. Voted in 1929 by Idaho school children as the Idaho State Bird, the mountain bluebird is sometimes seen flitting busily about along the Lochsa River and in other sections of Clearwater Country. The male is brilliant blue with a paler belly, while the female is a dull brownish color with a splash of blue on her rump, tail, and wings. Mountain bluebirds live in holes in trees, snags or cliffs and sing a soft, subdued warbling song. (Mountain bluebirds are not to be confused with the more common and larger black-headed, tuft-bearing Stellar's bluejay.)

Mile 143.0 The suspension bridge located here is the Mocus Point Pack Bridge. Every autumn Clearwater Country is invaded by hunters seeking a wilderness experience and the chance to bag one of America's most prized hunting trophies, a bull elk. The Highway 12 corridor then becomes a staging ground for pack trips to hunting camps. Packers load food and camping gear onto horses and mules at hitching posts such as those available two-tenths of a mile up the highway from here, and hunters from throughout the United States warily survey the mountain peaks above them as they leave modern modes of transportation behind and enter the wilderness. The Mocus Point Pack Bridge and Trail takes them to 5579-foot Mocus Peak, where on crisp September mornings the melodic bugle of the bull elk echoes from crag to ridgetop and back.

From Mocus Peak, the trail connects to other trails, one eventually descending from the high country to the Lochsa River at Eagle Mountain Pack Bridge (Mile 135.4). This connecting trail thus makes possible a trip from Mocus Point Bridge to Eagle Mountain Bridge or to Wilderness Gateway Campground.

The word "mocus" stems from Old West trapping days and, according to local usage, refers to a trapper's or mountain man's hankering for company of the feminine kind.

Mile 144.8 Post Office Creek, which empties into the Lochsa here, etches a long, winding route from Indian Post Office Lake which lies near a site along the Nez Perce Trail and Lolo Motorway known as the Indian Post Office. During earlier centuries the Nez Perces built rock cairns at various locations along the Nez Perce Trail. In his June 27, 1806, journal entry, Meriwether Lewis wrote,

> ...on this eminence [where they stopped so the Indians could ceremoniously smoke] the nativs have raised a conic mound of Stons of 6 or 8 feet high and erected a pine pole of 15 feet long.

A Ceremonious Smoke

Two such mounds above the headwaters of Post Office Creek were given the name Indian Post Office by early whites believing that the Indians left messages for one another at the cairns. Lewis was advised by his guides that the cairns where they smoked indicated that a side trail departed the main trail for travel to fishing sites on the Lochsa.

Mile 146.7 Bear Mountain Creek makes its appearance here on the south side of the river. The Lochsa drainage is home to a large black bear population. A hundred years ago river corridor black bears had company: grizzlies. Both thrived during earlier years on abundant salmon runs in area streams and rich plant life in high mountain valleys.

Today, however, there are no known grizzlies in North Central Idaho and grizzly reintroduction proposals have become cause for controversy. Some people stand adamantly opposed to such proposals. Others believe grizzlies are what true wilderness is all about. Interestingly, among those who favor reintroduction are resource extractors who recognize that reintroduction will classify grizzlies as *experimental* and, therefore, not subject to the same level of protection afforded endangered species and which could negatively impact logging and mining activities. Non-experimental reintroduction could happen naturally and inadvertently, however, if grizzlies wander into Idaho from Montana prior to a managed reintroduction of them here. Of course, Montana's grizzlies remain unaware of this debate.

The natives...classed the white, the deep and the pale grizzly red, the grizzly dark brown —in short, all those [grizzly bears] with the extremities of the hair of a white or frosty color, without regard to the color of the ground...under the name of hohost. They assured us that they were all of the same species with the white bear; that they associated together, had longer nails than the others, and never climbed trees. On the other hand, the black skins, those which were black with a number of entirely white hairs intermixed, or with a white breast, the uniform bay, the brown, and the light reddish-brown, were ranged under the class yackah, and were said to resemble each other in being smaller, in having shorter nails than the white bear, in climbing trees, and in being so little vicious that they could be pursued with safety.

Wm. Clark, May 31, 1806, Among the Nez Perces

Mile 147.7 Situated along a wooded loop drive here is Colgate Campground, which includes toilets and seven campsites. The campground derives its name from George Colgate, member of the 1893 Carlin hunting party. In late October of '93, desperate to escape heavy, early winter snows, the party constructed two cedar log rafts at this location in order to make what would turn out to be an ill-fated attempt to float down the Lochsa. (See Mile 148.0.)

Mile 148.0 This USFS rest stop is site of the twenty-five minute Colgate Licks National Recreational Trail. Signs along the path present information about the area's plants, trees, fires and elk. The term *lick* refers to a natural mineral salt deposit which typically attracts wildlife who lick the needed salts. The area gets its name from a man named George Colgate who was buried here in the spring of 1894.

Colgate had been cook for a hunting party of easterners, William Carlin, John Pierce, A.L.A. Himmelwright and their guide, Martin Spencer, with whom they rendezvoused at Kendrick, Idaho, seventy-five miles west. From there they rode on horseback to the Weippe Prairie and over the Nez Perce Trail to the location known as the Indian Post Office. It was late September and, in places, the trail was already covered with eight inches of snow. The party descended to the Lochsa where they found prospectors

> *We went down the river a long way this morning, and were horrified to find that we were absolutely 'stuck.' Half a mile below camp is a ledge of rocks, and a rapid through which we cannot take a raft. Below this are two more places still worse. Every one gave his opinion...that we could not get our rafts ...down the river. ...We have barely one week's short allowance of flour left. All our other provisions, except a few pounds of cornmeal and beans, and a handful of salt each, are exhausted. The shores of the river are a mass of irregular rocks. Numerous ledges or cliffs, some of them hundreds of feet high, rise vertically above the river and project into it. The hillsides...are steep and rocky and covered with dense brush. Many of the ledges are so precipitous that it is all an able-bodied man can do to hang to bushes and climb around them on narrow clefts or steps in the rock. Most of us are considerably weakened from exposure and are not in a fit condition to walk.*
>
> A.L.A. Himmelwright, Saturday, Nov. 11th, 1893

Jerry Johnson and Ben Keeley building a cabin. Colgate was feeling ill when he arrived on the Lochsa, and as his condition worsened, Spencer urged the party to begin their homeward trek. Jerry Johnson also advised them that they risked getting snowed in, yet the hunters continued their sport. After six inches of snow fell on October 10th, they did decide to leave. On the ridge above their camp, they soon discovered the snow was already three feet deep. The party reconsidered their planned exit route and returned to Johnson and Keeley's cabin. There they purchased a stock of food and hired Keeley to help Spencer build two rafts while the others passed the time hunting.

Finally on November 3rd, the party boarded the completed rafts and attempted to float the icy Lochsa. However, the larger of the rafts overturned in the fast water the first day, causing the group to advance only one mile. Plagued with further difficulties during subsequent attempts to float downstream, they continued to make little progress. In frustration on November 12th, they abandoned their rafts...and a very sick George Colgate...at a temporary camp a short distance below Eagle Mountain Creek (Mile 135.1). The three hunters, the guide, and Keeley then proceeded to claw their way through five-foot snowdrifts along the bluffs above the river's north bank. Fortune finally favored them when on November 22nd above Apgar Creek, starved and exhausted, they were met by a rescue party which had been sent out by Carlin's father. The following spring a military crew from Missoula located Colgate's remains eight miles from where he had been abandoned. Apparently his body had washed downstream. Speculation ran rampant regarding whether the Carlin hunting party was justified in breaking an unwritten law of the wilderness that one should never abandon a companion. The military crew brought Colgate's remains to this location, known now as Colgate Licks, and buried them on the north riverbank just below today's highway, where a grave marker remains today.

Mile 149 Mink Creek flows in here. Early day Clearwater Country trappers, like Jerry Johnson (see Mile 150.3), were attracted to this area for its furbearing animals, which included the pine marten and the mink. This area's habitats, of course, are still today the homelands of these and many other small mammals.

An animal of larger stature and today of larger import on the political as well as wildlife management scene is the wolf. Clearwater Country, along with much of the United States, was once home to the gray wolf, largest of the wild canine predators. A nationwide all out war against wolves throughout the nineteenth and much of the twentieth century led to decimated populations of this animal, and, as a result, the gray wolf was placed on the Endangered Species List. In 1995, the U.S. Fish and Wildlife Service reintroduced gray wolves to the Selway Bitterroot Wilderness and Frank Church River of No Return Wilderness. The reintroduced wolves have thrived so that they now number more than one hundred animals. Numerous subadults have begun dispersing into new territory, including crossings of the Lochsa River and Highway 12. Campers around their evening fires at campgrounds along the highway listen, hoping to hear the rare, sonorous howls of wolves coming from within the wilds of North Central Idaho. Of course, some campers may be hoping to not hear wolves.

Mile 150.3 Jerry Johnson Campground is named after the late 1800s prospector and trapper Jerry Johnson. He was

A Hot Springs Bath

spending the winter here with fellow prospector Ben Keeley when the Carlin hunting party became trapped in the canyon by autumn snows. (See Mile 148.0.) The campground includes picnic tables, toilets and fifteen campsites.

Mile 151.5 Warm Springs Pack Bridge serves as a gateway to the Selway Bitterroot Wilderness. The trail beginning here winds deep into the wilderness and connects with a network of other trails. An easy one-mile walk along Warm Springs Creek will take you to Jerry Johnson Hot Springs where, year-round and at times *au naturel,* bathers enjoy the mineral waters and the soothing glade and rush of creek water that make up the hot springs' surroundings.

Mile 153.8 A short distance up Squaw Creek, Doe Creek Road leaves Squaw Creek Road and climbs Deep Saddle to join the Lolo Motorway about two miles east of the cairns known as Indian Post Office along the centuries-old Nez Perce Trail. The Motorway is now over sixty years old, but, initially, was a long time in coming.

Back in 1854, the original trail was considered a possible route along which to lay a military road. That year, Capt. John Mullan, who sought a roadway to run from Fort Benton on the Missouri River to Walla Walla, Washington, made an exploratory trip along the trail. Of the trip, he wrote,

> In September of 1854, I determined to proceed to the coast by a new route, and the only one left unexplored, namely, via the Lo-Lo Fork Pass. This route I found the most difficult of all examined. After eleven days of severe struggle with climate and country, we emerged into the more open region where 'Oro Fino' [two miles south of Pierce]... stands, glad to leave behind us so difficult a bed of mountains.

Mullan soon concluded that a road along the Clark Fork River farther north could be built with much greater ease.

With the discovery of gold at Alder Gulch in Montana in 1863, and the decline of gold fields at Pierce and Elk City, Idaho, merchants in Lewiston, Idaho, hoped to compete with Salt Lake City, Utah, as a supply point for Montana miners. To facilitate such commerce, Lewiston merchants appealed to the U.S. Congress for funds to build a wagon road over the Nez Perce Trail. In 1865, fifty thousand dollars was appropriated. The following year, project director Wellington Bird began construction. He and his crew soon discovered what those before them had learned: the terrain forbade the building of a road. Instead, project members turned to surveying and to relocating portions of the existing trail to improve grades. The rerouted trail became known as the Bird-Truax Trail, which was itself replaced in 1935 by the Lolo Motorway, a narrow, curvy, crude dirt road that some folks still refer to as a *trail*.

Should you wish to travel on Squaw Creek Road or the Motorway, first check with USFS personnel at Kooskia or Powell about road conditions. Squaw Creek Road is narrow, soft-shouldered, and may at times be closed to through traffic.

Mile 158.3 Badger Creek enters from the north here. Like Papoose Creek at Mile 159.3, the Badger Creek area is a nesting and rearing habitat for the harlequin duck, a *sensitive* species.

Mile 158.3 Wendover Campground, here at the base of Wendover Ridge, marks the point along the Lewis and Clark party's 1805 route through the Bitterroots where the explorers left the Lochsa to travel northward before turning west again along the Nez Perce Trail.

When the Nez Perces traveled this their trail to buffalo country east of the Bitterroots, a small group would sometimes leave the trail and descend into the canyon to catch fish from the Lochsa. The mouth of Wendover Creek was one of their fishing sites. The fishers would rejoin the main party near Packer Meadows, close to Lolo Pass. The route they followed to the pass is approximately the same route Lewis and Clark followed westward mid-September, 1805.

From here the expeditionists zigzagged up the spine of Wendover Ridge which reaches an elevation of 5615 feet. They ascended the ridge, as Clark noted in his journal,

> winding in every direction to get up the Steep assends & to pass the emence quantity of falling [fallen] timber which had [been] falling from dift. [different] causes i e fire & wind...Several horses Sliped and roled down Steep hills which hurt them verry much the one which Carried my desk & Small trunk Turned over & roled down a mountain for 40 yards and lodged against a tree, broke the Desk the horse escaped and appeared but little hurt...

Clark would later use his desk as kindling for a fire at a cold and wet campsite. The accident caused a two hour delay before the party was able to continue.

> [We] proceeded on up the mountain Steep & ruged as usial...when we arrived at the top...we could find no water and Concluded to Camp and make use of the Snow we found on the top to cook the remns [remnants] of our Colt & make our Supe, evening verry cold and cloudy.

The following morning the party awoke to four inches of new snow and by nightfall six to eight inches more had fallen. As Joseph Whitehouse wrote in his journal,

> when we awoke this morning to our great Surprise we were covred with Snow...we mended up our mockasons. Some of the men without Socks raped rags on their feet, and loaded up our horses and Set out without anything to eat...

Wendover Campground, Ridge and Creek are named for a nineteenth century fur trapper who once lived and tended a trapline in this area. The campground includes toilets, drinking water and twenty-eight campsites.

Mile 158.6 Joseph Whitehouse, one of the Lewis and Clark party, noted in his journal on September 15, 1805, that the expedition had passed a pond at this point along their Lochsa route. Visible on the north side of the highway, the pond bears his name, as does the campground on the opposite side of the highway.

Sometimes moose lumber into the pond to cool off and nibble aquatic plants. An average male moose, sporting palmate antlers, a dark brown coat and long legs, measures to around five and one-half feet at the shoulders and nine feet in length. They can weigh up to twelve hundred pounds. While moose are typically not aggressive with humans, when provoked they have been known to attack. Unharassed, they are likely to nonchalantly provide passersby with several minutes of exciting observation.

Whitehouse Campground, located here, includes fourteen campsites. At the time of this writing, the U.S. Forest Service had proposed an information and staging area a short distance upriver from the campground for visitors who may wish to travel the Lolo Motorway during the

Lewis and Clark Bicentennial years, 2003-2006. Travel on the Motorway may be limited during those years in order to protect natural, historical and cultural resources and to ensure human safety along the narrow, rough Motorway. You can get information regarding the Motorway and possible limitations to travel from Forest Service personnel.

Mile 159.3 Papoose Creek enters the Lochsa from the north here. This is another of the many Lochsa tributaries that have provided spawning grounds for spring Chinook salmon and steelhead trout. Fast-moving mountain streams such as Papoose Creek also provide nesting habitat for harlequin ducks, a species whose decline in numbers has warranted its designation as a *sensitive* species. The males are beautifully colored by white and chestnut-red patches on an overall bluish-gray plumage. The female, for protective purposes, only bears the highlights of three white patches on each side of her head and a brushing of grayish-white on her breast feathers.

Mile 161.4 This point marks the upriver boundary of that stretch of the Lochsa bearing an official Wild and Scenic designation. The boundary also, of course, draws a line demarcating different river and forest management practices. (See related entry at Mile 171.3.)

Mile 161.8 POWELL [All services available.]

The side road which leaves the highway here leads to Lochsa Lodge, Powell Campground, Powell Ranger Station and the location of a Lewis and Clark Expedition campsite.

On September 14, 1805, the expeditionists had finally reached a tributary of the river system that would take them to the Pacific Ocean. Wet and tired after a day of climbing up and down forested hills and crossing fast-flowing streams in a full day of rain, hail and snow, Lewis and Clark "were compelled to kill a Colt for our men & Selves to eat for the want of meat & we named the South fork Colt killed Creek..." Today this creek is called White Sand Creek. The main stream, the Lochsa, the explorers later called Kooskooskee, a version of the Indian word for *clear water*. They used this name to refer to the entire stretch of river that runs from here to Lewiston.

Taking the side road, you may turn left in one-tenth mile onto the driveway of Lochsa Lodge, where visitor services are available. Staying on the side road, you'll reach the campground drive in three-tenths mile. The campground includes thirty-seven sites. In six-tenths mile on the side road, you'll be at Powell Ranger Station. A sign at the far end of the station parking lot draws attention to a short walk to the riverbank and the Lewis and Clark campsite.

Mile 162.0 Parachute Hill Road climbs north from this location to the Nez Perce Trail, intersecting the trail near a side road which leads to Rocky Point Lookout. On June 28, 1806, during their return trip, Lewis and Clark camped just west of Rocky Point, near Papoose Saddle. Although they had only covered thirteen miles that day, their horses were...

> ...hungry and much fatigued and from our information no other place where we could obtain grass for them within the reach of this evening's travel, we decided to remain at this place all night...

The next day they headed over Rocky Point to the Lochsa's Crooked Fork and up the slope, across which the highway now lies, towards Packer Meadows. Papoose Saddle camp is now called Camp Thirteen. The Lolo Motorway (Forest Road #500) begins near Camp Thirteen; however, before embarking on the Motorway, check at the ranger station for road information and possible permit requirements during the Lewis and Clark Bicentennial years of 2003-2006.

Through the Bitterroot Mountain stretch of their journey, Lewis and Clark, for the most part, followed the Idaho segment of the Northern Nez Perce Trail. For that reason, the Nez Perce Trail is, through this region, also referred to as the Lewis and Clark Trail.

Mile 163.4 Here, Elk Summit road runs to White Sand Campground and beyond. One mile down the road, five campsites comprise the campground, which lies near the point at which White Sand Creek (*aka* Colt-Killed Creek) and the Crooked Fork join to form the Lochsa River. A short distance further, the main road crosses a bridge over the Crooked Fork. A left turn just after the bridge will take you (about one mile) to White Sand Creek Trail, which parallels beautiful White Sand Creek for many miles. Continuing on the main road, one fork leads to Tom Beall Park (a high mountain meadow) and the other to Elk Summit (a campground). Both of these mountainous routes provide access to the Selway Bitterroot Wilderness.

Mile 165.0 The western red cedars in the Bernard DeVoto Memorial Grove are centuries old. The grove was named in honor of author and western historian Bernard DeVoto, who often camped here while working on his well known edition of THE JOURNALS OF LEWIS AND CLARK. In keeping with his request, his ashes were scattered in the upper Lochsa area, and the grove was later named in his honor.

Mile 168.0 The Lewis and Clark party traversed the ridge on the north side of the Crooked Fork (and of this stretch of today's highway) on June 29, 1806. They were traveling eastward and had camped the previous night near Papoose Saddle (see Mile 162.0). They left Rocky Point at the upper end of the ridge, traveled down into the draw you see here, crossed the Crooked Fork and then ascended the slope upon which you now travel. They ended the day out of high country snow at the hot springs now called Lolo Hot Springs with fresh venison for themselves and grass for their horses. They felt relieved that evening at being once again safely across "those terrible mountains," the Bitterroots. They also enjoyed a hot springs bath. (See related entry at Mile 7.2 on the Montana side of the border.)

Many of the conifers in this area are western larch, also called tamarack. The tamarack annually performs the unusual act, for a conifer, of losing all its needles, as if it were a leafy deciduous tree. Also like the deciduous trees, the tamarack turns color, yellows and golds, in the autumn. In the winter, you might assume the forest was dotted with dead, needleless conifers, but in the spring fresh needles emerge and grow to once again create lush summer greenery.

Mile 171.3 An interpretive sign at this location provides information related to the checkerboard appearance of the land in this area. As a means of encouraging westward expansion during the last quarter of the nineteenth century, Congress provided enormous incentive to railroad companies: ownership of every other section of land on both sides of any new railroad track. (A section equals one square mile or six hundred forty acres.) Railroad companies, of course, planned lines and were granted section ownerships, sometimes including sections of Federal property granted in lieu of less attractive or unavailable sections along the rail line right-of-way. The companies then either formed their own timber subsidiaries or sold some of their traded sections to established timber companies in order to benefit from rich timber resources obtained through the section grants.

As a result, many sections were clearcut, and those clearcut sections created a checkerboard effect on the landscape. Clearcutting has been a controversial method of logging because *all* trees of any size are removed. Clearcut proponents favor cutting all trees in a given area because doing so is economically efficient. They say that damage to streams and soil (loss of stream shade and increased soil erosion, including landslides) is not as severe as opponents suggest and that clearcut plots can be replanted. Clearcut opponents, however, decry the eradication through cutting of entire sections of forest and the resulting degradation of streams and soil stability. They point out that even when replanted, the growth of a new stand of trees all exactly the same age does not comprise a forest, but merely a tree farm. They feel that economic efficiency must not weigh more heavily upon the decision-makers than forest diversity and health. Readily apparent in the checkerboard landscape that lies before you here is the essence of this controversy.

The old Nez Perce Trail intersected the highway near this location. From 6280-foot Rocky Point a short distance to the northwest the trail dropped into the valley, crossed the Crooked Fork and ascended again to Packer Meadows, near present day Lolo Pass (Mile 174.4). In the spring of 1806, traveling east, the Lewis and Clark party's three Nez Perce guides led them along this route to the meadows. On this their return journey they were well mounted with sixty-six horses, some of which carried maps, records and scientific data that would significantly expand the horizons of a young nation. On their westbound trip the previous fall the Lewis and Clark party took an alternate and more difficult route from Packer Meadows to the Lochsa.

Seventy years later, during the Nez Perce War of 1877, about seven hundred Nez Perce warriors, elders, women and children, led by Chief Looking Glass, sadly traversed this trail in flight from their homeland. When the Indians emerged east of the Bitterroots, General O.O. Howard and his troops, also numbering about seven hundred, had barely begun their pursuit of the Indians at the trail's westward end in the Kamiah Valley. On August 5, 1877, with fifty-two trail-breaking axmen preceding them, General

> *We had passed the last tine [Crooked Fork] of the Clearwater where, after twenty-one miles of the roughest country...we came into camp in the twilight. We heard loud echoes of firing by the advanced scouts and thought they had come upon [Chief] Joseph's rear guard. Then we spurred the weary animals into a tired trot and along this narrow trail descended for miles through the almost impenetrable forest till we came to the narrowest of valleys. Here we found not a mouthful of food for horse or mule — but the nicest of salmon for the men, in water about knee-deep and clear as crystal, rushing and splashing over the rocks. The echoes which deceived us into thinking the enemy near were from the scouts' carbines shooting the bigger of the fish as they were swimming up the Clearwater.*
>
> Gen. O.O. Howard

Howard, two hundred cavalry and twenty Bannock Indians reached and made camp at the point where the trail crossed Crooked Fork Creek, below today's highway. Hauling ponderous amounts of supplies, ammunition and howitzers across the rugged country, the remaining soldiers and packers struggled up the steep hillside two days later.

Mile 174.4 LOLO PASS and THE MONTANA-IDAHO BORDER, where the highway mile numbers change:

Going east, Lolo Pass is Mile 0, and the Highway 12 miles run to Mile 32.6 at Lolo, Montana.

Going west, Lolo Pass is Mile 174.4, and the Highway 12 miles run to Mile 0 at the western edge of Lewiston, Idaho.

Trails in the Lolo Pass area offer pleasurable walks, vigorous hikes and, in the winter, cross country skiing. A road leads (one mile) to Packer Meadows, traditional camping area for Nez Perce Indians crossing the mountains to and from buffalo country to the east and, also, for Flathead Indians traveling to the upper Lochsa for salmon fishing.

On September 13, 1805, Lewis and Clark and company camped near Packer Meadows on Glade Creek. That September day would be one of the last comfortable days of their trek for awhile, as they were about to embark on the roughest section of their eight thousand mile journey.

In 1998, the Glade Creek campsite of the explorers and the surrounding one hundred sixty acres (then private timber land) was purchased by the Idaho Heritage Trust and donated to the State of Idaho for preservation. Like many of the other Lewis and Clark sites in Idaho, the Glade Creek campsite remains today much as it did at the beginning of the nineteenth century.

The Forest Service Visitor Center located here provides information about the forest, the Nez Perces, Lewis and Clark campsites and the north central Idaho region in general. Available are maps, books and information brochures. By 2002, the visitor center will have been expanded. Information at the new center will focus on the Nez Perces, the Lewis and Clark Expedition, the natural history of the region's wild lands, and the Nez Perce National Historic Trail/Lewis and Clark National Historic Trail/Lolo Trail and historic trail uses.

Mile 5.9 Lee Creek joins Lolo Creek here at Lee Creek Campground where twenty-two campsites lie amongst lodgepole pines, the trees used by the Indians as tipi supports. A two and one-half mile walking tour in the campground vicinity includes twenty interpretive stops detailing information about area logging activities.

The campground serves as trailhead for the Nez Perce Trail/Lewis and Clark Trail, which leaves Lolo Creek here, runs parallel to the highway over the ridge to the east and emerges on Packer Meadows near Lolo Pass six miles distant.

On September 13, 1805, the Lewis and Clark expeditionists passed through here on the trail and proceeded to Packer Meadows. One member of their party, Joseph Whitehouse, wrote in his journal,

> We could not git along the Indian trail for the timber which had been down in a thicket of pine. ...the mountains rough and rocks which appear above the timber like towers in some places.

Mile 7.2 Lolo Hot Springs A mineral lick for wild game, home to Indian spirits and an ancient bathing spot, the hot mineralized springs that rise on the north side here must have been welcome indeed to all early travelers of the Nez Perce Trail. William Clark of the historic Lewis and Clark Expedition recorded in his journal on Sept. 12, 1805,

These Springs issue from the bottom and through the inter-stices of a grey freestone rock, the rock rises in irregular massy clifts in a circular range, arround the Springs on their lower Side. imediately above the Springs on the creek there is a hand-som little quawmash [camas] plain of about 10 acres. ...in this bath which had been prepared by the Indians by stopping the river with Stone and mud, I bathed and remained in 10 minits it was with dificuelty I could remain this long and it causd a profuse swet. two other bold Springs adjacent to this are much warmer, their heat being so great as to make the hand of a per-son Smart extreemly when immerced. both the Men and the indians amused themselves with the use of the bath this evening. I observe after the indians remaining in the hot bath as long as they could bear it run and plunge themselves into the creek the water of which is now as cold as ice can make it; after remaining here a fiew minits they return again to the worm bath repeeting the transision several times but always ending with the worm bath.

William Clark, June 29, 1806

I...passed several springs which I observed the deer and elk had made roads to...I tasted the water and found it hot and not bad tasted. I found this water nearly boiling hot at the place it spouted from the rocks...

On their return trip, the expeditionists camped along the creek near here on June 29, 1806, and Clark enjoyed a good soak. The explorers were glad that evening to have safely crossed the rugged Bitterroots and to realize the journey yet ahead of them would be less difficult.

Years later, during the Nez Perce War of 1877, Gen. Howard and his cavalry camped here on August 6th. The two hundred blue-coated cavalrymen grazed their mounts and rested from their difficult journey over the Bitterroots. With them were twenty scouts from the Bannock tribe, tra-ditional enemies of the Nez Perces and eager for Nez Perce scalps. Howard's main military force was farther west on the Nez Perce Trail, two days behind this advance group.

Today visitors share in the history of this place by enjoying a hot soak. Also available at Lolo Hot Springs are food, lodging and a campground.

Mile 9.2 On September 12, 1805, during their westward journey, after descending "a long, steep mountain" which proved to be "verry bad passing," the Lewis and Clark party camped on a creekside slope near here — the "Party and horses much fatigued." While the horses carried most of the explorers' supplies, the men and their Shoshone companion Sacagawea and guide Toby and his son spent much time walking as they crossed this country and continued westward through the Bitterroot Mountains.

Mile 14.0 One-tenth mile north of Highway 12, along the road to Howard Creek Meadows, lies the Howard Creek Picnic Area with tables and trail access. At this point, the Nez Perce/Lewis and Clark Trail ascends a steep ridge to the west, inviting hikers to experience some of what Lewis and Clark described in 1805 as those "intolerable roads on the sides of the Steep Stoney mountains." Early Indian travel was common over this route, once known to the Indians as Q'u seyna Iss Kit, or the *trail to the buffalo*.

Mile 16.2 An early 1800s trapper named Lawrence, but called Lou-Lou or LoLo by the Indians, lived with his Nez Perce wife in a cabin near the mouth of the creek which flows here. Attacked by a grizzly one unfortunate day, LoLo shot the bear but only wounded it. A companion carried the severely mauled Lolo to his cabin where he died shortly thereafter. The name of the creek, Graves Creek, commemorates the area where he was buried. His own name was given to nearby Lolo Creek and colloquially to Lolo Trail, which is officially known both as the Nez Perce National Historic Trail and the Lewis and Clark National Historic Trail. Generally, the three names refer to the same trail.

The trail crossed Graves Creek a short distance up the creek from this point. Westward, the trail climbed a ridge to higher ground and then joined Lolo Creek again near Lolo Hot Springs (Mile 7.2). To the east, the trail likewise led travelers to higher ground, emerging into the Lolo Creek Valley at the upper end of Woodman Meadow (Mile 23.5). A major fork in the trail followed Graves Creek north to the Clark's Fork River near Alberton, west of Missoula. On September 12, 1805, the Lewis and Clark expeditionists crossed Graves Creek on their way to what would become the friendly welcome of the Nez Perces in Clearwater Country.

In 1877, when the Nez Perce War was being waged over a fifteen hundred mile stretch of country, five hundred or so weary Nez Perce women, children and elders camped on Graves Creek Meadows, visible a short distance up the good side road which turns to the north here. Young boys tended the two thousand horses grazing up and down the valley, while scouts kept an eye on the trail behind them. About two hundred warriors had ridden down the valley. All remained alert, ready to flee northward to the Clark's Fork should they become caught between Gen. Howard's troops from the west and other troops posted to the east.

Mile 17.0 The Lewis and Clark Campground here includes a parking lot adjacent to a picnic area with six picnic sites, and, via a bridge across Lolo Creek, seventeen campsites.

Mile 25.3 To the south, Lolo Peak rises to 9096 feet, making it one of the highest peaks in the Bitterroot Range that defines the Idaho-Montana border. The broad valley to the east is Montana's Bitterroot Valley. From the September 11, 1805 campsite of the Lewis and Clark Expedition (at Mile 23.5), William Clark noted that the day's route had been "bordered by high and rugged hills to the right [north], while the mountains on the left were covered with snow."

The interpretive sign that stands here identifies this as the September 11th campsite location, but the sign is placed here for easy vehicle access. See Mile 23.5 below for more accurate placement of the site. Several of the USFS interpretive signs throughout Clearwater Country are geographically misplaced, but with the good intention of facilitating convenience for passersby. At times, too, the signs may include inaccurate information simply because they were placed prior to the most recent historical research, which may have uncovered new, more current information.

Mile 23.5 On September 11, 1805, having delayed their departure from the Bitterroot Valley until 3 p.m., the Lewis and Clark Corps of Discovery stopped at this location, now known as Woodman Meadows, after traveling only seven miles from their previous camp. They turned their horses out to graze and camped "at some old Indian lodges," at the end of a warm and somewhat frustrating day mostly spent searching for two lost horses. That search resulted in the finding of the horses, but also in a great loss of time. A knowlegeable Nez Perce man, brought into camp the day before by one of the Corps' hunters, had offered to guide the Corps over the mountains, but hiked on alone — impatient with the expeditionists' slow departure due to the horse search. His leaving meant that the Corps had to rely on the Shoshone guide, Old Toby, already with them. Toby, however, knew little of the mountain route, and, thus, the explorers' westward Bitterroot Mountain journey took eleven days and a severe toll on the explorers' endurance. The following spring's return trip, under the guidance of Nez Perces, took half that number of days.

In 1877, during the midst of the Nez Perce Indian War, a large contingent of Nez Perce warriors camped on these meadows for four days while awaiting a resolution to the problem of a log and brush barricade which had been constructed and manned four miles downstream. They had reached these meadows after having trekked through the mountains to the west with a main body of five hundred women, children and elders, who camped in a meadow about one-half mile up Graves Creek (Mile 16.2). They were known as the *non-treaties* because of their resistance to being confined to a small reservation within the vast region of their traditional homeland. The warriors who waited here maintained close observation of the white soldiers blocking the Indians' way and debated what course of action to take in response to this obstacle. Some argued for battle. Others speculated on means of avoiding both battle and the military blockage. The Indians were no doubt anxious, for they thought Gen. Howard and his troops were in pursuit along the mountainous trail from Clearwater Country. Actually, Gen. Howard had not yet begun the trek across the mountains and would reach this site more than two weeks later.

Mile 28.0 On July 24, 1877, upon learning via the telegraph that the Nez Perces were fleeing their Clearwater Country homeland west of the Bitterroots after several skirmishes and battles with Gen. Howard's troops, Capt. Charles Rawn, four officers, twenty-five enlisted men and a group of Flathead Indians rode south out of Fort Missoula. Their destination: Lolo Creek. Their objective was to block the creek valley in order to halt the Nez Perces and thus prevent any threat to Montana citizens. They were joined by approximately one hundred civilian volunteers from Missoula and the Bitterroot Valley.

The Nez Perces, however, traditionally accustomed to warring with only certain bands of other Indians, did not surmise that whites other than those of Gen. Howard's *band* were also now enemies. Having no desire for general warfare with the whites, the Nez Perces, under a flag of truce, negotiated with soldiers and citizens at Woodman Meadows (Mile 23.5) and indicated that no whites would be harmed if the Indians were allowed to pass. Reluctant to engage in battle with the well-equipped and skilled Nez Perces and having had for years observed the Nez Perces peaceably pass through the Bitterroot Valley, many of the civilian volunteers accepted the Indians' promise and turned towards home. Badly outnumbered, Capt. Rawn may have wanted to concede, but he could not disobey his orders. He refused to allow passage and demanded a surrender.

As an uneasy dawn broke on July 28th, the bemused Rawn and his soldiers looked up on the ridge to the north to see a line of Nez Perce warriors well out of rifle range. The line of Nez Perce elders, women and children was traveling up a draw about a half mile west of this location. Guarded by warriors, they passed the *corral*, as they referred to Rawn's entrenchment, on the north side of the visible ridge and emerged back on the valley floor a safe distance downstream from this location. Uninclined, as they had said, to spill white man's blood, the Nez Perces had cleverly found a means of avoiding a battle they could have easily won. Capt. Rawn and his men were left guarding an arrangement of logs. This site of the-battle-that-might-have-been was later jokingly dubbed "Fort Fizzle."

We do not want to fight. I tried to surrender in Idaho, but my offer was rejected. The soldiers came upon my camp and the first thing I knew, the bullets were flying around my head. [See Mile 75.9.] The soldiers lie so that I have no more confidence in them. They have had their way for a long time; now we must have ours. We must go to buffalo country. If we are not allowed to go peaceably we shall do the best we can. If the officer wishes to build corrals for the Nez Perces, he may, but they will not hold us back. We are not horses. The country is large. I think we are as smart as he is and know the roads and mountains as well.

Chief Looking Glass, Woodman Meadow, 1877

On the Trail

Today it is a picnic and rest stop for travelers. Interpretive signs explain the Fort Fizzle story. A path leads to a replica of the soldiers' entrenchment and breastworks, and south of the parking lot, another leads to Lolo Creek.

Mile 31.0 After hoodwinking the Fort Fizzle soldiers (see Mile 28.0), the line of non-treaty Nez Perces wove down a ridge between the two forks of Sleeman Creek to the north and here rejoined the Nez Perce Trail. An extraordinary sight they must have made — papooses snoozing in cradleboards attached to the sides of saddles or on their mothers' backs, buckskin fringes wagging at their hems as women padded along in hand sewn moccasins; tipi skins, blankets, and woven grass baskets tottering on horses' backs; horses herded along by boys wearing buckskin leggings and bearing willow switches; gray-haired oldsters holding fur robes or blankets around their shoulders and trying to keep pace; and in the lead, stalwart warriors carrying guns.

Mile 32.4 The Lewis and Clark Expedition camped on the south side of Lolo Creek on both legs of their epic westward journey. On September 9, 1805, having been outfitted with horses by the Shoshone Indians, the explorers arrived from

105

the south. The expedition consisted then of thirty-five individuals: leader Meriwether Lewis, who shared his command with William Clark, twenty-six hand-selected regular army troops, Capt. Clark's black slave York, interpreters Charbonneau and his wife Sacagawea and their infant son Baptiste, and two of Sacagawea's fellow Shoshones — a man called Toby and his son.

After the party's journey northward along the Bitterroot River, they spent a day and a half at rest on a small flat approximately three-fourths mile south of this location, which they named Travelers' Rest. On September 11th, they set out along the Bitterroot section of the ancient trail of the Nez Perces for what would prove to be the most difficult segment of the expeditionists' 8000-mile odyssey which had begun sixteen months earlier in St. Louis, Missouri.

Nine months later, on their homeward trip, they arrived back at Travelers' Rest on June 30, 1806. Their return trek through the mountains had been easier and faster than the initial crossing, thanks to three Nez Perce guides, good weather and the excitement of the homeward journey. Nevertheless, when they arrived here on the 30th, they were delighted to have the Bitterroot Mountains once again behind them.

As they discussed parting with their Nez Perce guides on July 2, 1806, Lewis gave the Chief among their guides a Jefferson Medallion and the two exchanged names, which was a tradition of friendship and respect among the Nez Perces. Lewis was given the name *Yo-me-kol-lick* after the grizzly bear, an indication of the Indians' high regard for him. The explorers dried meat and readied arms in preparation for the upcoming journey.

Junction of Highways 93 and 12 LOLO, MONTANA [Population: 2800. All services available.]

Lolo Creek enters the Bitterroot River about a mile southeast of here. Although the origin of the name Lolo Creek is a secret of history, the best document-supported theory is that the creek was named after a trapper the Indians called Lou-Lou or LoLo, who lived in a log cabin upstream at the mouth of Graves Creek in around 1810 (Mile 16.2). Later, here just north of Lolo Creek's juncture with the Bitterroot River, a small community sprouted and also acquired the name Lolo. Because the ancient Nez Perce Trail ran through the area of the trapper's home, the Bitterroot Range portion of the trail west of here has come to be colloquially referred to as the Lolo Trail.

The Nez Perces, who live in the foothills and valleys west of the Bitterroots, used the trail during earlier centuries to travel to buffalo hunting grounds on this side of the mountains. These early travelers formed small but complete communities of hunters and families, who toted tipi skins, fur robes for beds and shoulders, baskets for gathering and cooking, hunting equipment and other provisions. Their stay on the eastern side of the Bitterroots might last up to two or three years before they would make the return trek to Clearwater Country. Once home they would trade some of their buffalo skins for food and other items with those Nez Perces who had not made the hunting journey.

Indians such as the Flatheads, who lived on the eastern fringes of the Bitterroots, traveled west on the trail to reach the salmon streams of the upper Lochsa River. Highway 12 follows this river's route and escorts today's travelers past the former fishing sites of the Indians. The Blackfeet Indians also used the trail, but for less peaceable endeavors. They followed it to Clearwater Country in order to raid the Nez Perces and capture horses, asundry loot and hostages.

The trail has also become well known because it was traversed by the Lewis and Clark Expedition. The Corps of Discovery, as the expedition was referred to by President Thomas Jefferson, traveled much of the trail in September 1805, and again in June of 1806. In honor of their historic trek, much of the Nez Perce/Lolo Trail is also referred to as the Lewis and Clark National Historic Trail, and Highway 12 is called both the Lewis and Clark Highway and the Northwest Passage Scenic Byway.

During the Lewis and Clark Expedition's return trip, Lewis, nine of his men and five Indians traveled north into the Missoula Valley, while Clark and the others trekked south. Lewis' group followed the Bitterroot River to its confluence with the Clark's Fork River where they constructed rafts, loaded themselves and their provisions, and crossed the Clark's Fork. Lewis noted that,

> ...the Indians swam across their horses and drew over their baggage in little basons of deer skins which they constructed in a very few minutes...

Lewis waited till last with two men who were poor swimmers.

> ...with these men I set out on the raft and was
> soon hurried down with the current a mile and
> half...on our approach to the shore the raft sunk
> and I was drawn off the raft by a bush and swam
> ...the two men...fortunately effected a landing at
> some little distance below.

The group continued up the Clark's Fork to Grant Creek, on the western edge of present-day Missoula, and made camp. Concerned about the horses' being pestered by "excessively troublesome" mosquitoes, the men kindled large fires and moved the horses into the drifting smoke.

The next day, July 4th, Lewis and his men left their guides and proceeded towards the "great falls." The passage of the Lewis and Clark Expedition through the Missoula Valley, Clearwater Country, and parts of Washington and Oregon, had etched an indelible trail across our nation's history and would powerfully affect her destiny.

MISSOULA, MONTANA [Population: 58,000. All services available.]

On Highway 93, eleven miles north of Lolo, sprawls Missoula, site of a colorful western history.

The Flathead Indians were the first residents of the valley upon which the city grew. One of the tribes with whom they interacted was the Nez Perce tribe, whose homeland lay to the west. The two tribes exchanged ideas and goods and found their lives in many ways alike. Both groups were subsistence hunter-gatherers, family oriented, independent individually and tribally, steeped in ancient rites and beliefs, and as intimate with the earth mother as all living things.

Within a few years of Lewis and Clark's passing through the country in 1805-1806, English and French explorers, traders and trappers filtered through the *Porte d'Enfer* (Gates of Hell), a narrow canyon just east of Missoula where Blackfoot ambushes frequently terrorized them. Others pushed up the Clark Fork from Kullyspel House, the Hudson's Bay post on Lake Pend O'reille in today's Idaho established by David Thompson in 1809. The following year Saleesh House, near present-day Thompson Falls, Montana, moved the center of trading with the Flatheads even closer. Soon to arrive as well were twenty

Iroquois Indians led by Ignace La Moussee, who shared with the Flatheads not only trade goods but their Catholic religion. This influence paved the way in 1841 for Father Pierre-Jean De Smet and his missionary endeavors among the region's Indians and further set the stage for the rapid cultural changes that would soon envelop the Flatheads.

The Indians came under the increasing influence of the United States government with the creation in 1848 of Oregon Territory, which included the Missoula Valley, and in 1853, when the valley became a part of the new Washington Territory. Settlers were by this time slipping into the area, claiming land that wasn't legally open to them, and nudging the U.S. Government towards ownership by any possible means. A treaty negotiated with the Flatheads, Pend d'Oreilles, and Kootenais in 1855 established a reservation and opened the remainder of the region to settlement by whites.

Many came. Among them were Lyman Worden and Christopher Higgins, who in 1860 established a store in a tent about four miles west of present-day Missoula. When Missoula County was delineated in December of that year, their store became the county seat, and the community of Hellgate was born. The population grew with the discovery of gold in the valley in 1861, and soon rich strikes in Virginia City and Alder Gulch, in Southwest Montana, quickly established demand for the agricultural products that could be produced in the neighboring Bitterroot Valley.

In the spring of 1862, Hellgate folks were accused of putting on "States Airs" by pioneer Granville Stuart when he learned that Hellgate had a justice of the peace and was about to hold its first trial. It seems that Tin Cup Joe had allowed his horses to find their way to Baron O'Keefe's haystacks, whereupon O'Keefe shot one horse. Frank Woody, newly appointed prosecuting attorney, was to face self-defended O'Keefe before Judge Henry Brooks. Stuart was no doubt amused to learn that Woody's accusations caused O'Keefe to attack both prosecutor and judge, and that a general melee had broken out in the courtroom. "When the dust of battle cleared away it was considered to be a draw," wrote Stuart in his journal. The jury later delivered a verdict for the plaintiff, recorded Stuart, "but I do not know that anyone ever tried to collect money from Baron O'Keefe. I do know that I would not have cared for the job."

> *Along the valleys of both the Hell Gate and Bitter Root, there is a great abundance of excellent timber — pine, hemlock, tamarack or larch predominating. Beautiful prairie openings occur at frequent intervals, with good soil inviting the hand of the husbandman. At the settlement called Hell Gate, situated at the junction of the river by that name and the Bitter Root, are several farms, which yield all the cereals and vegetables in great abundance, bringing good prices, such as would astonish farmers in the States, as parties are constantly passing through that region on their way to the mines, and glad to purchase supplies.*
>
> J.L. Campbell, 1864

Idaho Territory was created in 1863, and Hellgate swelled with promise as word of the vast natural resources of this huge region reached gold-hungry adventurers and land-hungry farmers in the eastern United States. However, when Higgins, Frank Worden and David Pattee formed Missoula Mills Company in 1864 and erected a sawmill about four miles east on Rattlesnake Creek, Hellgate was destined for demise. In 1865, the mill owners built a flour mill and moved the Worden & Higgins store to the mill site. Soon two hotels, a carpentry shop, and several log houses were axed into existence and the place acquired the name Missoula Mills. In 1866, the county seat, already unofficially drifting towards the newer community, was officially moved from Hellgate. From then on, Missoula flourished — the first school in '69, first courthouse and jail in '71, first bank and hospital in '73, first fire department in '77, first library in '78, and the first water plant in '80.

During the 1870s, white citizens of the region became concerned about Indian hostilities and, in 1877, as the Nez Perce War was about to begin west of the Bitterroots, pressured the government into building Fort Missoula. By the time the warring Nez Perces entered Montana, construction of the fort was barely underway. Nevertheless, by then troops were in place at the fort, and Capt. Charles Rawn with a contingent of soldiers and volunteers was dispatched in late July to Lolo Creek where they set up the Fort Fizzle barricade. (See Mile 28.0.) Other official endeavors were conducted out of the fort over the years, but its relatively safe location led to its becoming as much a social and recreational outpost as a military one. The men engaged in fishing, hunting, riding and saloon-hopping, and upper class Missoulians attended dances and other social functions at the fort. The fort exists today as a thirty-two acre historical walking tour and museum open year-round to visitors. The museum houses about eleven thousand artifacts and twelve historic structures, and its coverage, which begins with the period of early exploration, includes forestry, agriculture, transportation, the military, mining and community life.

The Northern Pacific Railroad laid line to Missoula in 1883, connecting the community to new markets and bringing an influx of people with it. New businesses soon opened, and community prosperity continued. In 1886, the railroad was extended south into the Bitterroot Valley where logging, agriculture and mining had created a demand for improved means of transit.

In the fall of 1895, the University of Montana opened in Missoula in a small renovated building known as Southside School. Cultural consciousness no doubt padded in on polished shoes with the prominence Missoula gained by becoming a university town. Such consciousness continues today in the city's Museum of the Arts, a multitude of cultural events each year, bookstores and galleries, and, of course, the aforementioned Historical Museum at Fort Missoula.

You may enjoy a biking or walking tour along Missoula's Riverfront Trail, which is dotted with historic markers and the Missoula Millstone Display. The markers trace the old main line of the Chicago, Milwaukee and St. Paul Railroad and cover much of the history of the valley in which Missoula lies. You can access the trail at several points, but if driving into the city from the south, you'll be traveling on Highway 93, which becomes Brooks Avenue and then Higgins Avenue. When you reach South Fourth Street, just before crossing the Clark Fork River, turn right. Drive ahead a couple blocks to John Toole Park, where you can park, get out and start your self-tour.

To reach the Missoula Chamber of Commerce visitor's center, continue into town on Higgins. Downtown, turn right onto Broadway. Drive one-half mile to Van Buren and turn right again. Drive ahead one block. The Chamber building is on the right. You may wish also to stop at the Missoula County Courthouse to view eight historical paintings by

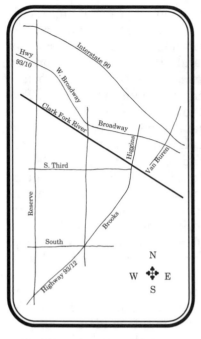

Skeletal Map of Missoula

nineteenth century artist Edgar S. Paxson. The paintings cover Flathead Indian history, the Lewis and Clark Expedition, a roundup, and early transportation. You can easily spot the white courthouse dome just west of Higgins Avenue in downtown Missoula. Upon reaching Broadway, turn left and drive one block to Ryman Street.

You'll find in Missoula, as throughout the Missoula and Bitterroot Valleys and North Central Idaho's Clearwater Country, the story of the West as it was and is — either brought to you with a ten-gallon handshake by the big-hearted folks who live in the country or by the land itself. Much here is free, offered in plentiful amounts by Mother Nature; much is as inexpensive as the price of this book; and by following your particular fascinations you can purchase with two bits of effort as much more of the story as you want to find. Like the skilled reinsman of a nineteenth century stagecoach, CLEARWATER COUNTRY! THE TRAVELERS' HISTORICAL AND RECREATIONAL GUIDE leads the way.

> **If you are beginning your Clearwater Country tour at Missoula, take merged Highways 12 and 93 south to Lolo and turn west on Highway 12. As you travel, read the entries in this self-tour in reverse numerical order.**

Clearwater Country Recreation

No lesser word than *extraordinary* describes the possibilities for outdoor recreation throughout Clearwater Country. Whether you're young, old or in-between; alone, with a companion or children, you'll find excitement, challenge and fun — in many forms and during all seasons. Yet quietude, pristine beauty and peacefulness are also ever present. The region's blend of streams, terrain, wildlife and climate create an exceptional outdoor environment.

The **rivers** that run through Clearwater Country are among the world's clearest and finest. Whitewater rapids challenge kayakers and rafters, while deep dark pools and shallow riffles lure fishermen. Hot sandy beaches summon swimmers and sunbathers. Crystal veinlets dribbling down mountainsides beckon dayhikers, backpackers and horseback riders along cool, shadowy creekside paths. Indeed, intricate traceries of water and trailways weave and wend throughout the whole of Clearwater Country.

In October of 1968, the U.S. Congress designated the Lochsa, Selway, and Middle Fork of the Clearwater one of the nation's first Wild and Scenic river systems. Defined by Public Law 90-542, such rivers "with their immediate environments, possess outstandingly remarkable scenic, recreational, geologic, fish and wildlife, historic, cultural...values." The law functions to protect those values. Of Clearwater Country's five major rivers, the Selway remains the most hidden. It is the focal stream of one of the longest stretches of virgin watershed in the contiguous United States.

In addition to the designated wild river system, the South Fork and upper North Fork of the Clearwater, both of which also wind through forested mountainous country, are similarly scenic. And while the main Clearwater River flows through a more populated and less forested area, it too offers much beauty and recreation. Then, to make this incredible river system even more astounding, the famed Salmon and Snake Rivers are within easy reach.

Those modern-day explorers who like remoteness will find pristine mountain lakes tucked away midst mountain peaks and talus slopes. For those who want a bit of company with their outdoor excursions, Lolo, Red River, and Jerry Johnson Hot Springs provide still another form of wet entertainment.

Clearwater Country's **terrain** is likewise magnificent because of its diversity, breadth and accompanying climate. The region includes sections of Idaho's Nez Perce, Lewis, Clearwater and Idaho Counties. Idaho County alone covers 8,539 square miles, area enough to contain eight Rhode Islands! Yet it is home to only 16,000 people. Varying natural environments lie within these counties — high alpine mountains, arid sagebrush hills and canyons, grassy prairies, lushly forested foothills, wetland sanctuaries for birds — and elevations ranging from seven hundred to over nine thousand feet.

These elevations and diverse terrains create multiple climates within any one season. In early fall and late spring, for example, you may fish for steelhead on the Clearwater in sixty to seventy degree warmth or don sweaters to camp on the cool upper Lochsa. Late summer you may float the Salmon with temperatures over one hundred degrees and the next day head to a high mountain lake where your water bucket may have ice in it by morning. You may hunt high country elk in snow in September or pheasants at lower elevations in sixty-five degree sunshine in early November. Most years you can cross-country ski and snowmachine at Red River, Dixie or Lolo Pass in March and even April, and along some mountain roads, still make snowballs in July. Yet during some years, golfers in Lewiston enjoy their game in November and February.

While the Lewis and Clark expeditionists camped beside the Clearwater River in the Kamiah Valley on May 15, 1806, William Clark commented on the area's variable terrain and climate in his journal. He wrote,

> ...as the days are worm &c. we have a bowry made to write under which we find not only comfortable but necessary, to keep off the intence heet of the sun which has great effect in this low bottom. on the high plains off the river the climate is entirely different cool, some snow on the north hill sides near the top and vegetation near 3 weeks

later than in the river bottoms, and the rocky Mountains immediately in view covered several say 4 & 5 feet deep with snow. here I behold three different climats within a fiew miles.

Wildlife in Clearwater Country, both flora and fauna, is as diverse as its topography. Among plants, variations run from the most delicate of wild flowers, to scruffy sage and thorn brush, to immense old cedars. In their journals, Lewis and Clark noted varied plant growth around them as they rode through area foothills on their homeward leg.

The country through which we passed...is well timbered with several Species of fir, long leafed pine and Larch. the undergrowth is choke cherry near the watercourses, black alder, a large species of red root now in blume, a Growth which resembles the poppaw in its leaf, and which bears a berry...two species of shoemate, seven bark, perple haw, service berry, Goose berry, wild rose, honey suckle...and a species of dwarf pine which grows about 10 or 12 feet high.

Among animals, Clearwater Country's habitats support big game herds, smaller forest animals, a multitude of songbirds and many larger birds as well, and other critters typical of the West, such as coyotes and rattlesnakes.

Many of Clearwater Country's wild flora and fauna are noted below and/or in the Mile-by-Mile section of this book. Brief descriptions are sometimes provided to aid identification. Let's look then at the myriad of recreational resources offered by the region's streams, terrain and wildlife.

Birds

Whether or not you have ever held a birder's field guide in your hands or focused binoculars on feathered wings, Clearwater Country will introduce you to many birds. Naturally, your elevation, the terrain and the season will determine which birds you will likely see.

In WINTER, for example, **bald eagles** frequent the river corridor, often perching on dead tree limbs or lighting on the river's edge to feed on carcasses of winter-killed whitetail deer. Now and then that river's edge delicacy will be a fish dropped hastily by a river otter who thought that a dive-bombing eagle was after a meal of otter meat. Similarly large-sized, but without the white head, juvenile bald eagles may accompany their elders or find their own lookouts.

Another winter scavenger is the all black **raven**, a football-sized cousin of the smaller crow. Ravens favor forested areas along the Lochsa. So do **Steller's jays**, which are a bit larger than a robin and have black heads and shoulders, fading to blue on the body and tail, and sport a distinctive head crest. The long tails of **blackbilled magpies** will help you identify these black and white residents of the area. You may also spot a four-foot tall **great blue heron** with a whitish neck or a two-foot **little blue heron** motionlessly hunched on the shore ice watching the water for a morning meal. **Finches**, **pine siskins** and several varieties of **sparrow** call the valley their home, and a white snow background makes the **blackcapped chickadee** and **Oregon junco** very discernible. And if the unusually tall snowcap atop a farmer's fencepost suddenly turns its head, a **snowy owl** has just spied you.

In SPRING, romance disbands flocks and disperses pairs of birds across the landscape as the first snow-melt swells the rivers. **Geese** now take to the nesting boxes provided on the islands along the lower Clearwater or seek more natural nesting spots throughout the river corridor. **Robins** and their slightly larger cousin, the **varied thrush**, return to Clearwater Country, as does the **red-tailed hawk** and sleek-winged **osprey**. The latter birds can be seen sprucing up their bulky, stick nests atop bare tree snags or power poles or diving at great speeds into the river in search of rainbow trout. The red-tails, near eagle size and with broader wings than the osprey, are most often seen high overhead riding thermals. You might spot white **tundra swans**, among the largest of the birds that inhabit Clearwater Country, sitting like long-necked patches of snow on a mid-river gravel bar. In the early morning, the songs of Audubon, MacGillivray's and yellow **warblers** may harmonize against a backdrop of **mourning dove** coos, while wild tom **turkeys** gobble gobble in reaction to the zip of a tent flap. And if strange sounds enter your campground from the nearby woods suggesting that someone out there is attempting to start an outboard motor, you are listening to the drumming of the male **ruffed grouse** attempting to attract a willing mate.

With the hot weather of SUMMER, more visitors spend time beside or on Clearwater Country rivers, where the rattling call and uneven flight of the white-breasted **belted kingfisher** quickly draws attention. Larger than a robin, this blue-gray river traveler has a large head topped with a bushy crest. **Red-winged blackbirds** nest in the willows at shore's edge — the red epaulets on the male's shoulders provide a distinguishing mark. Several varieties of **hummingbirds**, their wings ablur, hover at blossoms to drink floral nectars. Slate-colored **water ouzels** dart and bob along the shoreline and dip into the water for food as their stubby tails reach skyward. Among the most colorful birds you may see are the yellow and black, but red-headed, **western tanager**; Idaho's state bird, the **mountain bluebird**; the black-backed and white-breasted **rufous-sided towhee**; the blue, gray and white-breasted **lazuli bunting**; and the mottled and striped **red-shafted flicker**. On occasion the kik-kik call of the **pileated woodpecker**, or its stacatto drumming against a tree trunk, echoes from the forests along the Middle Fork. Clearwater Country's **owls** vary in size from the great horned to the mid-sized barn owl and to the tiny saw-whet.

Several of the birds that draw notice in Clearwater Country in the AUTUMN are year-round residents. A variety of ducks float the river's edge, splash three-foot high water showers over their bodies, and quack conversationally at each other. Black and white-bodied male **common mergansers** and their lady friends, the more colorful **hooded mergansers**, shimmery green-headed **mallards**, rusty-headed green-winged **teal**, and once in a while an iridescent **wood duck** with its unusual facial patterns may be sighted. Local populations of such waterfowl are of course temporarily increased by migrating cousins. Ruffed and spruce **grouse** are also plentiful throughout the region and in lesser numbers blue grouse. You're likely, too, to see coveys of three varieties of **quail** scampering up ditch banks and an occasional long-tailed, rust-colored ring-necked **pheasant** visiting the road's shoulder to replenish the food-grinding gravel in its craw. Flocks of gray-bodied **Western Canada geese** cluster in coves and eddies along the rivers till time to fly off for daily feedings in area wheatfields. You can't miss the communal honking that accompanies their movements. **Grosbeaks** and **cedar**

waxwings migrate through as well, feasting on the abundant berries still clinging to trees and bushes.

Lewis and Clark fans may be on special watch for **Clark's nutcrackers** and the **Lewis woodpecker**. If that isn't enough for a roster of Clearwater Country birds, keep looking. Here come the **meadowlarks, killdeer, swallows, yellow-bellied sapsuckers** and many many more. So do remember your binoculars and notebook!

Wild Flora

Clearwater Country is also home to a stunning array of greenery and blossoming plants woven into a sometimes rugged, sometimes lush, and almost everywhere *wild* tapestry of land. There is much to appreciate in the flora of Clearwater Country, and appreciation is the most sensitive and satisfying recreation related to the area's plant life.

Acres upon acres of **trees** — firs, pines, tamarack, cedar, alder, Pacific yew, river birch, maple, black cottonwood, quaking aspen, hemlock, spruce, Pacific dogwood, wild fruit and others — are reason enough to carry your field guides and your camera. Often beneath the trees you'll find **ferns.** You may spot the four to twenty-four-inch high maidenhair ferns in cedar draws or the similarly sized horsetails in more open country. Towering over them, up to seven feet, may be a group of feather-like ladyferns or equally tall bracken fern. In the mid-size range, you may spot dark green sword ferns.

Like so many Clearwater Country visitors since Lewis and Clark's coming into the country, the explorers admired the beauty of the **wildflowers** that paint bold splotches of color across spring hillsides and summer meadows. On June 12, 1806, for example, Clark wrote,

> The quawmash [camas] is now in blume. at a Short distance it resembles a lake of fine clear water, so complete is this deseption that on first Sight I could have sworn it was water.

A long growing season throughout much of the area — an average of one hundred ninety growing days on the lower Middle Fork, for example — provides a hospitable habitat for a wide assortment of plants. The differing environments of north and south-facing slopes and variations in temperature according to elevation further enable the wildflower enthusiast to observe within a short time span the blooms of a sequence of springs and summers.

Earliest in the spring you're likely to spot a few **buttercups** and slopes full of yellow **ivesia**, **biscuit root** and **arrowleaf balsam root**. In more wooded areas, three-petaled white **trilliums**, curly yellow **fawn lilies**, bluish **mountain kittentails**, lavender **shooting stars**, and yellow and purple **violets** unfold. As the earth continues to warm, the delicate blossoms of **wild plum, Pacific dogwood** and **apple** trees will scent the air. Gradually the open slopes and meadows will become embroidered with colors — deep pink cut-leaved **geraniums, yellow pea**, purple **delphiniums**, blue **triteleias**, giant red **paintbrushes**. Narrow clusters of pale blue **common camas** will bloom alongside their poisonous cousin, the **death camas,** with its small cluster of white blossoms atop a short stem ringed at the base with thin spear-like leaves. Don't touch! Yellow **daisies**, sweet pink **Nootka roses**, and at higher elevations the tall, white and bulbous **bear grass** clusters bloom. Early summer will also bring the blossoms of the state flower, the **syringa**, which is a variation of the mock orange. The poisonous skunk cabbage, or **corn lily**, will open into clusters of tiny white petals atop a thick tall stem ringed at the base with large, lined leaves. Also white – **woodland stars**, wild **candytufts**, **pearly everlasting**, and **Queen Anne's lace** will appear, along with **golden asters, blue chicory**, blue **miniature lupine**, lavender **teasel**, and **golden alexanders**. Fuzzy stars of **mullein** leaves will lay against the ground after emergence in the spring and then this plant will grow into four-to-six-foot towers of leaves with a central column of yellow blossoms by autumn. More elusive and unusual, **Columbia virgin's bower**, like miniature purplish chandeliers, will entwine themselves around bushes, as will vines carrying apricot-colored **honeysuckle** blossoms. **Mountain lady's slippers**, yellowish **seep-spring monkeyflowers** and pink-striped white **bank monkeyflowers** will show themselves here and there. Among the showiest of the summer wildflowers are the brilliant purplish **fireweed** and the **white-to-purple pea** which grow in thick beds along the Middle Fork of the Clearwater.

As you can see, there is a multitude of flora to discover, photograph, describe in your journal, sketch or paint or just enjoy in Clearwater Country. If you find a species that seems abundant, a fresh blossom might make a fine specimen for your flower press. If you find a single specimen or just a few of one plant, taking a snapshot or doing a sketch will be a more sensitive way of recording your discovery and delight. Then the plant should be left to propagate.

Just as the Nez Perces and early pioneers found sustenance in the wild plants of Clearwater Country, many visitors today enjoy gathering what nature offers in the way of wild fruits, berries and other **edible plants**. **Blackberries** provide a fine example. Should you travel along the Middle Fork in late August or early September you may notice cars parked alongside the highway and local folk bearing buckets and wading hip deep into briar patches. The object of their pursuit is a large, juicy blackberry, and then another and another, until enough for juice, jelly and a winter's supply of blackberry pies have been captured. In April and May the hills along parts of the river are spotted with blossoming trees, marking the locations of an easy harvest of wild **plums** later in the summer. The tart jellies and jams these plums produce make prize-winning entries at county fairs. At higher elevations the odor of ripe **huckleberries** drifts through open car windows in August and September. These low-bush berry delights, which can be found right along Highway 12 in the area of Lolo Pass or along various mountain roads, will turn morning pancakes or muffins at a nearby campground into a special treat. Also in September, hanging from twelve-foot high bushes, large clusters of purple **elderberries** can be gathered to create a pleasing wine or syrup. If your gathering instincts include true foraging, you may wish to seek out the likes of **rose hips**, **camas roots**, or **wild celery**, **carrots** or **onions**. Some treasured **mushrooms** await the gourmet gatherer as well — shaggy manes in the fall moistness of an old logging road, springtime morels in an old forest burn, or chanterelles poking through fir needles on a dark forest floor. If you haven't the time or inclination to gather some of the wild edibles along your way, we invite you to enjoy them in the form of homemade pies featured at area restaurants or in gift packs of jams and jellies you can purchase along your route.

Rocks and Gems

Clearwater Country has witnessed numerous gold rushes, including one in the 1970s as this long sought metal soared to eight hundred dollars an ounce. Many **gold** claims are still active in the area, but for most modern day prospectors a few flecks of color in the pan are reward enough for some recreational labor. Many streambeds in the national forests are open to recreational prospecting. However, care must be taken in some areas, such as along the South Fork and in the Elk City basin, not to trespass on a miner's claim. Also, of course, when you leave a streambed, it should look pretty much just as it did when you arrived.

Idaho is known as *The Gem State*, and Clearwater Country's rock and gem deposits prove the name's appropriateness. **Smokey quartz crystals**, for example, wash out of roadcuts west and north of Lolo Hot Springs. Sections of the Lochsa and Middle Fork yield bronze and blue **sapphires**, as do some of the old gold diggings in the Pierce area. **Sillimanite** hides in Selway River pools and mountain streams north of Dworshak Lake as well as in the main Clearwater River. **Agate**, **jasper**, **opal** and **petrified wood** are buried in basalt along canyon walls. In addition, the Idaho state stone, the **star garnet**, hugs the bedrock of Emerald Creek and tributary streams on the northern edge of Clearwater Country. Among these stones can be found some true gems by anyone's standard.

Land Animals

Clearwater Country's vast and primitive wilderness areas provide the perfect environment for wild animals, ranging in size from a pesky noseeum barely visible on your arm to as large as a thousand-pound bull **moose**. Bull, cow and calf moose are sometimes seen in marshy areas and ponds along the upper reaches of the Lochsa River and eastward to Lolo Pass, but less often downriver.

More populous among the large Clearwater Country animals is the **elk**. A large bull can top eight hundred pounds. Elk sightings occur throughout the river corridor, but particularly along the stretch from Kooskia to Montana. The months that run from winter through late spring provide the likeliest time for human onlookers to see elk enjoying sunshine and fresh browse on south-facing slopes.

Smaller in size but even greater in number are **deer.** Whitetail deer are common along the Highway 12 corridor, while the nearby Snake and Salmon River breaks provide habitat preferred by the branch-antlered **mule deer.** Although not in great numbers, **Rocky Mountain goats,** the *white buffalo* of the Nez Perces, reside along the Lochsa, in the upper North Fork drainage and in high-bluff areas along the Clearwater's South Fork. **Black bears** are common throughout the region and sometimes can be spotted on open grassy slopes in the springtime, especially along the Middle Fork, Lochsa and Selway Rivers.

Beautiful, more secretive residents are the mountain lions, or **cougars.** These streamlined predators can weigh over two hundred pounds with a body length up to six feet not counting a three-foot tail. Cougars are regular inhabitants of the hills along the Lochsa and Middle Fork in the winter; thus a cougar may be enjoying a meal of fresh venison within a hundred yards of the highway as you drive by during that season. In recent years the **gray wolf** has joined the cougar in the wilds of Clearwater Country via reintroduction at high elevations and remote locations, thereby retaking its historic place in the Bitterroot ecosystem.

Smaller animals also live in Clearwater Country. Going about the daily business of survival within the region's forests, prairies and wetlands are **raccoons, bobcats, porcupines, beavers, badgers, skunks, foxes, coyotes** (listen for their night howls)**, otters, mink, martens,** occasionally a **fisher,** and an assortment of yet smaller creatures.

One of the region's most frightful critters isn't a mammal: the poisonous **diamond-back rattlesnake.** Like other snakes living in Clearwater Country, the rattler is actually quite reclusive and not likely to show itself. Yet, on a hot summer's day, you may catch sight of a sleepy-looking rattler sunning itself on a rock, particularly along the Selway River.

Of course, a wide assortment of other land animals live here too — from frogs and toads to moles and mice, worms and slugs to honeybees and ladybugs. If you take your time as you travel through Clearwater Country, you're likely to see many land animal residents, each playing a specific role in the life cycles and food chains of the natural environment in which they, and we, live. For most people the deep pleasure of silently watching central Idaho's wild creatures offers the most satisfying means of enjoying them.

Fish

More Americans pursue the sport of fishing than any other form of outdoor recreation. Clearwater Country rivers and lakes afford anglers an exquisite year-round menu from which to choose wilderness food fare.

One of the true delicacies of the culinary world is a fresh **trout** prepared at a mountain campsite. Pan-sized brook trout are common catches at high mountain lakes, and at some, large rainbows are plentiful. The Lochsa River provides a fishing location for summer and autumn trout seekers — here both rainbow and cutthroat trout abound within casting distance of a U.S. highway! Much of this river is managed on a catch-and-release basis to assure continued quality angling for all. Parts of the Selway River are similarly managed, with the quality of the river and its trout fishing matched by the canyon's exquisite scenery. The Middle Fork lures fishermen in early June to trout feeding on bug hatches beside river willows and again on cool September mornings in a framework of autumn colors. The upper North Fork of the Clearwater is equally rewarding trout country. A North Fork tributary, Kelly Creek, for example, is widely known as a fine fly-fishing stream.

Now imagine a rainbow trout weighing twenty pounds flashing out of the water...and you're in for an unforgettable Clearwater sight: **steelhead**. Each fall the anadromous steelhead, the most famous of Clearwater Country's trout, begin arriving from the ocean. These fish are pursued throughout the fall, winter and early spring.

Along the upper branches of the Clearwater drainage, the Rocky Mountain **whitefish** also provides winter fishing. Typically eleven to fifteen inches long, these small-mouthed fish run in schools and tend to hit maggots baited on small hooks. The whitefish offer rewarding rod-and-reel fun for fishers who just can't wait for spring fishing, or those who know the secrets of turning these fish into smoked or pickled delicacies. The main Clearwater is also home to **smallmouth bass**, deep-bodied fish that love to hide out in dark holes or near water's edge willows.

Popular on Dworshak Lake are the **kokanee**, a small land-locked salmon. May and June are the best months for pursuing this eleven-to-twelve-inch fish, and trolling is the method of choice.

Again, the best way to enjoy fish may be simply to watch them. When a hatch of yummy bugs hovers over the water, you may see fish feeding — watch for small splashes, fish-lip nips at bugs sitting on the surface, and larger splooshes with a flash of fish-silver in them. Also, because the area's river waters are so clear, onshore viewers can often see fish swimming in quiet pools or riffles.

Beaches and Water

During the hot summer months, you may prefer to jump into the water! Sandy beaches abound in Clearwater Country. Hot summer days and the available shade of towering pines, firs or cedars make the beaches of the Clearwater especially inviting to swimmers, sunseekers and picnickers. If you're a strong swimmer, you may discover a secluded beach etched with deer, wild turkey or bobcat tracks on the south side of the Middle Fork or Lochsa. Fed by mountain snows, the rivers are high and frigid in May and June, but in July and August provide superb swimming. A book of poems and the solitude of a beach in seventy-five degree September or April sunshine can also be a treat, as can the lengthy stretches of lonely, trailside beaches miles up the Selway River beyond the end of the road and any signs of the civilized world. If snorkeling or scuba diving is a pastime of yours, Clearwater Country's clear water gives you a prime opportunity to explore riverbed worlds of stones, plants, fish and other smaller underwater creatures.

Especially popular beaches along the Highway 12 route are two on opposite sides of the river at Mile 53 near Greer, Tunnel Beach at Mile 56, Button Beach at Mile 71, Number One Beach at Mile 88, and Three Devils Beach at Mile 94. Also, you'll find several beaches of varying sizes along the Selway River and the South Fork.

Boating is also a popular form of outdoor fun in and near Clearwater Country. A jet boat excursion up the Snake River deep into Hell's Canyon, for example, or on the likewise tempestuous Salmon River can be an exceptional experience. Because of their proximity to some of the finest whitewater in the nation, the twin cities of Lewiston, Idaho, and Clarkston, Washington, have emerged as the jet boat building capital of the world. Half-day to multi-day jet boat excursions are available, providing thrills and fantastic scenery, and can be combined with fishing, hunting, camping or other recreational activities.

For those who prefer the calmer waters of a lake, during late May, June and early July, when the water behind Dworshak Dam is high, boating, swimming and camping may be enjoyed on Dworshak Lake near Orofino.

Few recreational activities in Clearwater Country provide more variety than river floating. River enthusiasts float in rafts, driftboats, kayaks, canoes and innertubes. The time of year of a float affects not only the clothing required, swimsuit to wetsuit, but also the height of the river and hence wildness of the run. Also, each river and section of river offers unique challenges and elicits reactions that range from exhilarating terror to serene bliss. The upper Lochsa, for example, is fast water but limits its leaps to class II rapids. Thus a day's run through high alpine Lochsa country in late spring and early summer will be full of action delightful to the guided beginner or experienced floater. The lower Lochsa in late winter through June lures to its rapids the most experienced, thrill-seeking kayakers and rafters because here the river offers some of the toughest whitewater in the nation. River runners on the upper Selway also face extreme challenges and achieve maximum thrills before completing their runs in the Selway's less turbulent lower waters. If you'd like a more relaxing run, in July and August, the Middle Fork and main Clearwater will glide you beneath an osprey nest, gently jostle you through light rapids, and carry you to a sandy beach for an afternoon picnic. Float trips are also possible through the magnificent Salmon River Canyon, exceeded in depth only by one other river gorge in the United States — the nearby Hell's Canyon of the Snake. Licensed guides, who'll work closely with you to provide the kind of floating experience you will enjoy, are available for all area rivers. To arrange a float trip, stop at Lowell (Mile 97.0), Orofino (Mile 44.0), Grangeville (See Side Trip #5 in the Side Trip chapter.) or Lewiston.

Even the historical self-tour covered in the Mile-by-Mile section of this book could be taken via Clearwater Country's waterways. Your floating experience might be along a moving museum of rivers — water routes of the Nez Perces, the trappers and traders, the miners, the settlers, and, of course, of those famous 1805-'06 explorers who rode rough-hewn log dugouts down the Clearwater on an always-to-be-remembered Clearwater Country float trip.

Picnic Areas and Campgrounds

Another way to enjoy Clearwater Country's beaches and waterways is to picnic or camp beside them. There are many picnic areas and campgrounds along the river corridors. Beginning on the western edge of Clearwater Country, you'll find picnic and campground areas along Snake River Avenue in Lewiston. (See Lewiston in the Mile-by-Mile section.)

On the main Clearwater River, picnic tables are available at a large rest stop at Mile 27.5. West of Orofino, Pink House Hole Recreation Area includes a few undeveloped campsites (Mile 39.1). There are riverside benches and a table at the Canoe Camp interpretive site at Mile 40.0. Big Eddy Recreation Area alongside Dworshak Lake near Orofino provides picnic tables. (See Side Trip #3 in the Side Trips chapter.) In Orofino itself, just across the Clearwater River bridge at Mile 44.0, you'll find a large city park.

Likewise in Kamiah, picnic tables are provided in a groomed park setting at Riverside Park (Mile 66.9), where overnight RV camping is allowed. Kooskia, too, provides a picnic area and RV sites in its City of Kooskia Lion's Park alongside the South Fork. (See Kooskia at Mile 73.9 in the Mile-by-Mile section.)

Main Street in Kooskia is also state Highway 13. If you continue south on Highway 13 and then, fourteen miles later, turn onto Highway 14, you can follow the South Fork to Elk City. Along Highway 14, there are several campgrounds and picnic areas, all in lovely streamside settings. (See Side Trip #6 in the Side Trips chapter.)

Back on Highway 12 and the Middle Fork upriver from Kooskia, you'll arrive at Tukatesp'e Picnic Area at Mile 76.3 and Three Devils Picnic Area at Mile 94.3. Wild Goose Campground lies at Mile 95.3. At Mile 97.0, Lowell, you may turn south onto the Selway River Road to locate picnic and camping sites. See Side Trip #7 in the Side Trips chapter for a guide to those sites. Upriver from Lowell along the Lochsa, you'll find nine beautiful USFS campgrounds. On the east side of Lolo Pass (Mile 174), you'll find two more campgrounds and Howard Creek and Fort Fizzle Picnic Areas.

Some campers enjoy a forested, riverside setting and the recreation such a setting allows, but still appreciate the amenities of a cabin, inn or motel. These lodging accommodations also can be found throughout Clearwater Country, — from Lewiston to Lowell, at Powell, and from Lolo Hot Springs to Missoula — and offer you most satisfying means of enjoying the country.

Trails

Over two-thirds of Clearwater Country is federal land and hence shared by all Americans. Thus, a few million acres of forest and wilderness lie available nearby for outdoor pleasures. This vastness is crisscrossed by hundreds of trails, some that have existed since time immemorial and others that are brand new; some that are annually maintained and others that have become nearly obliterated.

For those of you who prefer to put your camping equipment on your back — or your gear and you on the back of a horse or mule — a broad and beautiful natural world awaits you. The Selway Bitterroot Wilderness alone consists of over a million acres laced with hundreds of miles of trails. The Gospel Hump Wilderness area covers another two hundred thousand acres. Add in the 2.3 million acres of the neighboring Frank Church River of No Return Wilderness and those of the nearby Hell's Canyon National Recreation Area and you'll find enough trails to take you around the next bend or over the next hill for the rest of your life.

Many fine hikes and pack trips are also available in areas not officially designated as wilderness. Your source of information regarding all trails in the region are the USFS offices in Orofino, Grangeville, Kooskia, Elk City, near Lowell and Powell. The following are a few of Clearwater Country's favorite trails readily accessible from Highway 12 that can provide a fine introduction to hiking in the region.

Selway River Trail

At the end of the Selway River Road a major trail continues upriver into the Selway Bitterroot Wilderness. (See Selway River Road Side Trip #7 in the Side Trips chapter.) If you wish, you could follow the Selway River Trail and connecting trails for a hundred-plus miles to the south or swing east and end up in the Bitterroot Valley. Assuming that you intend to spend less than a couple of weeks in the wilderness, however, the Selway River Trail can introduce you to more of the beautiful Selway River canyon. You'll enter the wilderness a couple of miles upstream from the trailhead. The trail generally follows a river grade, traverses open hillsides at times, and passes by several white sand beaches before reaching Moose Creek twenty-one miles upstream. Here the trail forks, with one branch heading east up Moose Creek and the other continuing up the Selway. A day hike should be considered as a minimum amount of time to devote to the Selway River Trail, for you'll hate to turn around wherever that decision must be made. In the spring, the lower stretches of the Selway are replete with wildflowers and with usually cautious rattlesnakes, so be on the alert for both.

Meadow Creek Trail

Eighteen and a half miles up the Selway River Road (see Side Trip #7), a bridge crosses the Selway. Shortly after crossing the bridge, a left turn will take you along Meadow Creek for about two miles to another bridge. Enroute, this stretch of road passes a campground. Across the bridge, Slim's Camp, a two-site campground, serves as a trailhead for the Meadow Creek Trail, which follows this beautiful mountain stream in a westerly direction. The first three miles are level and at stream side. The trail then climbs up out of the canyon and continues west with occasional overlooks into the canyon below. Eventually Meadow Creek Trail climbs to Anderson Butte a few miles northeast of Elk City. At Slim's Camp, a road climbs fourteen miles to Indian Hill and to a series of hiking trails referred to as The Highline. The road that leaves the valley to the right before reaching Slim's Camp winds through the mountains to Elk City. This slow route is for rugged vehicles and people with plenty of time.

Fish Creek Trail

A half mile up the road running north from Highway 12 at Mile 120.1, the Fish Creek Trail begins following Fish Creek northward. The trail soon winds a fairly easy up-and-down hill grade away from the creek and, in about an hour's walk, returns to the creek upstream. From that point, the next three miles of the trail again leave the creek and take hikers to Hungery Creek's intersection with Fish Creek. Past Hungery Creek, the Fish Creek Trail continues westward into higher country. An unmaintained and largely obliterated trail follows Hungery Creek into a rugged canyon in which the Lewis and Clark Expedition camped. Parts of the Fish Creek Trail are along southern exposures, making for hot walking in summer months, but nice viewing.

Lochsa River Historical Trail
Idaho Centennial Trail

The Lochsa River Historical Trail provided USFS personnel a means of supplying the Lochsa Ranger Station prior to the road's reaching that location in 1952. You can begin the Lochsa River Historical Trail, a relatively easy trail, at Sherman Creek near the Wilderness Gateway Campground at Mile 122.6, at the Lochsa Historical Ranger Station at Mile 121.6, a short distance up Fish Creek Road at Mile 120.1, or opposite Split Creek at Mile 111.9. The trail parallels the highway from Split Creek to Sherman Creek, covering a total distance of about ten miles. It affords beautiful views of the Lochsa River and canyon, much of the time without a sense that a highway is in the vicinity. You can leave the trail at several points and drop down to the highway. Near the middle of this route, Snowshoe Falls drops into an unforgettably lovely glade — lush enough for a kiss, a poem, a picnic — or perhaps all three!

The Historical Trail is part of the Idaho Centennial Trail, which will eventually traverse the state north to south. Emerging from the Selway Bitterroot Wilderness, a portion of the Centennial Trail crosses the Lochsa River from the south via Split Creek Bridge, then proceeds upriver along the Lochsa River Historical Trail. At Sherman Creek the Centennial Trail climbs north for seven miles to Noseeum Meadows, where it joins the Nez Perce National Historic Trail and proceeds east before angling again northward.

Jerry Johnson Hot Springs Trail

Warm Springs Pack Bridge at Mile 151.5 enables hikers to cross to the south side of the Lochsa River and embark upon the one-mile, mostly level trail to Jerry Johnson Hot Springs. There are no amenities other than those provided by Mother Nature at the hot springs, so take snacks, towel, toilet tissue and a baggie in which to carry used tissue out, and so forth. The hike to the pools takes about twenty minutes. The trail continues up the Warm Springs Creek valley and into the Selway Bitterroot Wilderness.

White Sand Creek Trail

At Mile 161.8 near Powell, White Sand Creek joins the Crooked Fork to form the Lochsa River. One mile from Highway 12, on the Elk Summit Road and just across the bridge over the Crooked Fork, the Beaver Ridge Road heads east toward Lolo Pass. About a mile up this road you will find the trailhead for White Sand Creek Trail. This trail follows the creek south for as far as you may care to walk, including the possibility of crossing Blodgett Pass into Montana. It can also provide a lovely, easy leg stretch for a weary traveler or a fine day hike or overnighter. Spring chinook salmon spawn in White Sand Creek in late summer.

Nez Perce National Historic Trail
Lewis & Clark National Historic Trail

In large part, these two major trails share common tread and are included in what is referred to as the Lolo Trail. The Nez Perce National Historic Trail is an ancient trail long used by the Nez Perces, and its *historic* designation commemorates the flight of the non-treaty Nez Perces from Clearwater Country during the Nez Perce War of 1877. This trail actually begins in eastern Oregon and ends in the Bear Paw Mountains in northern Montana. That portion of the trail the Nez Perces followed from Weippe to Lolo, Montana, was the original Nez Perce *road to the buffalo*. Lewis and Clark took an alternate route into the upper Lochsa on part of their westward journey through this area but stayed on the main trail traveling east the following summer. For most people, these trails can best be enjoyed in segments, some of which are included here:

a. At the Howard Creek Picnic Area at Highway 12 Mile 14.0 on the Montana side of the Idaho/Montana border, the trail crosses the road a tenth of a mile north of Highway 12. Enroute to Lolo Hot Springs, the trail ascends the mountains to the west and allows a hiker to experience, like the members of the Lewis and Clark

Expedition, those "intolerable roads on the sides of the Steep Stoney mountains."

b. Lee Creek Campground (Mile 5.9 on the Montana side of the border) serves as trailhead for that part of the Nez Perce/Lewis and Clark Trail running from the campground to Packer Meadows near the top of Lolo Pass. The distance to Packer Meadows is about six miles.

c. The Parachute Hill Road (Mile 162.0 on the Idaho side) provides access to USFS Road #500, otherwise known as the Lolo Motorway. The Motorway closely parallels many segments of the Nez Perce/Lewis and Clark Trail, and literally shares tread with some trail segments. In other words, the Motorway provides direct access to some stretches of trail that have been to an extent maintained and can be located without too much difficulty. Finding more obliterated sections of the trail, however, calls for exceptional orienteering skill and historical knowledge. The Lolo Motorway traverses the divide between the Lochsa River on the south and streams flowing into the North Fork of the Clearwater on the north.

Vehicles may exit the Motorway and return to Highway 12 Mile 139.7 via Saddle Camp Road), to Highway 12 Mile 153.8 via Squaw Creek Road, or to Highway 12 Mile 88.4 from the west end of the Motorway via Forest Road #101. By studying a forest map, you'll also see that other forest roads on the west end of the Motorway lead to Road #100, which joins Highway 12 at Kamiah. Many people are expected to visit this area during the Lewis and Clark Bicentennial years of 2003-2006. Due to the rich historical, cultural and natural resources along the Motorway and the area's limited capacity for large numbers of visitors, the USFS may find it necessary to restrict access to the Motorway during the peak years of the Bicentennial celebration. Visitors are thus urged to check with personnel from the Clearwater National Forest before planning a motor or hiking trip on the Lolo Motorway between the years 2002- 2007.

d. The trail Lewis and Clark took from the Lochsa River up Wendover Ridge to the main Nez Perce Trail leaves Highway 12 near Wendover Campground at Mile 158.3. The USFS intends to clear this trail prior to the year

2002 and offer it as access to the main Nez Perce/Lewis and Clark Trail along the Lolo Motorway. This portion of the trail may be included in any permit system implemented during the Lewis and Clark Bicentennial Celebration.

e. Portions of the Nez Perce/Lewis and Clark Trail are identified and improved from the Musselshell Meadows area southeast of Weippe and north of Kamiah (MP 66), running eastward to the west end of the Lolo Motorway. Access to these portions can be made from forest roads in the area. Some signage guides drivers, but forest maps, available from the USFS, are essential.

It is anticipated that much information will be available by 2001 regarding the Lewis and Clark route through Clearwater Country, including more detailed guidance on hiking opportunities following this historic trek.

The Nez Perce/Lewis and Clark/Lolo Trail and all area trails wend through wild regions. Enjoyment of the wilds is every hiker's focus, but do hike with appropriate equipment and do stay alert.

Remember that one of the best defenses against any potentially dangerous animal is easy to implement: make noise. Human voices and walking noises forewarn wild animals that you are approaching, and, typically, the wild ones will move away before you actually reach them. The hundreds of folks who safely hike Clearwater Country trails every year have discovered that most often a trail hike will end without sightings of dangerous animals, so don't hesitate to take a walk.

However, if noise doesn't work as well as you hope, and you do meet a potentially dangerous animal, folks familiar with the wilds usually recommend slowly, quietly but deliberately backing off. In other words, give the animal **its** space. Of course, you'll have to rely on your own judgment in all cases, but the general rule is: don't run. (You could suddenly look like something fun to chase — just what a predator likes.)

Some warning signs: A *coiled* or *rattling* rattlesnake may be preparing to strike. (Move back.) Believe it or not, the snake is scared too. A *quiet, steadily pursuing* bear may be stalking you. (Act and look BIG, move away. If you can get to your vehicle, do so.) A *huffy, noisy* bear is probably trying to scare you off. (Leave.) A cougar is likely to follow a walker from behind and not show itself until it is attacking. Yet, an attack is highly unlikely, for cougars are fairly reclusive. (If you do see a cougar, slowly backing away is likely to be the best response. Never turn and run.) Mountain goats, elk and deer are not thought of as dangerous. (Typically, it is safe to just stop and silently watch.) Moose usually are not threatening either, but a harrassed or surprised moose or a mother moose with a calf can be. (Move quickly away from any aggressive moose. To watch one, stand at a distance, still and quiet.)

Take care to prepare yourself fully for the duration of your hike with food, drinking water, companions and appropriate clothing, including suitable shoes or boots. Remember that summer months can be quite hot and that, in the mountains, unexpectedly cold temperatures and rain or snow squalls can occur in any month. Realize, too, that trails are often crossed by other trails, for there is quite a network of walkways in the forest. Perhaps you need a trail map or firsthand information from someone who knows the trail. If so, stop at a Forest Service station.

As you hike the trails of Clearwater Country, you can maximize your enjoyment by maintaining a sensitivity for the natural world. While the wild environment may appear to possess the might of a bull moose or black bear, it is at the same time fragile. Please tread lightly by sticking primarily to maintained trails, respecting the rights of animals and carrying out everything you carry in.

Boots padding along a pine needle path, fingers brushing grass tips and leaves, eyes feasting on greenery and flower-strewn mountainside beauty — walking a trail is very possibly the most pleasurable way for anyone to visit the true depths of Clearwater Country.

Snow

While most hiking and horse trails are closed by snow in the winter, many mountain roads are converted by the snow into winter-fun trails. Then cross-country skiers and snowmobilers take to miles of winter-abandoned woodland roads and open spaces. From mid-November until late March, Lolo Pass offers eighteen miles of groomed ski trails for the beginner and another nine miles for more advanced skiers. Fish Creek Meadows near Grangeville is also a popular cross-country ski area and, like Lolo Pass, is part of the USFS park and ski program. If you'd like to take a winter side tour into the mountains for cross-country skiing, snowshoeing or snowmobiling, you could also head to Elk City and Dixie via Highways 13 and 14. (Side Trip #6)

Three area downhill ski slopes add to Clearwater Country's winter recreational opportunities. Ski lifts south of Grangeville, at Cottonwood Butte, and near Pierce provide downhill skiers with snow-time fun and thrills.

Community Events

All Clearwater Country communities offer events to which travelers are invited. You may, for example, be here at the right time for a rodeo in Lewiston, Grangeville, or Kamiah; a loggers' competition in Orofino; a Lewiston-to-Kamiah jet boat rally; Orofino's old-fashioned Sunday crafts fair; the Dogwood Festival in Lewiston; county fairs, fishing derbys, Christmas tree lighting ceremonies; a music festival in Kamiah or Kooskia. You may walk along the levee in Lewiston for an afternoon refresher and then drive to Kooskia for an evening of on-stage drama at the popular Old Opera House Theatre, which the owners and local volunteers have turned into a Victorian showcase of local talent. You may tour the Camas Prairie throughout your day and then drop down into the valley to catch a concert in Orofino. You could enjoy a Labor Day free barbeque at Kamiah or head upriver to Kooskia in April for an evening of readings by local writers or in the winter for a pre-Christmas art show. Look for special events and ongoing displays at art galleries in Grangeville, Orofino and Lewiston and museums in the same three towns and at Kamiah and Spalding.

The gist of it is that there's a lot going on and a lot to do *just naturally* in Clearwater Country throughout the entire year. Enjoy!

Clearwater Country Side Trips

After enjoying the scenery, historical sites and recreational opportunities found along Clearwater Country's Highway 12, there are several side jaunts you may consider. All of the side trips suggested below can be completed in a day or less. Since North Central Idaho is bisected east to west by just one highway, U.S. 12, each side trip is oriented to Highway 12 and its mileposts. This orientation enables you to use U.S. 12 as a constant reference point while enjoying your Clearwater Country wanderings. You may wish at times to refer back to the large Clearwater Country map at the beginning of this book to reorient yourself to the whole region.

Gas, food and lodging are available at Missoula, Lolo, Powell, Lowell, Kooskia, Grangeville, Kamiah, Orofino and Lewiston; gas and food at Weippe, Pierce and Elk City. USFS campgrounds are located along the South Fork, Middle Fork, Selway and Lochsa Rivers. RV sites with services are available at Lewiston, Orofino, Kooskia, Grangeville, Harpster, Lowell and a few miles east of Kamiah.

Side Trip Menu

Side Trip 1: Lewiston Hill Scenic Viewpoint

Side Trip 2: Nez Perce National Historic Park Museum, Spalding Mission and Fort Lapwai

Side Trip 3: Clearwater Fish Hatchery and Dworshak Hatchery, Dam and Lake

Side Trip 4: Weippe Prairie, Weippe and Pierce

Side Trip 5: Northwest Passage Scenic Byway Extension to Grangeville

Side Trip 6: Elk City, Red River and Dixie

Side Trip 7: Selway River Road

Side-Trip #1 Lewiston Hill Scenic Viewpoint
Via Highway 95 North

To reach the top of the Lewiston Hill, from which you may view the valley below (and, if you wish, tour the Palouse Prairie and the university town of Moscow), turn north on Highway 95 from Mile 312.0 in North Lewiston. You will reach the viewpoint in five and one-half miles (and Moscow in thirty miles). Watch for signs guiding you to the viewpoint. At Mile 317.4 turn off Highway 95 onto Old Spiral Highway. When you come to a stop sign (in one-eighth mile), turn right. The overlook is one-tenth mile ahead.

As you stand at the overlook, to the southwest you'll see the Blue Mountains of southeastern Washington and eastern Oregon. To the south you'll see the breaks of the Snake River Canyon and a plateau region stretching south and southeast towards the Craig Mountains. To the east runs the Clearwater River Valley. At the base of the Lewiston Hill lies the business area known as North Lewiston and the Ports of Lewiston, Clarkston, and Wilma. Lewiston proper lies on the south side of the Clearwater River. Along the fringes of the plateau lies Lewiston Orchards, largely a residential section of the city.

You may wish to return to Lewiston via the Old Spiral Highway, a route of about eight miles considered an engineering marvel in its day. You'll enjoy the valley view all the way down the hill. Off to the west as you drive the Old Spiral, you'll notice traces of the wagon road that, prior to 1912, folks followed to travel back and forth between the valley and the Palouse Prairie. (For wagon road information, see Mile 312.0 in the Mile-by-Mile section.)

Side-Trip #2: Nez Perce National Historic Park
Museum, Spalding Mission and
Fort Lapwai Via Highway 95 South

At Highway 12 Mile 11.2 (which is also Highway 95 Mile 305.0) turn onto Highway 95 South. In seventh-tenths mile, you'll cross the Clearwater River. At just under two miles, you'll come to the entrance to the Nez Perce National Historic Park Headquarters and Museum, which are open 8 a.m. to 4:30 p.m. daily. The museum houses Nez Perce artifacts and dioramas depicting Nez Perce life, a gift shop, and a theater where informational videos are sometimes shown. The Nez Perce National Historic Park is a collection of thirty-eight sites located from eastern Oregon to northern Montana that commemorate Nez Perce history, particularly the flight of the non-treaty Nez Perces from the United States Military in 1877.

On the parking lot's northeast corner, a road leads to the Spalding Mission site. The grounds were once the site of a Nez Perce village, later of the Spalding Mission of 1838-1847, and still later of the Nez Perce Indian Agency. Four historical buildings can be viewed. Two are the still active Nez Perce Presbyterian Church, dating back to 1886, and Watson's General Store, operated from 1911-1964. During its heyday, the store functioned as a store, post office, pharmacy and gathering place. Nearby stands the one-time home of the Indian Agent and, on the northeast corner of the grounds, a rebuilt Indian Agency building. Interpretive signs describe the old Spalding mission, sternwheelers that once plied the river, the Indian Agency once housed here, and the layout of the old mission buildings, from which two fireplace hearths remain visible. In addition, a still used cemetery lies on the grounds and includes the gravesites of mission founders Henry and Eliza Spalding among others. Picnic tables and restrooms are available.

Back on Highway 95 South, drive 2 1/2 more miles to a left-side (east) pullout where you'll find an interpretive sign marking the site of the original 1836 Spalding Mission, which was in 1838 moved north to the location of the current park discussed above.

Drive one-half mile further south to reach the town of **Lapwai**, location of the Nez Perce Tribal Headquarters and of old Fort Lapwai, used by the U.S. Military during the second half of the nineteenth century. To visit the old fort site, continue south one mile beyond the entrance to the town of Lapwai and turn right. Drive ahead one-tenth mile to view the one-time military parade ground and location of Gen. O.O. Howard's council with the non-treaty Nez Perces in May of 1877, the year of the Nez Perce War. On its southwest corner stands one of the original fort buildings and an interpretive sign detailing the layout of the fort in 1877.

Return to Highway 12 by retracing your six-mile Highway 95 route.

Side-Trip #3: Dworshak Fish Hatchery, Dam, and Lake Clearwater Fish Hatchery

You'll find introductory information about the Clearwater Fish Hatchery, Dworshak Hatchery and Dam and the Big Eddy Recreation Area on Dworshak Lake in the Mile 40.0 entry in the Mile-by-Mile section of this book.

To visit these sites travel to Highway 12 Mile 44.0 and cross the bridge into **Orofino**. Immediately after the bridge, turn west (left) on Riverside Avenue. After driving west three miles on the avenue, glance at the hills across the river to the south. In May of 1806, the small prairie atop those hills became the eastward route of the Corps of Discovery, following their Clearwater River crossing at Bedrock Creek (Mile 26.0). On May 9th, the explorers camped on the prairie along a branch of Little Canyon Creek south of this section of Riverside Avenue. Along the ridge that you can see dropping down to the valley floor near Canoe Camp (Mile 40.0) ran a trail long used by the Nez Perces and, in 1806, likely used by Chief Twisted Hair and one of the explorers when they left the main party to retrieve the horses Lewis and Clark had left in the valley in the care of Twisted Hair the previous fall.

In 3 1/2 miles, you'll come to the entrance to Dworshak Hatchery. Visitors are welcome from 7:30 a.m. to 6 p.m. A self-guided tour includes access to the egging room and to the holding and rearing ponds. The size of fish you'll see varies according to the season. Most adult fish enter the hatchery from the Clearwater River during late winter and spring. Available, too, is information about the anadromous fish life cycle and the hatchery's role in that cycle.

Continue on the avenue, crossing the North Fork of the Clearwater River, once one of the West's most pristine rivers. The Nez Perces called this fork *Ah sah kah*, a name also applied to those Nez Perces who lived in this vicinity and later to the small community that exists here now. The road that runs north (right) immediately after the bridge ends abruptly a mile upstream just below the 717-foot high Dworshak Dam.

A left turn after the bridge leads to the Clearwater Fish Hatchery. At a small interpretive center in the hatchery's main building, procedures for spawning and rearing salmon and steelhead, and fish migration patterns are explained. The height of spawning activity occurs in mid-April. Most adult spawners are trapped in late February and early March. Egg collection from an approximate 3500 fish annually results in 6.5 million fertilized eggs, which will in turn result in smolts that will be released the following spring for their journey to the sea.

Continue west on the avenue one-half mile, at which point you'll see a Dworshak Dam sign on the right. Turn right and continue heeding the signs. The dam's visitor center is open 10 a.m. to 4 p.m., Wednesday through Sunday, autumn through spring, and seven days a week in the summer. At the center, you'll find a series of interpretive displays on the North Fork, including information about the area's original human inhabitants back nine thousand years, the early days of the Pierce gold rush, the 1890-1930 era of white pine logging, and early white settlement of the area. A small natural history display includes the golden eagle, bald eagle, wild turkey, cougar, osprey and fall chinook salmon. The center includes a theatre and lake/dam viewing room. Walking tours of the inside of the dam are available. Also, you can drive across the top of the dam to reach boat launch sites on the east side of the lake.

To reach Big Eddy Recreation Area alongside the lake, continue past the entrance to the visitor center 1 1/2 miles. Big Eddy is a day-use area with picnic tables, toilets, marina and boat launching ramp. This is also the location of the Dworshak State Park administrative office, which oversees the lakeside campsites.

Dworshak Lake extends fifty-three miles north and east of the dam. Along the lake's shores sit more than seventy campsites accessible by water. However, when drawdown makes the lake level low, campers must hike up the steep, muddy banks of the lake to reach those campsites.

Why, you may ask, is the lake drawn down so low? Under normal, pre-dam river conditions, spring highwater run-off effectively flushed salmon and steelhead smolts down the Clearwater, Snake and Columbia Rivers to the sea in two to three weeks. The establishment by the dams of slack water for navigation on this river system created slow-current lakes. The slower current causes the flushing of smolts to the sea to take twice as much time as it did under natural conditions, and this, in turn, exposes the smolts to greater stress and predation. Increased water temperature due to slower currents is also believed to negatively affect fish health. In an attempt to address these problems, Dworshak Lake water is now released in large quantities when smolts begin swimming downstream into the main Clearwater River, usually in early July.

When full, the reservoir measures 1600 feet above sea level. At full drawdown, it measures 1445 feet. The reservoir is usually drawn down in early spring to prepare for snow melt, then gradually allowed to fill in April and May in time for summer recreation. A lake level of 1580 feet or more is considered *attractive*. Below 1500 feet, *ugly*. For recreationists, June is the best month. Drawdown begins again shortly after the Fourth of July weekend. To inquire about the current week's lake level, call the visitor center at 208-476-1255.

Side-Trip #4 Weippe Prairie, Weippe and Pierce
Via Highway 11

Travel along Highway 12 to Mile 51.6. Cross the bridge into **Greer** and continue on Highway 11, which coils uphill on an eight-mile route referred to as the Greer Grade. Take your time — the Grade is steep and includes several hairpin turns. At the top of the hill, Highway 11 unrolls across the Weippe Prairie to the towns of Weippe (seventeen miles) and Pierce (twenty-nine miles).

Two to three miles up the Grade, pullouts allow you to stop to survey the valley below. If you look across the river at the facing hillside, you'll see the route of an old wagon road winding down to the river. Years ago, the road enabled travelers from Lewiston and other points downstream to reach Greer, where the Greer Ferry waited to take travelers across the river. The ferry was the only means of reaching the north side at this point, and, in turn, to make the trip uphill to the gold rush towns of Pierce and Oro Fino.

At Mile 3.5 on the Grade, looking east, you'll see the lower end of rugged Lolo Creek Canyon. If it were possible to walk upstream on the creekbed, you would see the walls of the canyon gradually grow steeper and higher until they became sheer cliffs. In centuries past, a Nez Perce trail connecting the Kamiah Valley (eleven miles east) to the Weippe Prairie crossed the upper reaches of Lolo Creek. In 1806, after an extended wait in the Kamiah Valley for mountain snows to melt, Lewis and Clark and company used the trail to reach the Weippe Prairie before heading eastward again on their homeward journey.

At Mile 8 at the top of the Grade, you'll reach the **Weippe Prairie** yourself. Highway 11 now takes you through an area of farmland known as Fraser after a small community once located in the area. At Mile 9.3, looking to the east, you'll again see the breaks of Lolo Creek Canyon. At Mile 12.5, a turn to the left will take you into pleasant Fraser Park, where you'll find picnic tables, toilets, a playing field and ponderosa pines.

In late September 1805, during the westward leg of their journey, the Lewis and Clark party traveled across Weippe Prairie to the west of Fraser on their way to the stream now called Jim Ford's Creek. (See Miles 47.3 and 47.8 in the Mile-by-Mile section.)

Weippe Prairie is a registered national historic landmark, a designation commemorating the 1805 meeting of the Nez Perces with Lewis and Clark's Corps of Discovery. To reach the site of that meeting, drive into **Weippe** (Mile 17.3) and don't make the 90-degree turn on Highway 11 to Pierce. Instead, drive straight ahead onto Musselshell Road. Drive three-tenths mile to Cemetery Road and turn right (south). Drive 1.8 miles to Larson Road. Turn left (east) and ahead a short distance to a pullout and interpretive sign. The area just north of this sign was the location of Nez Perce lodges to which Clark and his advance party were led on September 20, 1805. Lewis and the rest of the party were still traveling the ridges visible to the south and east of the pullout. Approximately a mile south of the pullout, three Nez Perce boys first saw Clark and his men. What followed was the first meeting of Euro-Americans and Nez Perces in the Nez Perces' homeland.

Back in Weippe, you'll find travelers' amenities, such as a laundromat, cafe and RV park. To continue on to Pierce, follow Highway 11 northward.

At Highway 11 Mile 27.4, an interpretive sign describes the September 18, 1885, hanging of five Chinese residents of Pierce by vigilantes. A short trail leads to the actual site of the hanging. Following the early boom years of the 1860s gold rush in this area, many folks living in and near Pierce were Chinese miners and shopkeepers. In mid-September of 1885, a white merchant named D.M. Fraser, with whom the

Chinese had had many disagreements, was brutally murdered. Seven Chinese were suspected and jailed, but attempts to elicit confessions, including threats of hanging on Main Street's *confession tree*, failed. Due to a lack of confession or sufficient evidence to hold the two oldest of the prisoners, they were released. The five others were to be taken to another court for trial. Having identified Lewiston, Walla Walla and Murray as possible locations for such a trial, authorities and prisoners began the journey. However, three miles into the trip, they were intercepted by vigilantes, who promptly hanged all five prisoners.

At Mile 28.6, you'll pass through the vicinity of what was once the gold rush town of Oro Fino City. In 1861, gold had been discovered in nearby Canal Gulch and Pierce City had etched itself into the wilderness. Then, rich strikes on Rhodes Creek and upper Orofino Creek for a short time moved much of the population out of the already established Pierce City and into Oro Fino. That short migration resulted in the sprouting of hotels, a Wells Fargo express station, blacksmith shops, sixty houses, the Miner's Restaurant, Pat Ford's saloon and several other drinking establishments, all nestled together near the mouth of Rhodes Creek. Rhodes Creek was named after the highly successful miner Billy Rhodes, known locally as Black Bill, reputably the district's most generous miner. Of the estimated four-to-six thousand inhabitants of the two towns during the gold rush's peak, fewer than two thousand actually engaged in mining. The rest sold provisions, handsawed lumber, hauled freight, dug ditches, constructed buildings and provided whiskey and entertainment. The population of Oro Fino dwindled rather quickly as new rushes lured miners to Elk City and Florence to the south, and some of Oro Fino's buildings disappeared when it was discovered they had been built on placer ground. An 1867 fire removed most other physical signs of the town.

You'll enter **Pierce** at Mile 29.0. Shortly thereafter, you'll come to an RV dump station and a map of the area. In town you'll find several travelers' amenities, such as a gas station, cafe and grocery store.

On the left side of Main Street, next to the library, rests a forty-foot long bateau commemorating early-to-mid-twentieth century log drives on the North Fork of the Clearwater River north and west of Pierce. About a half block further down Main, you'll come to Courthouse Street. Turning up it and driving one block will take you to an 1861-1862 vintage courthouse and jail, the oldest in the state of Idaho.

Back on Main Street, you'll soon reach a fork in the road. The right fork runs through famous Canal Gulch. On October 1, 1860, William Bassett made *a find* in the gulch and sparked gold fever throughout Clearwater Country. The miners who worked the gulch dug a canal along the creek to provide water for their placer operations. Thereafter, townsfolk referred to the place as Canal Gulch.

The left fork is a continuation of Highway 11 to the village of Headquarters, a former center of regional logging activities. Five and a half miles north of Pierce on Highway 11, the Grangemont Road runs south to Orofino, but this road is heavily potholed for about ten of its twenty-six mile length. We suggest that you turn around at Pierce and retrace your Highway 11 route back to Weippe, Greer and Highway 12.

For additional information, see Mile 51.6 and Mile 52.3 in the Mile-by-Mile section of this book.

Side-Trip #5: Northwest Passage Scenic Byway
Extension to Grangeville
Via Highway 13

Travel to Mile 73.9 on Highway 12 and turn south onto Highway 13, which runs through Kooskia and follows the Clearwater's South Fork 13 1/2 miles and then winds uphill ten miles to Grangeville. This route comprises a branch of the Northwest Passage Scenic Byway (also Clearwater Canyons Byway). From Highway 12, the mileposts on Highway 13 run backward from Mile 25 at Kooskia to Mile 0 at Grangeville. You'll find information about the colorful town of **Kooskia** at Mile 73.9 in the Mile-by-Mile section.

Three and one-half miles south on today's Highway 13 you'll come to the small town of **Stites**. In 1897, a homesteader named Jacob Stites settled on recently opened Nez Perce Reservation land. He soon sold part of his holdings to three businessmen, who in turn platted a townsite. When the town became the terminus for the Clearwater Short Line, the jumping off place for gold strikes at Thunder

Mountain and Buffalo Hump as well as the closest rail shipping point to Grangeville, the community dubbed Stites blossomed. But the inevitable decline of a mining boom and the completion of a rail link between Lewiston and Grangeville via the Camas Prairie saw the blossom wither. Stites did have the distinction in 1905 of becoming the first upriver location of telephone service when a crude but clever system of smooth wire was fastened to the top strands of barbed wire fences which ran between Stites and Grangeville, a new link in the Bell System.

About a mile south of Stites (east of the pullout at Mile 21.2), the high basalt bluffs of the Clearwater Battlefield are visible. From these bluffs on July 11, 1877, troops and volunteers under Gen. O.O. Howard's command began volleying canon balls and howitzer fire across the South Fork toward the more than seventy lodges of non-treaty Nez Perces camped on the flat alongside the mouth of Cottonwood Creek. Warriors quickly crossed the river and rode horses up the steep ravines lying a short distance north and south of today's pullout. On a plateau atop the bluffs, the more than five hundred soldiers and volunteers quickly formed a circular front of over two miles, and both they and the Indians dug in.

Despite much smaller numbers and the disadvantage of not holding the higher ground, the warriors held the troops in place with deadly accurate rifle fire. As night fell, each side maintained fortified positions, though the army was without water. A charge at dawn, however, by troops with a gatling gun, secured the only spring in the area for the army.

About 3 p.m. on July 12th, a company of cavalry escorting a pack train of supplies approached from the south. Col. Miller and four cavalry companies were sent out to escort the supply train to the army lines, and the Nez Perces made no counter moves. When Miller's troops were almost safely back within the main defensive perimeter, they wheeled and charged the main Nez Perce position. This bold move stirred the rest of the military force to action, and a rout began. The South Fork between Mileposts 21 and 22 was soon witness to mounted warriors dashing across the river, followed shortly by two hundred U.S. Cavalry. The cavalry had originally been ordered to charge the retreating Indians, but that order was countermanded, and instead some of the cavalry took up a defensive position along the riverbank, while others ferried across the infantry. The Nez

Perces had earlier in the day decided to move their camp. Thus their main group was already following Cottonwood Creek into the hills enroute to Kamiah. Only a few lodges, some food and camp supplies, and an aged Nez Perce woman remained at the creek's mouth by the time the main body of military crossed the South Fork.

If you would like a panoramic view of the battlefield bluffs, return to Stites and turn west on Bridge Street. One block ahead, you'll cross the South Fork. Turn left and drive eight-tenths mile to Cottonwood Creek, then left to cross the creek on a one-lane bridge and pull to the side of the road. On the east side of the river, you'll see the battlefield bluffs and the draws on either side of the bluffs used by the Nez Perce warriors during the battle as routes by which they could approach the troops. Running north and south on the east side of the river is Battle Ridge. Here on the west side lies the flat where the Nez Perce village under attack was located. To return to Highway 13, retrace your route to Stites.

At Highway 13 Mile 15.1, Sally Ann Creek enters the South Fork from the east. The creek was named for a Nez Perce woman who lived in the area. The paved road that follows this creek eastward leads to the hamlet of **Clearwater**, which was in the 1800s a stage station on the Elk City Wagon Road running between Harpster and Elk City. The wagon road is still traversable today by foot, horse, bike or vehicle. Those wishing to learn of the Wagon Road and road conditions can get information at area USFS offices.

Harpster, at Mile 13.5, was another link in the route

> *At the 'Clearwater' the opposing forces were about equal. If anything, the troops had the advantage in numbers as well as position. And yet, strictly speaking, the Indians were not defeated. Their loss must have been insignificant and their retreat to Kamai [Kamiah] was masterly, deliberate and unmolested, leaving us with victory barren of results. Their strategy and fighting qualities, whether opposed to two troops of cavalry or to General Howard's command along the Clearwater, or to General Miles' troops in Montana, where they were so largely outnumbered, commanded the attention and admiration of all.*
>
> Major W.R. Parnell, U.S. Army, 1877

between the Elk City gold fields to the southeast and the Camas Prairie towns of Mt. Idaho and Grangeville to the southwest. Abe Harpster participated in the gold rush of 1861, but decided not to follow the next rushes to Warrens and the Boise Basin. He eventually selected a homesite on the South Fork, and an early post office here bore his name. Sometime in the '60s William Jackson built a waystation and toll bridge here across the South Fork on the main trail to Elk City. The Nez Perces burned the station and partially destroyed the bridge during the War of 1877, but Gen. Howard and his army managed to cross here on their way to what became the Battle of the Clearwater. During the late 1800s, a series of townsites sprouted at various locations along this section of the South Fork. Brownsville, named for Loyal P. Brown of Mt. Idaho, once existed here, and a community called Bridgeport enjoyed a brief life, as did Riverside. The post office moved among these early towns, but always retained the name of Harpster. Hopes that quartz veins in the area would prove heavy with gold or that the Clearwater Short Line would extend up the South Fork gradually floated away, but the post office and its name remained.

At Mile 11, Highway 13 leaves the South Fork and climbs to the Camas Prairie, eventually merging with Grangeville's Main Street and ending at Highway 95. (To follow Highway 14, which branches south from Highway 13 at this point, see Side Trip #6 below.)

Grangeville is the county seat of Idaho County and hub of the grain-producing Camas Prairie. Grangeville also serves as a recreational gateway to the Salmon River twenty-seven miles to the south, and to the White Bird Battlefield, site of the first major engagement of the Nez Perce War of 1877. To reach the Salmon and the Battlefield site, drive through Grangeville and turn south onto Highway 95. (A right hand turn on Highway 95 leads to Lewiston, a distance of seventy miles.)

In the 1860s, settlers and ranchers followed the miners into Clearwater Country and particularly to the prairie on which Grangeville now sits. The town which first emerged in this area, preceding Grangeville, was Mount Idaho, which lies a few miles southeast. In 1874, prairie settlers and cattlemen founded Charity Grange No. 15 at Mount Idaho. When the men sought a plot of land on which to build a grange hall, the corner of a farmer's field was selected, and it became the location of the future town of Grangeville. During the Nez Perce War, both Mount Idaho and Grangeville were centers of activity for the white citizens who lived just over the hilltop from the scene of the first battle. The newly built grange hall served as a refuge.

In 1994, at Tolo Lake seven miles west of Grangeville, the Camas Prairie historical record took a new twist. While deepening an old lake bed to improve fishing and waterfowl nesting habitat, local workers uncovered the first of a large number of mammoth bones in the silt. Ice age relatives of today's elephants, mammoths stood up to fourteen feet tall and weighed between ten thousand and fifteen thousand pounds. The find sent excitement rippling through prairie residents and among paleontologists across the state and nation. Archaeologists soon uncovered parts of at least six different mammoths along with the bones of an ancient bison. Tolo Lake, it was realized, had once been the gathering place for these creatures, who perhaps at times got bogged down in the shallow waters of the lake and couldn't get back to firmer ground. During ensuing years, excavation efforts continued and community interest in these exceptionally early residents of Camas Prairie remains strong.

Today Grangeville serves as a hub for in and out-of-town residents, including Camas Prairie farm families. The surrounding rich soils of the prairie have supported agricultural activities since the late 1800s. Elements of the town's history may be viewed at the Bicentennial Historical Museum (305 North College), which is open Wednesday and Friday afternoons during the summer months. Nez Perce artifacts and an early mining exhibit are on display.

The prairie plateau's winters are a bit colder and snowier than those in the river valleys. Thus about seven miles southwest of Grangeville, city-owned Snohaven (downhill) Ski Area and one of Idaho's first Park'n Ski Areas, Fish Creek Meadows, for cross-country skiers, provide outdoor winter fun for area folks. There are also ninety miles of trails for snowmobilers and off-road vehicle users at the Park'n Ski site. Also, Fish Creek Campground offers eleven campsites, including RV spaces, and a picnic shelter.

Highway 13 ends where Grangeville's Main Street ends, at that point at which Main Street meets Highway 95 on the western edge of town. Turning north on Highway 95 and driving a half mile ahead will take you to the Grangeville Visitor Information Center.

On the other end of town (east), the Nez Perce National Forest headquarters sits on the north side of Highway 13.

Side-Trip #6: Elk City, Red River Hot Springs, Dixie
Via Highway 13 and Highway 14

To reach the backcountry locations of Elk City, Dixie and Red River Hot Springs, travel on Highway 12 to **Kooskia** at Mile 73.9. Turn south onto Highway 13 and follow Side Trip #5 above to Mile 11, at which point Highway 14 junctures with Highway 13.

Turn south onto Highway 14. The mileposts along Highway 14 begin here at Mile 0 and run to Mile 49 at Elk City. Near Elk City, another road leaves Highway 14 and follows the Red River to Red River Station and Dixie. An offshoot of that road runs from the station site to Red River Hot Springs. Highway 14 is a narrow, shoulderless, fully paved roadway through gorgeous wild canyon country. There are plenty of vehicle pullouts along the way, a number of picnic areas and campgrounds, a few horse staging areas and trailheads. Those sites:

Mile 8.7 Entering the Nez Perce National Forest; Picnic Area and Area Map.

Mile 9.5 Cotter Bar Picnic Area

Mile 11.5 McCallister Picnic Area (includes a one-mile interpretive trail to Earthquake Basin, with nine interpretive stops featuring the area's flora and fauna)

Mile 14.6 Castle Creek Campground (eight campsites)

Mile 15.0 South Fork Campground (eight campsites)

Mile 17.0 Meadow Creek Campground (three sites)

Mile 19.3 Johns Creek Trailhead/Horse Staging Area

Mile 20.2 Cougar Creek Trailhead/Horse Staging Area

Mile 47.0 Crooked River Campground (five campsites — two miles south of the highway on Crooked River Road)

At Mile 15.5 you'll see tailing piles across the river from old mining days. Unfortunately, while the miners were drawing gold from these lands, they accumulated piles of leftovers that altered and scarred the natural landscape.

The high bluffs in the Miles 21.0 to 22.0 vicinity are a winter and spring hangout for mountain goats. In the summer, the goats will typically graze at higher elevations.

At Mile 30.7, a dilapidated concrete structure and miner's cabin mark the location of an old mining operation. If you look up the hill, above and to the right of the concrete structure, you'll see an old flume used to transport water for mining processes. Servicing the miners of old were merchants and ladies at the one-time town of Golden, now pretty much a ghost town at Mile 31.2.

Newsome Creek enters the South Fork at Mile 36.5. Road 1858 runs uphill alongside Newsome Creek and past the gold rush ghost town of Newsome and to the Elk City Wagon Road.

At Mile 47.0, you will have reached Crooked River and Crooked River Road, which takes off to the south. If you drive this road, you'll soon see that Crooked River's unnatural landscape today makes a dramatic statement about the effects on the environment of placer mining with large-scale dredges. Further, the road takes travelers to Orogrande summit, then branches off into the Gospel Hump Wilderness Area or to Dixie. The route up the Crooked River and on to Dixie, then back to Elk City via Red River comprises what is called the Gold Rush Loop, described in a USFS brochure available at Grangeville and Elk City Forest Service offices. The sixty-two mile loop, including eight interpretative signs and a total of eighteen special locations, offers visitors a side trip into North Central Idaho's mining history.

Continuing on Highway 14, you will drive into **Elk City**, where you'll find several traveler's amenities, such as gas stations, grocery stores and cafes. If you turn left on Schoolhouse Street, in the town's center, you'll soon come to the Elk City Ranger Station, where you can get information about the Nez Perce National Forest, the Elk City Wagon Road, the Gold Rush Loop Tour, the Magruder Crossing into Montana, and other roads, trails and points of interest.

In August of 1861, the second major gold rush in Idaho began at the headwaters of the South Fork in the vicinity of Elk City. Hundreds of miners hastened to the area, many from the declining mines at Pierce City to the north, all lured by the newest eldorado well within Nez Perce Indian lands supposedly protected from such encroachment by the United States' 1855 treaty with the Nez Perces. Within three weeks of the first strike, Elk City's population was nearing one thousand, and during the next few years its gold production totaled 3,500,000 dollars. Much of the upper South Fork, incidentally, is still mined today.

Elk City is also the terminus of the Elk City Wagon Road, a historic mountain route that begins at Harpster, Mile 13.5 on Highway 13. The Wagon Road allowed pack-train and wagon travel to Elk City from the South Fork communities of Stites and Harpster, and from the Camas Prairie communities of Mount Idaho and Grangeville. Many a mule load passed over the road, carrying a wide assortment of goods — ranging from foodstuffs and socks to opium and pianos. For winter travel, pack animals were sometimes outfitted with snowshoes. Today interpretive signs and a descriptive brochure highlight twenty-nine points of interest, such as road house sites and the Southern Nez Perce Trail, and tell of the difficulties and unusual events that made the route both a blessing and a curse. You can access the Wagon Road from Elk City, Newsome Creek or Harpster. Total distance of the route is fifty-three miles, with estimated traveling speeds of fifteen miles an hour. Again, first check road conditions with Forest Service personnel at Grangeville, Kooskia or Elk City.

In 1867, as a result of another gold strike, the village of Dixie was founded. The 1860s, of course, were witness in the United States to the Civil War, which became a hot issue of discussion amongst miners throughout Clearwater Country. We can guess which side, the Union or the Confederacy, claimed the most sympathizers in Dixie, Idaho.

To reach Dixie and Red River Hot Springs from Highway 14, return two miles to the South Fork, then turn onto Red River Road. Nearby, the American River (running toward Elk City) and the Red River merge to create the South Fork. At a distance of twenty miles on Red River Road, you'll arrive at the now closed Red River Ranger Station. From the station, Forest Road #234 leads to Ditch Creek Campground with four campsites, Red River Campground with forty sites and all amenities, and Bridge Creek Campround with five campsites. Eleven miles from the Red River Road, #234 ends at Red River Hot Springs. There, like the Indians and miners of old, you can soak. It was at the hot springs in earlier centuries that the Nez Perce Indians would stop for a soothing, hot bath on eastward journeys along the Southern Nez Perce trail to buffalo grounds or westward journeys back home to Clearwater Country. Late nineteenth century miners also made special trips to the hot springs for similar comfort.

Back near the station, Forest Road #468 also branches off. It generally follows the route of what is known as the Southern Nez Perce Trail. This mountainous road traverses the divide between the Clearwater River drainage and the Salmon River drainage. Eventually crossing Nez Perce Pass, the road winds all the way to Montana, where it connects with Highway 93 south of Darby. Road #468 is today referred to as the Magruder Crossing or Magruder Corridor and serves hunters, fishers, hikers, horse riders and backcountry enthusiasts of all other sorts during the mid-to-late summer and early autumn months. This ninety-five mile road is curvy, narrow, at times steep and is suited only for experienced mountain road drivers who have asked localites or Forest Service personnel about road conditions. The Corridor also serves as a dividing line between the Frank Church River of No Return Wilderness to the south of the road and the Selway Bitterroot Wilderness to the north. The country through which the Corridor runs is wild and spectacular.

Back at the Red River Station again, the main Red River Road (paved) continues another fifteen miles over Dixie Summit to Dixie. According to some travelers, the road to Dixie also spans a time warp — running backwards into the nineteenth century. A short distance south of the village, the road loops back north and continues to Orogrande Summit and Crooked River as described in the Gold Rush Loop Tour information above. This road is open in the summer and autumn months.

Today the Elk City, Dixie and Red River region is an all-season outdoor playground for many folks. Swimmers, fishers, campers, horseback riders and hikers lavish themselves in the lush summertime beauty of the place.

As the name "Elk City" suggests, the basin in which Elk City sits and the surrounding mountainous region is home to herds of elk, which lure hunters to the backcountry in the autumn. In the winter, visitors are likely to be carrying cross-country skis or snowshoes, or towing snowmachines. Many just bring matches, to light a fire in the fireplaces or woodstoves of their getaway cabins in Dixie, which can come as alive in winter as in summer with folks who have relaxation and recreation on their minds. Of course, anytime of year, soakers come; that is, people in search of the hot springs to be found at Red River.

In general, while the Elk City, Dixie and Red River area has enough of a feel of civilization to make anyone comfortable, it is marvelously wild country, worthy in itself of visitors.

Side-Trip #7: Selway River Road

Travel on Highway 12 to Lowell at Mile 97.0. Turn south onto the Selway River Road. Services are available in the Mile 97.0 vicinity, but not further along the Selway Road.

For most of its one-hundred-plus miles, the Selway River flows through the Selway Bitterroot Wilderness. The Selway River Road parallels the river's lower twenty miles. Eighteen miles up the road, fifty-foot high Selway Falls roars over giant rocks. Beyond the falls sits the Selway Falls Pack Station, an information and staging site for backcountry horseriders and hikers. A second staging area is located at Race Creek an additional 1 1/2 miles, where the Selway River Trail begins. The road ends at the head of this trail, which is a horseback and hiking trail lacing its way through the wilderness. (For Selway River Trail details, see Trails in the Recreation chapter.)

The first 6.8 miles of the Selway Road are paved; then the road continues on as a sometimes rather bumpy dirt road. USFS picnicking and camping sites, sandy beaches, trails, Fenn Ranger Station and the Pack Station await road and trail travelers. Those landmarks:

Mile 4 Johnson Bar Campground (seven campsites, large beach)

Mile 4.5 Fenn Ranger Station

Mile 4.7 Fenn Nature Walk and Fish Pond

Mile 6 CCC Campground (for tent campers)

Mile 6.5 Horse Trail #734

Mile 6.8 O'Hara Campground (thirty-four sites, suitable for RVs)

Mile 7.9 Rackliff Campground (six sites)

Mile 9.6 Twenty-Mile Bar (for tent campers)

Mile 10.8 Boyd Creek Campground (five sites) West Boyd Horse and Hiking Trail

Mile 15.1 Glover Campground and Trailhead (suitable for RVs)

Mile 18.2 Selway Falls

Mile 18.5 Selway Falls Pack Station

Mile 19.5 Race Creek Campground (three sites, horse staging area for horse trips, and the Selway River Trail trailhead)

A half mile up the Selway River Road, the Coolwater Ridge Road leaves the Selway, and at almost three miles, the Swiftwater Road does so too. Eighteen miles up the Selway, Fog Mountain Road begins its thirteen-mile *rugged* climb to Fog Saddle from which one can view grand scenic vistas or head out along mountain hiking trails.

The Indian Hill Road crosses the Selway via a bridge at mile 18.6 and runs to Indian Hill (to the left) or to Elk City (to the right), about fifty miles (and several hours) distant. (Note: Upon reaching Elk City, travelers may return to Highway 12 at Kooskia via Highways 14 and 13.) Selway Falls Campground (seven sites) and Slim's Camp (two sites) are located along the lefthand road within a couple miles of the bridge.

While the Selway River Road itself is usually accessible year-round, mountain roads reachable from the Selway Road are only open in the summertime and early fall, some not until July. Stop at Fenn Ranger Station to get information regarding road conditions.

Flight-seeing

Finally, to close this chapter, if you'd love to see Clearwater Country from the perspective of a grand overview, try flight-seeing. In little more than an hour, for example, you can fly with one of the area flying services, such as those in Grangeville and Orofino, over parts of the

Selway Bitterroot Wilderness and the Nez Perce National Historic Trail, or head just south of Clearwater Country for an aerial tour of the White Bird Battlefield, the Seven Devils Mountains, down Hell's Canyon and back up the River of No Return. You'll discover an entirely new perspective on the land and its history — and experience a tour you'll never forget!

Nee Mee Poo

The Early Nez Perces

Sixty million years ago, insects, flowering plants and the forerunners of present-day mammals were newcomers to Clearwater Country. During the next several millions of years the configuration of the land itself began a period of change, so that by about ten million years ago the surrounding mountains and foothills were born and began their rise into the range which today comprises the Bitterroots. And the earth gradually cooled until glaciers crept across the land to remain for close to a million years an age of ice — out of which, according to archeological discoveries and records, man appeared in Clearwater Country.

Among the Nez Perce Indians, legend tells of the creation of the people *Nee-Mee-Poo*. Coyote, a cunning and magical creature, met in the Kamiah Valley a monster which reputably sucked all other animals into itself. Coyote cleverly tricked the monster into inhaling him as well, and once inside the monster's cavernous body he built a fire, enabling many of the animals inside to escape with the smoke through the monster's body openings. Then Coyote severed the monster's heart with a stone knife and made his own exit. From various body parts of the dead monster he made all the Indian tribes and flung them to their respective homes. Coyote realized he had not yet peopled the valley where he stood, and so wringing the monster's heart of its last drops of blood he created the *Nee-Mee-Poo*, now known as the Nez Perces, who since then have continuously inhabited Clearwater Country.

Scientifically, evidence of human life in the North Central Idaho region of North America dates back approximately twelve thousand years. As the ice age diminished in harshness, semi-nomadic humans, aided by crude spears, lances and traps, hunted the mammoth and other mammals of the period and gathered mussels and edible plants. These people found shelter in recesses in canyon walls or within the protection of other natural rock formations. Life expectancy was low by today's standards; perhaps thirty-five years constituted very old age.

By about 6000 B.C. the people were using weirs to catch fish in the region's rivers. Pestles and mortars enabled the processing of plant seeds into flour. Later the development of bows and arrows increased the efficiency of hunting. Fires were started by means of hand-turned fire-drills. Watertight, coiled willow baskets became cooking pots when hot stones were dropped into them to raise the contents to boiling.

By 4700 B.C. more sophisticated stone tools had been developed and large, side-notched hunting points to kill deer, elk, antelope, rabbit and beaver. Bone and horn were crafted into wedges, bows, whistles, awls, arrowheads, spoons and fish-spear points. Mussels, salmon, steelhead, eels, berries and ground wild plant seeds rounded out the native diet.

Within about two thousand years these people had begun to live in circular or oval semisubterranean pit houses and pole-frame huts covered with brush, bark or woven reed mats, some houses up to seventy-five feet in length. Permanent winter villages were established. Roots began to replace seeds as a staple plant food, and eventually bison were also hunted in the region. However, for these people who lived primarily in villages along the Clearwater, Salmon and Snake Rivers and tributaries, fish made up about fifty percent of the diet.

Fishing platforms were extended out over the rivers at prime fishing sites, where large numbers of villagers would gather during the summer and fall fishing seasons. The Indians used hemp dipnets, spears, harpoons, seines and hooked lines to catch fish from the platforms or from dugout canoes typically made from fir logs. Weirs and fish traps were also used. A ceremony of gratitude was offered upon the return each summer of the salmon. Thanks was given to the Creator and to the fish who *gave themselves to the people*. The fish were equitably divided, and what was not eaten immediately was smoked or dried for storage.

Other stored foods, gathered in the spring, summer and fall, continued to be seeds, berries and roots, such as those of kouse (biscuitroot), camas, kah keet, wild carrots, wild celery and bitterroots. These roots were eaten raw, boiled, baked, dried, ground or mashed. Similar to the first-day's fishing ceremony, a first-fruits ceremony offered thanks for the bounty. During periods of winter famine, the people also ate lichens, pine moss and the inner bark of trees.

Baskets remained important for gathering and cooking foods. Other woven items included cups, bowls, fez-shaped women's hats, winnowing baskets, basket worktops for mortars, pouches, and mats. Hemp, bear grass, birch roots, cattail and tule were commonly used basketry materials.

By A.D. 1700, the Nez Perce population had grown to about forty-five hundred persons living in permanent villages throughout the region. Anywhere from thirty to two hundred people lived in each village where the basic social and economic unit was the family. The village as a whole was governed democratically by a council composed of the male heads of these families. Although the council members selected an influential village leader who exhibited wisdom, generosity, diplomacy and bravery, and who was an experienced elder, he could not override council decisions. The council discussed matters of importance to the village or problematic situations and agreed upon common village activities, such as hunting and gathering treks. However, council clout was limited to persuasion, for the council did not have the power to force agreement or compliance. Impassioned, eloquent oratory was a well-developed and valuable skill upon which leaders frequently depended for power and prestige.

While the voices of the councilmen were highly influential, egalitarianism and individual freedom ruled throughout the village. Behavior that threatened or harmed others was responded to by relatives of the offender. The family carried out punishment among its own members, although in relatively few cases the village council might banish the offender from the village. A murder of a tribal member would usually be avenged by the victim's family, and adultery and rape were also sometimes punished by death. Severe public contempt was meted out to liars.

Villages within one area or along one stream interacted and functioned in some ways as a band, overseen by a council and headman. The band council planned joint endeavors involving food gathering, occasional feasts and festivities, and warfare. Within broader regions, bands were tied together by common heritage, language and inter-group marriages, and were overseen by regional councils and leaders. One such composite Nez Perce group lived in the Kamiah area, and a second near the confluence of the Snake and Clearwater Rivers. Several smaller bands lived along the Middle, South and North Forks of the Clearwater as well as along the main river. Also, other Nez Perce bands lived in sections of what are now Eastern Oregon and Eastern Washington.

Through intermarriage and trade, the Nez Perces were closely associated with the Cayuses of the lower Snake River. They were also friendly with the Flatheads and the Crows, fellow buffalo hunters who lived to the east of the Bitterroots; the Umatillas to the west; and the Palooses with whom they shared camas meadows north of the confluence of the Snake and Clearwater Rivers. The Nez Perces interacted with the Shoshones, Spokanes and Coeur d'Alenes as well, sometimes trading goods but other times insults and arrows. The Sioux, Blackfeet and Bannocks were traditional enemies from whom the Nez Perces stole horses and took scalps to adorn their war attire. Bows and arrows, sometimes dipped in rattlesnake venom, stone clubs, eight-foot lances, and elk-hide shields and helmets were among Nez Perce battle gear.

Even within the regional bands, egalitarianism and individual freedom reigned, so that in effect no council or single leader held power over or spoke for all Nez Perces. Individual and village autonomy predominated, even though unified decisions and actions were often possible. However, during hunting trips or during warfare, an indisputable leader was selected by the council.

During this time the Nez Perces lived in lodges and semisubterranean longhouses roofed and sided with reed and grass mats and cedar bark. The longhouses, up to one hundred fifty feet in length, provided homes for several families and at times an entire village. Boys and girls might sleep in separate dormitory lodges. The number of fire pits laid out along the center of the longhouse told how many families shared each home, as usually two families used each fire. Beds made of grass and bark lay near the outer earthen wall, with the foot of each bed towards the center of the longhouse. Villagers used small steam huts for cleansing — both body and spirit. Tipis were used for during seasonal hunting, fishing, and gathering trips and when bands came together for ceremonies and other events.

Sometime during the mid-1700s, the horse came to Clearwater Country, and in time the Nez Perces became proficient riders and herders. They also were at one time the only Indians known to geld and selectively breed horses. While the Nez Perces have become known as breeders particularly of the Appaloosa, they in fact bred all types of horses with no one as a favorite. In the early 1800s, the Lewis and Clark expeditionists did notice some horses pied "with large spots of white irregularly scattered and intermixed with the black brown bey or some other dark colour." Both Lewis and Clark commented on the quality of the Indian horses, noting that they resembled "our best blooded horses in Virginia" with respect to fleetness, form and color. With horses the Nez Perces were able to travel farther and carry more supplies, trade goods and lodging provisions. They expanded their hunting range to the buffalo prairies of Montana and learned more of the many worlds beyond Clearwater Country. Additionally, a whole new arena of

Nez Perce Woman Who as a Child Visited Lewis and Clark
Note the root digging stick, basket and rush mat tipi covering.

sport and recreation developed involving horses. In time, large herds were acquired by some members of each village, and these herds became symbols of wealth and status.

The hides of mountain sheep, deer, elk, antelope, mountain goat, bison, wolf, bear, coyote and smaller mammals provided blankets, leggings, breechclouts, shirts, gown-like dresses, hats, moccasins, and other accouterments. Children wore little clothing in the warmer seasons, and babies were comforted in the wrappings of cradleboards. An infant's umbilical cord, a good luck charm, was toted in a small bag attached to the board. Decorations and accessories worn for special occasions typically were made of such items as elk teeth, bear or eagle claws, shells, porcupine quills, feathers, stone disks or beads, ermine and otter skins. Pouches holding good-medicine objects might also be worn. During the early summer 1806 return trip through Clearwater Country, Capt. Clark described the Nez Perces, who by this time had added to their ornamentation items evidently obtained from white Pacific Coast traders:

> ...orniments consist of beads, shells, and pieces of brass, variously attached to their dress,...ears, ...necks, wrists arms... A band...usually serounds the head...most frequently, of the skin of some fir animal...The ornament of the nose is a single shell of wampum. Pearl and beads are suspended from the ears. The hair is queued in two rolls, which hang on each side in front of the shoulders. Collars of bear claws are common, but the article on which they bestow most pains and ornaments is a kind of collar or breastplate. This is commonly a piece of otter skin. ...On the front of this skin are attached pieces of pearl, beads, wampum,...red cloth...whatever they conceive most valuable or ornamental....I observed a tippet worn by Hohhostillpilp, which was formed of Human scalps and ornemented with the thumbs and fingers of several men which he had slain in battle.

Men and women wore their hair long, parted in the middle, often braided. The men wore bangs and sometimes wove ornaments into their braids. Grooming tools, such as wooden combs and hair tweezers, and facial paints made of clays, minerals, fish oil, mud and tallow were carried in skin pouches. Face painting met several needs — protection from sun, cold or insects, to express a mood, for spiritual use, as a matter of style, to imitate animal colorings during dances, or simply for attractiveness. According to reports by Lewis and Clark and other white travelers, for a period of time some Nez Perces pierced their noses through which they then poked dentalium shells. This short-lived practice, which is not reported in the oral histories of the Nez Perces themselves, caused French-Canadian fur trappers in the early 1800s to call them the *pierced nose* Indians, or Nez Perces.

The Indians raised their children with the help of relatives. Grandparents imparted the legends and histories of the people and traditional skills. During these interactions the values of the Nez Perce culture were indirectly taught — bravery, self-reliance, generosity, withholding emotions, individualism, independence, and the significance of the supernatural in guiding one's life. All natural objects and beings were thought of as spiritual and therefore able to offer guidance, warnings, persuasion, and to lend the listener some of the spirit's natural skills. Visions and visits from these spirits were welcomed and at times sought.

Some youngsters, for example, would set out alone on a quest of several days to seek a visitation and acquire a *wyakin* or guardian spirit. Possession of a wyakin provided a person with a sacred name and an intimate link to the spirit world from which he thereafter drew strength. The guardian spirit imparted to the keeper of the quest vigil a sacred song later sung during the guardian-spirit dance. This dance became a fervent expression of faith in *Ip-noo't-se'lilpt*, the Nez Perce religion and was accompanied only by the spirit songs and animal calls of the dancers. Other ceremonies might be accompanied by musical instruments, such as stone or deer hoof rattles, wood and elk-hide drums, elderberry wood flutes and bone whistles. Some persons whose communions with a spirit were particularly intense were thereafter groomed to become shamans, spiritual leaders, wise and revered. A shaman might also become a medicine person, responsible for knowledge of medicinal plants and their application.

At appropriate ages, usually young teens, marriages were arranged after a courtship during which the boy might flute outside the girl's lodge at night and observe her daily activities. Usually the families of the couple were of similar social and economic status. If a marriage were imminent, a gift exchange was planned. The boy's family gift was in effect a purchase of the girl, and upon completion of the gift exchange, the couple was considered married. Polygamy was also allowed, particularly with sisters of a married woman and with women captured during battle.

The Nez Perces believed all creatures, plants and objects of nature, including humans, had souls which would live on in an afterworld. To ensure this, a person practiced certain rituals throughout his life, and upon death his body was bathed and dressed in his finest garments and adornments, his face painted, and he was wailed over. A deerskin was sewn around his body, and he was buried with objects that might be important to him in the afterworld. Funeral participants smoked pipes. Sometimes the person's name would be given to a newborn who might then develop some of the characteristics of the deceased, but otherwise the deceased person's house was torn down and his name never again mentioned. A new house was built with materials from the old, but before anyone moved in, a shaman blew away the ghosts by blowing pipe smoke into the corners of the home.

Cemeteries were located on benches of land in view of each village. Piles or rings of rocks marked each grave site. A horse might be killed either atop the body or the grave or perhaps skinned, stuffed and set upright alongside the grave. Thereafter, it was believed, the dead person's ghost rode the horse, wore the burial clothing and used the objects which buried with him.

As has been the case throughout the world, such beliefs have guided the behaviors of most people, as they did the Nez Perces. These Indians, longtime residents of Clearwater Country, developed actions, events and character traits stemming from ancestral legends and life needs.

The Nez Perces were highly regarded by Lewis and Clark as an admirable people. "We are poor," Nez Perce chiefs told the white Americans in council as recorded by Clark, "but our hearts are good." Sergeant Gass wrote in his expedition journal,

> It is but justice to say that the whole nation to which [the Nez Perces] belong are the most friendly, honest, and ingenious people that we have seen in the course of our voyage and travels.

Travail and Triumph

The Lewis and Clark Expedition

By the year 1800, the Nez Perces had indirectly made contact with outsiders in the form of trade goods. For a number of years American and Russian fur traders had been interacting with other Indian tribes along the Pacific Coast and lower Columbia River. Spanish trade goods had gradually worked their way north from a colony in New Mexico, with the chief contribution — the horse — reaching Clearwater Country about 1750. From the northeast had come the British and French fur traders who bartered with tribes along the way and provided them with ornaments as well as more utilitarian goods, including the gun. In turn, these tribes in areas surrounding the Nez Perces' ancestral home had introduced many of these same trade goods to the Nez Perces. During intertribal exchanges the white man was depicted, discussed and debated among the Indians, and thus the Nez Perces learned of this new band of light-skinned people drawing closer and closer to Clearwater Country.

Unfortunately, some news of the white man was deadly. Some came, for instance, in the form of gunshots leveled at Nez Perce warriors during battles with other tribes. An even more tragic result of the indirect introduction of whites to the Nez Perces was disease. In 1781-1782, for example, the Nez Perce population was reduced by nearly half due to smallpox introduced to them by tribes who had contracted it from the whites.

While a few members of the Nez Perce bands may have seen an American or Russian fur trader on the Columbia, the first white men to actually approach the Nez Perces in Clearwater Country were William Clark and six other men of the historic Lewis and Clark Corps of Discovery. Having moved ahead of the main body of explorers to seek game on

Capt. William Clark

a prairie they had spotted in the distance, Clark's group walked out onto what is now called the Weippe Prairie, high above the Clearwater River, on September 20, 1805. There they met three young Nez Perce boys who hurriedly hid at sight of the white men. But Clark lured two out of hiding and sent them running to their village with news of the newcomers. The boys returned with a Nez Perce brave who led the party back to his village. And, thus, the intermingling of the Nez Perces and the whites began.

The Lewis and Clark expedition had set out a year and four months earlier from St. Louis, Missouri. And one year after their first meeting with the Nez Perces in Clearwater Country they would return to St. Louis — having completed one of the most extraordinary odysseys this nation has known. They would have trekked two years and four months, approximately eight thousand miles, partly on foot (in elkskin moccasins), when possible by dugout canoes (hand hewn along the route), and at times by horses (purchased from the Indians). They would have overcome whirling rapids and overturned canoes, spine-tingling introductions to potentially unfriendly Indians, swarms of mosquitoes, attacking grizzlies, blinding snows, blistering heat, 6000-foot mountain passes, near starvation, exhaustion, and sickness.

The Corps of Discovery was the brainchild of President Thomas Jefferson, whose fondest fascination was the thought of unconquered wilderness west of the Mississippi. The Louisiana Purchase, supposedly stretching to the continental divide, intensified his vision of a possible water route, a northwest passage, that would take Americans to the Pacific Ocean. Then, the wild land, he was sure, would be a tremendous boon to the nation's fur trade and also be open to claim as an extension of America — across the entirety of the wide continent, from ocean to ocean.

Jefferson's dream began to take shape when he asked seasoned hunter and soldier, fellow Virginian and his own private secretary, twenty-nine-year-old Meriwether Lewis, to lead the expedition. Jefferson personally instructed Lewis in all that would need to be done. The journey would not simply be an adventure. Jefferson expected all terrain and land configurations characterized, flora and fauna identified or described, all Indian tribes approached and then depicted in detail, daily weather and regional climates logged, all mileages recorded accurately, and every westward waterway mapped.

Capt. Meriwether Lewis

Lewis selected as his co-commander a soldier named William Clark, who had served with Lewis in the Indian wars of the late 1700s. Together they enlisted twenty-three American soldiers, two French watermen, a half-breed adventurer named Drouillard (Drewyer), and Clark's Negro servant York. In mid-May, 1804, they headed up the Missouri River accompanied by nine French boatmen and seven additional soldiers who traveled with them as far as a village of Mandan Indians in today's North Dakota. There the expeditionists spent a frigid winter learning all they could about the near West from the Mandans and Minnetarees.

There they also met a Shoshone woman and her husband who would join the Lewis and Clark party on their trek to the Pacific. The woman, Sacagawea, had been born much farther west, in what is now Idaho, and would prove to be a stalwart traveler who would provide important, sometimes vital, assistance to the Corps, in large part as an interpreter. At thirteen years she had been captured by the Minnetaree Indians and kept as a slave. From the Minnetarees, with whom he had been living, a Frenchman named Touissant Charbonneau won her in a gambling game and made her his wife. He was officially hired as an interpreter for the expedition. Charbonneau, Sacagawea, and their infant Baptiste, born during Lewis and Clark's winter with the Mandans, set out on April 7, 1805, with the westward explorers as they resumed their trek.

In eight canoes the expedition pushed up the swollen Missouri, living off the land as they went and watching the horizon for sight of the Rocky Mountains. On the greening countryside game was plentiful. Vast herds of buffalo, deer, antelope and elk roamed the plain which, along with an abundance of beaver, provided a continual source of food. Grizzlies were also numerous...and pesky. Coming upon the Great Falls of the Missouri, the explorers could see that portaging was imminent — an eighteen-mile portage using cottonwood logs for wheels upon which to roll their heavy canoes across muddy terrain. Rain and mosquitoes plagued the party and prickly pear cactuses tore at their moccasins.

Eventually the explorers entered country familiar to Sacagawea – Shoshone summer campsites, the spot where she had been captured by the Minnetarees, and geographical landmarks, such as Beaverhead Rock. Lewis and Clark knew that the Shoshones were key to the party's reaching the Columbia before winter, because the explorers' canoes would need to be abandoned at the Missouri's headwaters and the next leg of their dramatic journey completed on horseback. The source of the needed horses was the Shoshones. When contact with this tribe was finally made and Sacagawea sat in the council circle to serve as interpreter, she was joyously overwhelmed to see that the tribe's chief, Cameahwait, was her brother. The continued success of the Corps was once again temporarily assured.

With Sacagawea's help, Lewis and Clark considered with the Shoshones which westward routes should be tried, purchased twenty-nine horses, and secured the guidance of a man they called Old Toby and his son. Toby led them from north through the Bitterroot Valley to the mouth of Lolo Creek about eleven miles south of present-day Missoula. On September 11th, mindful of approaching winter, they began their journey along an Indian trail connecting Bitterroot Valley and buffalo plains with Clearwater Country, home of the Nez Perces. Little did they guess, however, the difficulties that would beset them along the Nez Perce Trail.

Autumn storms had nudged game towards the lowlands so that the party, already on short rations, found little or no food. Their bodies low on calories, they struggled through rugged forested terrain, strewn with downfalls and dense brush, boulders and rock slides. Perilous cliffs, steep ridges, and tangles of creek bottom foliage sapped their waning energy. Winds, rainstorms, sleet, hail and fog further hampered them. Heavy snows blanketed and hid portions of their path, and coldness numbed them. Game remained scarce.

On September 18th, in search of food, Clark and six hunters advanced ahead of the main party. The next morning Clark's group was surprised to spot a lone horse in the woods. They killed and butchered it, roasted portions for breakfast, then hung the rest in a tree for the others to find. Energized by the food, the hunters trekked twenty-two miles through more rugged country till at day's end their bodies sank once again into sleep under blankets on the forest floor. Early on the 20th, they rose to continue westward. This day would bring them to the high prairie where a band of Nez Perces had set lodges for autumn root gathering.

Upon reaching what is today called Weippe (*wee ipe*) Prairie, Clark and his six fatigued and starving companions became the first European Americans to enter the Nez Perce homeland. Three young Nez Perce boys first encountered the expeditionists and, according to Nez Perce sources, ran to the village to report that they had seen strange creatures with large, fish-like eyes, pale skins and an unpleasant odor. In part because Nez Perce legend had prophesied the coming of strangers to their homeland, the Indians decided to welcome the expeditionists. Thus, with both curiosity and caution, the Indians greeted the strangers, offered fish and roots and housed the newcomers in the village for the night. The next evening, on the banks of the Clearwater River a short distance upriver from present-day Orofino, Capt. Clark met Twisted Hair, a Nez Perce headman. The two held a conference using sign language. Twisted Hair and his son accompanied Clark back to the Weippe Prairie the next day to locate Lewis and the main party. After a day's rest, the expeditionists gladly left the rugged mountains behind them and descended into the autumn warmth of the Clearwater Valley.

During their time with the Nez Perces on this the westward leg of their trip, the travelers distributed trade medals embossed with President Jefferson's likeness, medicine, two American flags, tobacco and trinkets. The Indians offered food so desperately needed by the whites, but when the

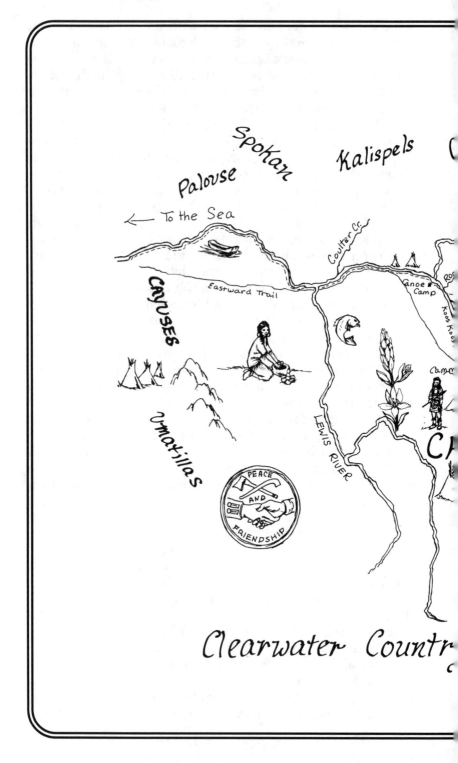

Clearwater Country

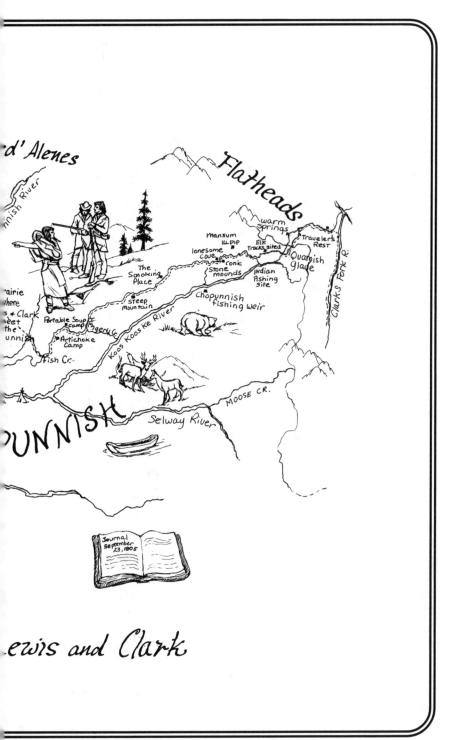

explorers' exclusive diet of red meat became in a single day replaced with fish, roots and berries they became instantly and seriously ill. However, despite being much debilitated by dysentery, the explorers hewed dugout canoes from large pines along the Clearwater River, opposite the entrance of its North Fork, at a site now known as Canoe Camp. During their twelve days at Canoe Camp, the explorers hunted, traded for food (including four puppies), cached their saddles and canisters of gunpowder and rifle balls, and consulted with the Nez Perces about the route to the sea.

Having arranged to board their horses with Twisted Hair until spring, on October 7th, the Corps pushed their canoes into the Clearwater for their journey to the Pacific. They exchanged curiosities with villagers along the way and were halted for a day near the mouth of the creek now called Potlatch Creek when a canoe crashed into rocks in and filled with water, soaking men and supplies. Toby and his son soon thereafter left the party to return to their Shoshone tribe, but Twisted Hair and fellow Nez Perce Tetoharsky had since joined the expedition. On the group paddled, through gentle flows and risky rapids, till they entered the Snake River. On October 16th, Clearwater Country well behind them, they reached the Columbia, the river they knew would take them to the sea. Twenty-two days later Clark jubilantly entered in his journal,

> Great joy in camp we are in *view* of the *Ocian*, this great Pacific Octean which we been so long anxious to see, and the roreing...made by the waves brakeing on the rockey shores may be heard disti[n]ctly.

After several days' reconnoitering taround the mouth of the Columbia, the party began constructing a fifty-foot square stockade near present-day Astoria, Oregon, which they named Fort Clatsop after the Clatsop Indians, whose country they had entered. By New Year's Day, 1806, the fort was completed, and the expeditionists settled in for a foggy, rainy winter's stay. They collected scientific specimens, worked on maps, and wrote in journals a few kept. Evenings from time to time, one member of the party would play his fiddle while the others danced, sang, laughed and talked to liven an otherwise wet and gloomy existence.

On March 23rd they left Fort Clatsop to head homeward. By early May they were back in Clearwater Country,

Evening's Entertainment

having replaced their canoes with horses they had traded for along the way. Friendly Nez Perces, including Cutnose and Twisted Hair, led them up the Clearwater Valley to the village of Broken Arm on the banks of Lawyer's Creek about four miles southwest of the present town of Kamiah.

The explorers remained in the Kamiah Valley from May 10th until June 10th, waiting for deep snows to disappear from the Nez Perce Trail. Lewis and Clark exchanged information with the Indians and told them about tools and gadgets the travelers carried, such as "the power of magnetism, the spye glass, compass, watch, air gun and sundery other articles equally novel and incomprehensible to them." Clark also increased his growing reputation as a healer, daily administering medicines and medical treatments to Nez Perce patients. In councils with the Indians, the whites described their own nation, the United States of America, and expressed a desire for peace among the western Indian tribes so trading posts might be established. The explorers drew maps showing proposed locations of the posts. The Indians, according to the explorers, at first doubtful that the tribes could establish peace, eventually declared "confidence in the information they had received" and gave their word of agreement with the proposals.

Lewis and Clark's amicable exchanges with these Indians had opened the way for years of continued peace between United States citizens and the Nez Perces. Among the Nez Perces the agreement held as a long-lasting promise of good faith and friendship until part of the tribe was drawn into war seventy-one years later.

On June 15th, after making final preparations while camped on the Weippe Prairie, the expeditionists, now in possession of sixty-six horses, set out to retrace their path across the Bitterroots, but after a few days of travel, deep snows turned them back. They tried again June 24th, this time with three Nez Perce guides, and in six days reached their previous autumn's camp, *Traveler's Rest*, near the Bitterroot River on the other side of the Bitterroot Range.

At this point Clark took one segment of the party south to their previously cached canoes at the headwaters of the Missouri River. Lewis led the other men northeast. Eventually, all the members of the expedition regrouped at the confluence of the Yellowstone and the Missouri. Lewis and three others in his party had a hair-raising adventure to recount — a hostile encounter with the Blackfeet. Two Blackfeet were killed before the Indians retreated, and Lewis and his men took advantage of the retreat to hurry eastward on horseback and avoid further fighting.

At the Knife River, one expeditionist named John Colter, requested a discharge. For him, the prospect of a hero's welcome in St Louis held little promise compared to the western wilderness. Upon his discharge, he joined two trappers headed upstream. Colter would later discover what would in time become Yellowstone National Park.

Charbonneau, Sacagawea and Baptiste remained with the Mandans in the Dakotas. The rest of the party reached St. Louis in triumph on September 23, 1806.

Their extraordinary journey was the talk of the American people and gave the United States claim to the breadth of the continent. Settlements of whites began creeping up the Missouri as word of the expedition's discoveries generated increased interest in the western regions, and fur trade between Indians and white traders expanded. Back in Clearwater Country that momentous happening which was the Lewis and Clark Expedition had catalyzed the events of the rest of the nineteenth century.

Cultural Conflict
in Clerical Clothing

The Missionaries

Just as horses and trade goods began crossing the mountain and river boundaries that defined Nez Perce territory, so too did ideas pass from tribe to tribe. Thus it is believed that during the 1700s, the Nez Perces heard about elements of Christianity and incorporated some of these ideas into their own religious views.

In the early 1800s, Lewis and Clark, as well as fur traders and trappers, did for certain speak of Christianity and of the Bible with the Nez Perces. As trading posts became established in eastern Washington and western Montana, the Nez Perces at times observed the whites practicing their Christian faith in daily prayer, in observance of the Sabbath and sacred days such as Christmas.

In 1825, the Hudson's Bay Company escorted two young Indian men from the Spokane and Kootenai tribes north of Clearwater Country to an Anglican mission school near what is now Winnipeg, Canada, for instruction in Christianity and the ways of the whites. Four years later the two returned to preach to area Indians — in English, in white man's clothing, with white man's haircuts, and toting Bibles. Their listeners were mightily impressed. With the aid of the Nez Perce interpreter Lawyer, one of the tribes among whom they preached was the Nez Perce. Since the Nez Perces themselves had always placed much faith in the supernatural for aid and influence in life, they saw the white man's religion as the supernatural source of the white man's economic dominance. So they came to feel that securing the book, the Bible, and all its teachings was vital to unlocking the secrets and power of the white man's economy. Thus in 1830, the Nez Perces sent two of their own young men to the Red River Mission.

Then in 1831, four Nez Perce warriors accompanied a group of white fur traders to St. Louis, where they met with the Superintendent of Indian Affairs — none other than expeditionist and Nez Perce friend William Clark — as well as with a Catholic priest and others who spread the word of the Indians' visit. Black Eagle, Man of the Dawn, Rabbit Skin Leggings, and No Horns on His Head jointly indicated to the whites that the Nez Perces wanted *the book* and teachers to teach them about the white man's religion. Two of the four became ill and died in St. Louis, and a third died on the return trip up the Missouri. Rabbit Skin Leggings reached his band on the plains east of the Bitterroots where he reported that teachers, as well as the Bible, would be coming to Clearwater Country. He was shortly thereafter killed in a battle with the Blackfeet and so never returned to his homeland, but his message did reach his tribesmen along the Clearwater. This unusual journey to find *the book* thus ended sadly and perhaps ominously with respect to the coming of the white man's religion to the Nez Perces.

Meanwhile, Nez Perce leaders had begun implementing several Christian practices which they had learned from the returned Red River Mission students, so that the ancient nature-based religion of the Nez Perces was becoming interfused with Christian elements. One American trapper, Benjamin Bonneville, having observed their adopted Christian customs, wrote,

> ...the fasts and festivals of the Romish Church ...
> have become blended with their own wild rites,
> and present a strange medley; civilized and bar-
> barous. ...the principal chiefs, who officiate as
> priests, instruct them in their duties, and exhort
> them to virtue and good deeds.

Strict observance of the Sabbath and morning, evening and mealtime prayers became commonplace. Indeed, the Nez Perces were ripe for Christian teaching, but their reasons remained economic — they hoped to maintain status as a people and increase their own success in trade and influence by absorbing the white man's religion, the white man's concepts of and communications with the supernatural.

Following the visit of the four Nez Perce seekers of the book to St. Louis, various religious organizations in the east scrambled to answer the call. Missionaries began to venture westward, and in 1836, Presbyterian missionary Henry Spalding, his wife Eliza and helper William Gray arrived to establish a mission in Clearwater Country. Two miles up Lapwai Creek near the village of headman Thunder Eyes, the Nez Perces helped the Spaldings and Gray construct a first mission building, a home and adjacent classroom. The Indians freely supplied food and other items of convenience to the missionary trio.

Rev. Henry Harmon Spalding

Thus the Spalding ministry began. Daily prayer sessions, Sunday services, hymn singing, sermons and Bible readings with accompanying illustrative paintings and translations became routine. Eliza Spalding taught the English alphabet, reading, writing, sewing, spinning and weaving, and other housekeeping skills. Henry administered medical remedies, as best he could, and taught the Nez Perces the medical procedure of blood-letting.

Spalding wanted to maintain regular attendance at lessons and services by large numbers of the tribe, whose population was now between three and four thousand. In order to provide consistent, regular teaching, he felt he needed to keep the Indians in the Clearwater Valley, reasonably close to the mission site. So he taught them to farm — vegetables and fruits, grains, cattle — in order to restrict their root-gathering and game-hunting in distant areas. This would further give the Indians a skill that might help them make the transition from the old ways to the new which Spalding believed would inevitably be ushered in with a white population. His efforts resulted in the first attempts at agriculture in present day Idaho.

For a time, Spalding's interactions with the Nez Perces reaped positive results for him and for the Indians, and he gained a sizable group of faithful followers. Gradually, however, good relations between the white missionaries and many of the Indians began to break down. A major problem apparently was Spalding's personality. He was dogmatic, intolerant, and severe, to the point of directly pronouncing sinners' damnation to hell and lashing disobedient members of the tribe. Several of his practices and teachings also contradicted long held beliefs and customs of the Nez Perces. For example, many of the Indians, who had always thought of the earth as their mother, were horrified at the sacrilege of scarring the earth with hoes. Some of the men of the tribe, who were asked to hoe along with the women, further considered this work demeaning because such manual labor had always been women's work. Moreover, roaming to hunt and gather had been basic to Nez Perce culture for centuries, so that it was contrary to the Indians' nature to stop. In addition, the Nez Perces had thought of themselves with pride as a good people, and found the concept of original sin unfathomable. Finally, the leaders and shamans had been threatened and riled by Spalding's ignorance of their importance and his luring the people away from their own leaders' influence.

These rifts in relationships between Spalding and the Nez Perces created a split among the Indians themselves. Many, still passionately desirous of the white man's supernatural power, remained loyal to Spalding. Others did not, although the interests of these would fluctuate, so that for the most part many remained in contact with the mission and its practices and continued receiving instruction. In 1838 the Nez Perces helped Spalding move the mission to a site on the Clearwater River near the mouth of Lapwai Creek. There the missionaries and their followers built a two-story house, new school, a blacksmith's shop, and two smaller houses. In time a church, sawmill, granary, gristmill, storehouse, and other farm buildings would be erected. Most of these buildings were the first of their type in present-day Idaho, as was the irrigation system Spalding designed and the printing press he eventually put to use.

Also in 1838, new Protestant missionaries arrived in the region. One couple, Asa and Sarah Smith, was requested by a few Nez Perces to establish a mission about fifty miles upriver from the Spalding mission at a site near present-day Kamiah. The couple was easily convinced of this move since they, like other Presbyterian missionaries in the Northwest, disliked the Rev. Henry Spalding from the outset. However, despite the help of a few accommodating Indians, the Smiths were not well received by the Nez Perces as a whole and were not happy with

Spalding Mission Printing Press

their new assignment. Sarah Smith, in fact, spent a great many days depressed, ill, and in tears, and became known to the Indians as "the weeping one." The couple remained only two years in Kamiah. Asa Smith did during that time, however, contribute to historical record much information about the Nez Perces. He also developed a written form of the Nez Perce language and wrote the first Nez Perce dictionary and grammar. He also assisted Spalding with the production of a Nez Perce alphabet book, enabling Spalding to print four copies of the New Testament in Nez Perce on his printing press.

Trouble between the Indians and Spalding intensified. Simultaneously, conflict brewed between the Cayuse Indians and the whites at a similar mission which had been established in 1835 in Oregon by Marcus and Narcissa Whitman. Exacerbated by the continual arrival at the Whitman Mission of white people who were traveling the Oregon Trail and by a devastating measles outbreak among the Indians, this conflict led to the Whitman Massacre of November 28, 1847. Marcus and Narcissa and eleven other whites were slain by the Cayuses. Three others later died, and forty-seven were taken captive. Among the latter group was the Spaldings' daughter Eliza.

During the dreadful hours of the massacre, Spalding himself was approaching the Whitman Mission, but was forewarned of the situation there. Fearing generalized unrest, he turned homeward. Hiding during daylight and stumbling through the chill of winter darkness, in four days Spalding made his way to the ridge just west of the Lapwai mission, from where he saw the buildings being ransacked by a cadre of young Nez Perces. He was discovered that evening by a Nez Perce woman who could barely recognize him due to his condition. Several loyal Indians then came to his rescue and took him up the Lapwai Valley to the home of mountain man William Craig and Craig's Indian wife who was a daughter of Chief Thunder Eyes. Spalding's wife and several other whites had already fled to the safety of the Craig home. For nearly a month thereafter Spalding and the others were held unmolested but nevertheless captive at the house. Finally a group of men from the Hudson's Bay Company, under the leadership of Peter Ogden, reached the region, began conferencing with the Cayuses and Nez Perces, and eventually managed to have the captives released for a ransom. The Spaldings were reunited with their daughter Eliza, and the early white missionaries temporarily left Clearwater Country.

In retrospect, despite pious intentions and honest efforts, what these early missionaries had generated among the Indians were disparity, disunity, disbelief in their ancient religion and culture and the breakdown of lines of authority. The damage would not be, could not be, repaired. Further missionary activity and increasing encroachment of the whites in general into Clearwater Country would only widen these ragged tears in the cultural fabric of the Nez Perces. In addition, the Christian *versus* non-Christian fracture inadvertently created among tribal members by the missionaries would have dramatic effects on the course of Nez Perce history throughout the remainder of the 1800s. Not until more than a century later would the Nez Perces begin again to draw strength from their cultural heritage and to pull together for economic and social gain – this time in interaction with the modern world of the white man. Yet, residual animosity exists to this day.

During the late 1830s and the 1840s, missionaries of various denominations in surrounding regions were also beginning to influence the Nez Perces who traveled to those regions for social and subsistence purposes.

In 1838, for example, Father Francis Blanchet and Father Modeste Demers, two Catholic priests, passed through Fort Colville in northeastern Washington and Fort Walla Walla on the Columbia River to the west of Clearwater Country. They informally preached, baptized about twenty-two Indians and halfbloods, and implored the Indians to recognize that Catholicism embodied the only true and effective spiritual power. This created confusion for the Nez Perces and other Indians who had until then heard only the preachings and learned only the rites taught by Protestant clergy. As the Catholic missionaries spoke out against Protestantism and began to win converts, the Protestant missionaries throughout the Northwest, including Spalding, countered with vigorous teachings against Catholicism. In time some of the Nez Perces would reject Christianity entirely, partly because they saw it as a religion of great conflict – between the Christian and non-Christian Indians at first, then between and among the Catholic and Protestant missionaries themselves, and eventually between the Catholic and Protestant Indians. One of the Nez Perce chiefs, Chief Joseph, who would later become well known during the Nez Perce War of 1877, stated that he was not interested in the white man's Christian schools because,

> ...they will teach us to quarrel about God. We may quarrel with men sometimes about things on this earth, but we never quarrel about God. We do not want to learn that.

Further Catholic influence came to the Nez Perces in 1840 during a buffalo hunting trip east of the Bitterroots. There a Nez Perce hunting party heard Father Pierre De Smet, who was visiting the Flatheads to discuss a possible mission site in their country. The Nez Perces brought news of De Smet's teachings back to Clearwater Country — causing increased religious confusion among the Indians and deep frustration among the Protestant missionaries who began to fear the Catholic encroachment on *their Natives*. During the next year's buffalo hunt and visit among the Flatheads, thirty Nez Perces were baptized by Father De Smet, and Catholic priests, east and west of Clearwater Country, continued thereafter to influence and convert many Indians.

More than two decades later, in 1866, Sicilian born Father Joseph Cataldo was sent to Lewiston, at the confluence of the Clearwater and Snake Rivers, to explore with the whites in the area the potential for a Catholic mission among the Nez Perces. The next fall he returned to Lewiston and with the help of Brother Achilles Carfagno built a clapboard church which was attended mostly by whites in the town. In 1868, he built a log cabin chapel on the north bank of the Clearwater River above the mouth of Lapwai Creek, and in the spring of 1873, another on Sweetwater Creek about ten miles south of the Spalding site. The following winter he established a mission nearby which became known as Slickpoo Mission, named after the first Catholic convert among the Nez Perce chiefs. By 1877, when the Nez Perces were on the brink of war with the United States and Father Cataldo was ordered out of the area, he had baptized three hundred Nez Perces. He would return to Clearwater Country in 1904 for a three-year residency at Slickpoo and then again in 1915 to an expanded mission which had by that time added an orphanage. Father Cataldo continued at Slickpoo until his death in 1925 at the age of eighty-seven.

The Protestants in the region remained active through these years of Catholic influence. Rev. Spalding had returned to Lapwai as a school teacher in 1863, but was dismissed due to his disagreeableness in 1865. He did, however, stay in the area, and he and a young missionary assistant, Henry Cowley, vigorously competed for converts with Father Cataldo, then in residence at Lewiston.

During the late 1860s, the United States endeavored with much difficulty to establish Indian reservations in the west. President Ulysses S. Grant determined in 1870 that reservations would be governed in accordance with a tribe's principal religious affiliation. The Presbyterians were granted administrative authority over the Nez Perces and in turn selected John B. Monteith as agent in 1871. That year Monteith directed young Cowley to establish a mission in the Kamiah Valley where the First Presbyterian Church had already been organized among the Indians. In 1873 Cowley was replaced by Spalding, who assisted the Indians in the construction of the church building in East Kamiah which today remains the oldest continually used church in Idaho. Spalding's stay in Kamiah was brief, but quite successful. He became ill in 1874 and was taken to Lapwai where in August he died at the age of seventy-one.

The selection of a Presbyterian administration of Indian affairs in the area had given credibility to that denomination among the Nez Perces. When the headman of a village became converted, he often drew all of his villagers into the church with him as a means of maintaining group continuity and of holding onto his position of leadership. Spalding alone, during his short time at Kamiah, brought six hundred converts into the fold. The strength of Presbyterianism continued at Kamiah following Spalding's death when the physically slight but spiritually determined Miss Susan McBeth arrived to take his place.

Miss McBeth had diligently studied the Nez Perce language and taught at the Indian school at Lapwai during the previous year, but saw in the 1874 missionary vacancy at Kamiah her opportunity to move to the position she had hoped from the beginning to occupy.

At her "happy vale... Kamiah" she lived simply in the tiny house left by Spalding. During a visit early in her tenure, Gen. O.O. Howard wrote of her situation,

Sue McBeth

> In a small house of two or three rooms I found Miss McBeth living by herself. She is such an invalid from partial paralysis that she cannot walk from house to house. ...[She had] a pale, intellectual face above a slight frame. How could that face and frame seek this far-off region? ...Her soul has been fully consecrated to Christ, and He, as she fully believes, sent her upon a mission to the Indians.
>
> ...She gathers her disciples about her, a few at a time, and having herself learned their language ...she instructs them and makes them teachers.
>
> There is the lounge and the chair. There the cook stove and table. There, in another room, is the little cabinet organ, and a few benches. So was everything about this little teacher — the simplest in style and work.

Two of her five students were particularly helpful as well as devout in their studies — brothers Mark and Robert Williams. Her other three Nez Perce students were James

Kate McBeth and Her Ladies Class

Hines and brothers Archie and James Lawyer, serious, intelligent, eager learners, but who were not entirely taken in by Miss McBeth's presumption of authority.

By 1876-'77, the stirrings of an impending Nez Perce — United Statea war whipped up anger and fright among many whites. Among the frightened, Miss McBeth fled to Portland. But at the war's end in the autumn of 1877, she returned to Lapwai. In 1879, her sister Kate joined her there, and together they moved to Kamiah. Sue reestablished her men's school, and Kate opened a school for Nez Perce women. Zealously the two McBeth sisters sought to further inculcate the Nez Perces with Presbyterianism and to rout *heathenism* out of its every hideaway.

They assigned important church positions to favored faithfuls and also ordained several of the Nez Perce men. These positions of leadership in the church continued the erosion of traditional leadership roles in the tribe. The conflict between Christian and non-Christian factions intensified as it had before.

Eventually the McBeth sisters were seen by Indian Agent Monteith as contributors to growing conflicts, and in July 1884, he angrily ordered Sue McBeth off the reservation and Kate McBeth to the Indian agency in Lapwai. Sue moved to Mount Idaho, in the vicinity of present-day Grangeville, where she continued to receive Nez Perce visitors who sought further teaching and assistance.

Robert Williams, who was the first Nez Perce ordained by Sue, became pastor of the Kamiah church. But in 1890 problems arose which caused a number of the Nez Perces to leave the church, move across the river, and establish the Second Presbyterian Church. Archie Lawyer, whose father had been a traditional chief, emerged as new minister of the second church.

Sue McBeth died in 1893. During her years as a missionary, she had written a 15,000-word Nez Perce dictionary which she had sent to the Smithsonian Institution, and she had ordained nine of her Nez Perce students. Her sister Kate continued to minister to the Indians and was joined by Kate's niece Mazie Crawford in 1899. Yet, throughout the 1890s, Christian fervor among the Nez Perces gradually waned; the number of non-Christians appeared to increase; and in the early 1900s, other sects entered the region. Nevertheless, Kate McBeth continued her work among the Nez Perces at Lapwai until her death in 1915, and Mazie Crawford until her death in 1932. The Presbyterian mission at Lapwai was then closed.

As a legacy from the mission period of Clearwater Country history, the rift between Christian and non-Christian Nez Perces lingers and taints the relationships of the two factions even today.

Treaty and Trust Betrayed

The Gold Rush

By 1859, many white settlers had claimed homesites and grazing lands on both sides of the Columbia and Snake Rivers west of Clearwater Country, but the most numerous travelers along these waterways were miners. Gold strikes in the Northwest were frequent, and each splash of sunshine on yellow metal had the potential for creating wide ripples of gold fever. A few strikes had caused rushes, but thus far they had been brief and small.

The miners ached to move eastward toward the Bitterroots where surely, they surmised, small strikes would lay glittering pathways to fountainheads. Thus now and then a miner or two sneaked onto the Nez Perce Reservation to secretively prospect and then returned to Walla Walla to quietly stir rumors about gold on Nez Perce lands.

One of these prospectors was a man named Elias D. Pierce, who had first explored Clearwater Country as a trapper in 1852 and claimed to have found gold in what was later called Orofino Creek, *creek of fine gold*, which enters the Clearwater at present-day Orofino, Idaho. In 1858, Pierce returned, but sensing Nez Perce hostility he again left the reservation.

Back in Walla Walla more rumors instilled even fuller confidence that gold could be found in Clearwater Country. Yet, it wasn't until February 12, 1860, that Pierce and fellow prospector Seth Ferrell, feigning to be traders, returned to the reservation. Accompanied by an Indian, Wislaneqa, whom Pierce had earlier befriended, Pierce and Ferrell traveled to the North Fork of the Clearwater River on the 20th. There Pierce panned for gold...and found bright flecks in every pool of water and gravel he swirled. He knew these golden specks would lead him to a *feeder* upstream, to more, much more, of the treasured metal.

185

Elias D. Pierce

Because the Nez Perces saw no inclination on the part of Pierce to settle on and farm their land, they thought his panning was harmless. But Pierce knew, as he wrote in his journal, that he could shape "...the destiny of that country, and that I could flood that entire region with good reliable men at my own option."

Indeed he could. He returned to Walla Walla in March, sought permission from the regional Indian agent to develop a claim, disregarded the agent's negative response, and traveled to The Dalles, Oregon, to gather mining equipment, supplies and a crew. Then, fully geared, the miners determinedly trekked back into Clearwater Country, where they hoodwinked a subagent into giving them a permit to travel throughout the reservation. On they went to Wislaneqa's village on the Clearwater. There they sought agreement from Lawyer and other Nez Perce headmen that the miners could prospect freely in the country. But when two government officials suddenly appeared at the village, Pierce and his group were turned back to Walla Walla.

Now Pierce grew more aggressive in his efforts to win approval from the Indian agent. He mobilized numbers of men eager to mine or to indirectly benefit from mining development in the region. As noted in his journal, Pierce slyly explained at mass public meetings that,

> the part I am desirous to prospect is not on the reservation but lays to the east...and going into the country to explore can not in any manner, shape, or form interfere with the rights of the Indians. ...I don' t even intend to pass through the reservation but will travel to the north.

The swelling power of public pressure swayed the Indian

agent so that he finally gave the go-ahead. Thus, in early August, Pierce and ten fellow prospectors left Walla Walla. By this time, however, the Nez Perces had become agitated at the likelihood of an influx of miners and turned back the persistent prospectors twice along the trail. Then, hoping to uncover a route to the mining area that would circumvent interception by Indian scouts, Pierce sought the help of friendly Chief Timothy. Timothy told of such a passage, but noted that a guide would be needed. Some believe his eighteen-year-old daughter then offered to guide the miners. In his journal Pierce wrote,

> On the 14th came to a dense forest in the mountains. 15th wound our way through heavy timber and chaperell; had to cut a trail for our animals. About sundown ...we had to make a heavy decent. ...we were in great danger of dashing our animals headlong over a perpendicular precipice. In the morning we rolled, sliped, and slid our animals to the river.

A few days later, after finding further travel along the river (North Fork) impossible, the party was forced to again enter the mountains, which Pierce described as,

> The most dark dense forest I ever saw. From this point we had to make a trail...and did not make more than two miles a day. In this way we worried through a rough, rugged, mountanious country for over a month.

But at the end of their difficult trail Lady Luck lavishly rewarded the party. Pierce's journal continues:

> On the 1st of October commenced our labor. Found gold in every place in the stream, in the flats and banks and gold generally diffused from the surface to the bedrock. I never saw a party of men so much excited. They made the hills and mountains ring with shouts of joy. The second [of October] we moved down and camped on the stream, afterwards called Oraphenia creek [Orofino Creek] ...We made our locations and then gave the country a more thorough prospecting. A nice town site was laid off in nice building lots; name of town, Pearce [Pierce] City.

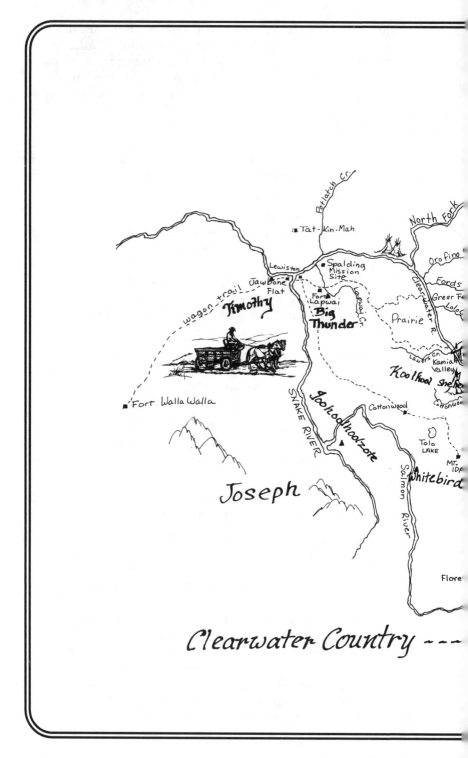

Clearwater Country ---

Hellgate

Lolo Hot
Springs

Lolo

Bitterroot River

ce

Fin

ie

Hungary Cr.

LOCHSA RIVER

rian
Mission

ing Glass

SELWAY RIVER

From the Light

Elk City

Red River
Hot Springs

outh Fork

---IN 1865

William Bassett had drawn the first rich slosh from the gulch, which later became known as Canal Gulch due to a canal which was dug along it to supply water to the placer miners. Canal Gulch was soon to be a familiar, even famous, place in the Northwest. Later in October, Elias D. Pierce left the country for unknown reasons, but a party of about thirty miners and one hundred twenty horses laden with camp gear and mining equipment arrived at the gulch in November. Lumber was whipsawed, hand hewn buildings hastily erected, canals dug, flumes and sluice boxes built, and, of course, claims staked. The ragtag miners even devised miners' laws and a government of sorts to oversee mining activities and disputes and they established boundaries for the Oro Fino Mining District.

By the summer of '61, Pierce City had not only been born, it flourished. Dozens of white canvas tents had popped up midst the log shanties, homes for two to three thousand miners and more than two thousand other folks — sawyers and builders, a smithy and a grave digger, barkeeps and store clerks, pack train outfitters and the inevitable ladies of ill repute. The likes of Whiskey Jim Johnson, Calico Jack, Deadshot Eugene Smith, Hot Footed Jack Ellis, Rolling Pin Jim Morrow, and Tobacco Juice George strode along the dusty main street in pursuit of a thirst-quencher at one of the new saloons, a pound of bacon at the general store, a replacement for a broken shovel, a long needed bath at one of the boarding houses, or a congratulatory slap on the back for packing out a pouchful of gold dust.

Provisions from Walla Walla normally kept the townsfolk and miners content and equipped to stay awhile, and what wasn't packed in was bought from the Indians, for the Nez Perces had established an ongoing and profitable economic exchange with Pierce City folk. Draw poker, bucking the tiger, chuck-luck, and chess occupied leisure hours amongst the miners, and even reading the few available books and days-old, dollar-a-copy newspapers kept people occupied evenings. News of the beginnings of the Civil War aroused some emotional polarization that from time to time sent bullets whizzing through the air. Even the first United States flag raised at Pierce City caught a slug. Confederate sympathizers wanted her torn down! The miners did suffer the hardships of living in the wilderness; of trekking on foot, heavily laden with supplies, for ten days or more to reach the mining district; and of losing companions along the way due to accident, snow blindness, misdirection, or falling into a drunken stupor on a freezing winter night because the whiskey barrel just couldn't be resisted. In addition, the continual threat of ambush by outlaws dogged the miners.

In the summer of 1862, what was to be the first courthouse in Idaho was built on a hillside just off Main Street, and on September 1st, with the arrival of Judge Ethelbert P. Oliphant, court convened. Pierce City soon witnessed its first murder trial, with others to follow in the months ahead, as the district continued to thrive.

However, by 1863, the easy to reach gold dust had diminished, and the miners had begun to leave. In their place came the Chinese. Yes, fortune-seeking Chinese miners sailed across the vast ocean to lease claims from the Americans and do the cleanup work — securing the hard to find remaining gold. The Chinese worked fastidiously to eke what they could from the abandoned claims, and a few did indeed make their fortunes. By 1864 Pierce City consisted of many more Chinese than Americans. The Chinese stayed on for years, and finally began moving out in the early 1900s when a new immigration law declared that they must become U.S. citizens or board a ship for home. Most, China bound, thus departed.

The Pierce City story was not an isolated one. Other strikes extended an equally vigorous Clearwater Country invitation to hoards of miners and townsfolk. In June of 1861, right next door to Pierce and Canal Gulch, the tiny town of Oro Fino was founded on Rhodes Creek, named for William "Billy" Rhodes, who supposedly took eighty thousand dollars worth of gold out of the area. While Pierce exists today, an ever-colorful remnant of gold rush days with the old courthouse still intact, the townsfolk of Oro Fino drifted away like the gold dust until only silent wooden shacks remained.

In late May of '61, fifty-two miners set out up the South Fork of the Clearwater, past the present town of Kooskia. Near present-day Stites they met Chief Red Owl and his band, who convinced thirty of the miners to turn back. The other twenty-two traveled around the Nez Perces and continued on into the wilderness. Near today's Elk

Early Day Elk City

City, about sixty miles from the juncture of the South Fork and main Clearwater, they struck gold. News of this new strike brought four hundred miners by July 1st and by August, two thousand!

Smaller strikes were made in the mountains surrounding and to the south of Elk City, but on August 20th the largest strike of them all was hit at what would become the town of Florence, about fifty miles south of present-day Grangeville. Some claims in the Florence area yielded up to eighty dollars worth of gold per pan. A man named Jacob Weiser is known to have once panned eighteen hundred dollars worth in just three hours. Miners, settlers and townspeople rode, walked and stumbled with the determined industry of ants across the Nez Perce Reservation until the population of Florence reached over five thousand.

Along the Salmon River in July of '62, another strike sparked a rush known as Warren's Diggings. Other strikes followed — at Buffalo Hill, in the Boise Basin, and along the Upper Salmon. As a result, miners who had taken all they could of the *easy dust* out of the Pierce, Elk City and Florence districts flocked to the new strikes along with thousands of others from throughout the West.

The Nez Perces watched the progression of the strikes with much wariness, in general, but also with an eye for profit. Many Nez Perces engaged in guiding, ferrying, and hauling in goods on pack trains, for example. Some supplied homegrown produce and beef to the mining towns. However, others engaged in harassment. Some delivered simple, forceful warnings to groups of miners that they must turn back and leave the reservation. In some instances, the Indians destroyed foot bridges built over streams the miners had to cross. Thus while some Nez Perces themselves earned money during the gold rush era in Clearwater Country and were, therefore, even eager to see miners arrive, clearly the Nez Perces as a whole could foresee Indian country turning white. They could also recognize that the gold which won fortunes for many white men was being removed from land that belonged to the Indians. In fact, estimates suggest that by the end of 1862, three million dollars worth of gold had been removed from the reservation. As an historical postscript, the United States government nearly a hundred years later paid a royalty to the Nez Perces for this gold.

Over the years, much change had also been brought to the entire region — mazes of trails and wagon roads, sternwheelers, ferries, mining towns that swelled to over five thousand during their heyday, constant pack train traffic crisscrossing the country, the destructive evils of alcohol abuse, and a gold-hungry, land-hungry fever dressed in white man's clothing. Also the stampede had indelibly trampled across the still freshly inked pages of the Nez Perce Treaty of 1855. In other words, powerful and permanent changes had swept in with the rush for gold to Clearwater Country.

Gold, Greed and Gallows

The Outlaws

Throughout the first half of the nineteenth century, as white trappers, traders, explorers, missionaries, settlers, and others appeared in the region, discord and disputes grew like stinging nettles among whites, among Indians, and between whites and Indians. Fist fights, armed skirmishes, murder, theft, revenge and counter revenge weren't uncommon. However, the real wild west outlaws of Clearwater Country, openly intent upon *doing bad*, didn't show up until the red wine of greed drooled down men's whiskered chins during the frenzied rush for gold.

Because laws did not exist, except those established by groups of miners to arbitrate mining disputes in their districts, underhanded characters of all sorts looked to the territory as either a refuge from more lawful locations or as a flush opportunity to pursue careers in crime...or both.

Claim jumping was one form of robbery which met with exacting disapproval by the miners. Take the old Setcher mine near Pierce City, for example. Three outsiders blundered in to jump the claim, but were quickly ambushed by townsmen Joe Wilson and Old Man Wheeler. When Joe's six shooter blast in the gut didn't down one of the intruders, Joe felt compelled to shoot the fleeing jumper in the back of the head — lest that varmint were to get away!

Two miles away at bustling Oro Fino nestled along Rhodes Creek, an 1861 gentlemen's duel over a gambling dispute turned to murder. When gamblers Finigan and Dorsey quarreled over a card game, they stood, took positions, and fired three shots each. Dorsey was evidently no marksman, for he took all three of Finigan's bullets without scoring even one of his own. Dorsey was rushed upstairs to a bedroom above the saloon where a doctor in attendance declared him "sufferin' but recoverin'." Upon hearing this report, Finigan strode upstairs, drew his knife, slashed Dorsey's throat, and returned to the bar to buy a round for the house. Now the townsfolk figured the knife-slashing was simply unjustified, so they sentenced Finigan to hang. Standing on the scaffold with a noose around his neck, doomed Finigan spoke powerful-touching last words. Some folks cried, and all looked mighty sad. The gallows trap was sprung ...why, lo and behold, Finigan fell right out of the noose and landed on his feet on the ground. The knot had not held. Amazed and still teary-eyed, some of the spectators drew guns to protect this *escaped* man. Others argued, till a vote was taken. Finigan, they determined, was to be set free. The citizenry passed the hat, bought Finigan a horse and saddle, and cheerfully waved him away as he offered the crowd a gracious farewell bow.

One of the Oro Fino saloon keepers, incidentally, used to sleep on the floor of his saloon so as to be out of the way of stray revolver shots that frequently whistled through his front door. He stated,

> Every morning when I opened my front door I looked out to see a dead man, and was disappointed on not seeing any, as we were ambitious to keep up a reputation for having a man for breakfast every morning.

Those sixties' miners and their fellow townsfolk were indeed a rough lot. During one two week period in 1861, four murders occurred in the fledgling town of Lewiston, which was outside the districts but in most respects a mining town — miners and miners' suppliers coming and going daily. Sunday afternoon strollers in the streets of Lewiston sometimes had to flee into doorways to avoid the wild pistol shots of young horsemen reveling through the town.

Into that scene in the spring of '61 stepped a dandy, a gentleman of stature and bearing and dignity, with a lady on his arm. He was Henry Plummer, a gambler by profession. And his lady had been kidnapped by seduction from an honest husband and three young ones. Within two days Plummer left her destitute and alone, a sorry state of life which left her with no choice but to ply her only wares from the doorfront of a crib.

Plummer took up his fortune-seeking at the poker table where the lowest of low desperadoes circled their chairs nightly. In time, a crass and cunning alliance grew out of their games, a camaraderie of crime...an outlaw gang.

The soon-to-become-notorious Plummer Gang had been organized by a bond of treacherous mutual honor and a code of killing and theft. Henry was its king. Cherokee Bob, a former Georgian in flight from a murderous foray in Walla Walla, joined him. And Bill Bunton, a double-dyed murderer and notorious horse and cattle thief entered the pact. A scoundrelous acquaintance of Henry's, Jack Cleveland, was also given the welcome handshake. And a number of others, evildoers and toughs, completed the gang's membership.

The vile deeds they visited upon the citizenry of the region would long be cursed...and remembered. One of the gang's main bases of operation, called a *shebang*, was located near the present town of Culdesac along what was one of the main trailways in the region. From there the ruffians set up ambushes and trickeries which allowed them regular infusions of gold dust and nuggets stolen from unlucky passersby. Hardly a week went by when some unsuspecting packer, miner, messenger, or pony expressman didn't unaccountably disappear in the vicinity of the Plummer Gang's shebang.

After months of such vicious harassment, some of the region's citizenry began talking of forming a group of vigilantes to capture and hang gang members. However, in a few cases, those who publicly encouraged such resistance

> *Bands of desperadoes... have rod roughshod, as it were, over the rights of the people, trampling upon both human and divine law, and so disturbing the quiet of the peaceful citizens, that not infrequently Judge Lynch has adjudicated, and a signpost or a neighboring tree has been converted for the time being into a gallows before which the doomed victim has plead unavailingly for mercy. However much may be said in favor of thus speedily ending the mad career of those who prey upon the innocent...it seldom, if ever, reforms any who escape its condign punishment, as they soon congregate in more remote localities, where new theaters of operation await the outburst of their pent up malice...and a new community is startled with the awful cry of murder in their midst.*
>
> THE BANDITTI OF THE
> ROCKY MOUNTAINS, 1865

were themselves murdered. One outspoken Lewistonian who went so far as to denounce gang members individually and in person was a man named William Patrick Ford.

One day some among the Plummer Gang overheard Ford's plans to travel with a cadre of dancing girls to a saloon he intended to open in Oro Fino. They then connived to kill Ford as he passed near the shebang. Ford, however, got wind of the plot and avoided attack by taking a more roundabout route. Angered at having had their murderous attempt foiled, Henry Plummer and two of his cronies, Charlie Ridgely and Charley Reeves, rode for Oro Fino. On the way they came upon two Frenchmen on foot, whom the rogues halted, held at gun point, searched and robbed. Then buoyed by one thousand dollars in new-found gold dust, the gang members whooped and hollered their way into Oro Fino.

There they made the rounds of the saloons, the last of which was Ford's. They hitched their horses, clomped into the bar, and sat to drink. Ford was nowhere in sight, so having slugged down several draughts, they proceeded to ravage the saloon. In a wild melee they destroyed much of the building's contents. Then, as a ghoulish finale, they cut the tail off a lap dog held by one of the women.

Then, departing, they suddenly heard Ford shouting curses and admonitions behind them. Brandishing his pistols, Ford ran through the barroom, followed the outlaws into the street and demanded that they get out of town. But one of the rowdies leveled a shot straight toward him as the other two took shelter behind their horses. A frenzied three-to-one bullet exchange ensued. Ford fired eleven bullets, hit Ridgely twice through the leg and pelleted Plummer's horse. Then Ford fell dead. Plummer and Reeves rode out of town, and Ridgely was taken to a ranch house nearby for medical attention. He recovered and later rejoined the gang. William Patrick Ford was planted in the ground.

By 1862, when the miner population at Florence was about five thousand and production at times reached fifty thousand dollars in gold per day, Florence had become the major base of operations for Clearwater Country's outlaws. Two or three dozen at a time, in loosely revolving bands, took up residence in this hub of impassioned gold-seekers, gamblers, and hurdy-gurdy girls, as well as of hundreds of honest and peace-loving merchants and other townspeople.

Charley Harper was chief of one outlaw band that had arrived fairly early in the boom days of Florence. He and fellow scoundrels Bill Peoples, Dave English, "Brockie," and Nels Scott picked up five purses of gold from a party of six miners just outside of town the first day of their arrival. Feeling flush, they galloped down Main Street, firing their pistols as they came, rode their horses into a saloon, and ordered a round of whiskey. Thus they had introduced themselves to the town that would grow increasingly fearful of these robbers who subsisted on the good fortunes of hardworking, unadulterated folk.

In the summer of '62, Cherokee Bob and a friend-in-crime from Carson City, Nevada, Bill Mayfield, and Mayfield's paramour, Cynthia, left Lewiston for Florence. During the course of the journey, Cynthia's eye was turned by the attentive Cherokee Bob. Indeed, soon after their arrival at Florence, she switched to the man "better able to take care of me" due to the fact that he'd just acquired a saloon from which he would be deriving a regular income.

During the heyday of violence and thievery ushered in by the likes of Harper, Mayfield, Cherokee Bob, and for a time Henry Plummer, Florence was witness to frequent scuffles and frays and atrocities. One particularly brutal act was the bloody slaying of an old German miner who lived alone a few miles from town. Having remained aloof from most folks thereabouts, the German had been the subject of much speculation — surely he secreted hoards of gold dust in his remote cabin. On the supposition that he did, the murderers violently broke into the shack. They tore apart every bit of furniture, bedding, and supplies in their efforts to find gold, lit a short-lived fire in a corner in an attempt to destroy evidence of their deed, and then left behind the mutilated carcass of the German. This crime incensed the miners and honest citizens of Florence, although they were unable to determine guilt.

Now and then the outlaws, to the satisfaction of law-abiding citizens, brutalized each other or were felled by intended victims. Within days of the German's murder, for example, a group of ruffians gambled at a local saloon. Near dawn, tired and boozy, they broke into an argument. One of them, the aforementioned Brockie, shot another and then surrendered to a justice of the peace. Delighted that at least one ne'er-do-well had been eliminated, the jury found

Brockie not guilty on the basis of his testimony that the shooting was an accident — that he'd actually intended to shoot someone else!

Brockie soon scuffled into a similar destiny. That same year while waiting for a river ferry with a group of others, he became angered at one Arthur Chapman. Brockie whipped out a pistol and a knife to begin an attack when Chapman clutched an ax and whopped Brockie, splitting his head wide open. Good folks in the region didn't call it self-defense; they called it justice.

Three other outlaws, Peoples, English, and Scott, who aroused citizen ire for the theft of eleven hundred dollars from a pack train, were captured shortly afterwards and taken to Walla Walla. There it was determined that their trial would be held in Florence. On their way back the prisoners were held in Lewiston, where the citizenry decided they should handle the thugs themselves. In response, the authorities imprisoned the three under heavy guard. The noise of an attempt to rescue Peoples during the night roused townsfolk from their beds. But seeing the failed rescuer wounded by a bullet, they went back to bed, content that the three thieves would be saved until daybreak. However, when a crowd of citizens found the guards dismissed and the jail door open in the morning, the crowd rushed in to find the prisoners. Alas...all three hung cold and stiff from the jailhouse rafters...the victims of vigilantes. Thereafter the town felt vindicated and a mite safer.

Charley Harper, hearing news of the hangings and feeling the heat himself, hot-footed out of the country. Henry Plummer was in other parts and had found himself a wife. Cherokee Bob and Cynthia remained in Florence where they had taken up a friendship with one Bill Willoughby.

Cynthia, despite her shady reputation in the town, wished to attend the upcoming New Year's dance. Cherokee arranged for Willoughby to take her. But when the couple sauntered onto the dance floor, the upright ladies of Florence huffed and scoffed until their husbands asked Willoughby to take his date and leave. Willoughby peaceably complied. However, upon hearing of this insult to Cynthia, Cherokee Bob vowed revenge. At first, general harassment of the citizens satisfied him, but then he and Willoughby decided to pursue a saloon owner named Jakey Williams, who had publicly spoken out against the outlaws.

Williams averted attack by fleeing from building to building until he tired of this cat and mouse game and returned to his saloon, picked up his shotgun, and began firing on his pursuers. Before long numerous citizens joined Williams, until Willoughby and Cherokee were far outnumbered. Willoughby took sixteen slugs before he finally dropped, mortally wounded, into the dust. Cherokee managed to fend off the townsmen awhile as he too attempted retreat. But soon a well-aimed bullet caught him and he too lay wounded.

Cherokee died three days later, a serious loss only perhaps to Cynthia, who quickly determined that she should go in immediate search of her one time lover Bill Mayfield. Not long after she rejoined him, however, Mayfield was shot dead by a gambler with whom he'd quarreled the day before. Cynthia wept over Mayfield's dying and then proceeded to set herself up in business — doing what most women of ill-repute and poor means did in the wild wild West of the 1800s.

Henry Plummer, ever a dandy, had for a short while taken up a life of modesty, honesty, and usefulness in Montana. The Honorable William C. Rheem, who knew him well during this time, described Plummer thusly,

> He was about five feet eleven inches in height, and weighed a hundred and fifty pounds. He was straight, slender, spare, agile...He was a quiet man and talked but little;...always in a low tone and with a good choice of language. He never grew boisterous, even in his cups, and no impulse of anger or surprise ever raised his voice above that of wary monotone. His countenance was in perfect keeping with his utterance. Both were under the same vigilant command...Affection, fear, hate, grief, remorse, or any passion or emotion, found no expression in his immovable face. No color ever flushed his cheeks. ...The observer beheld a well-cut mouth, indicating decision, firmness, and intelligence; but not a line expressive of sensuality; a straight nose and well-shaped chin, and cheeks rather narrow and fleshless, still, in their outlines, not unhandsome. But one might as well have looked into the eyes of the dead for some token of a human soul as

to have sought it in the light gray orbs of Plummer. Their cold, glassy stare defied inquisition. They seemed to be gazing through you at some object beyond, as though you were transparent.

Although peaceable for a time, Plummer was continuously mindful of the criminal element that mingled about and who might expose his vile life history. Midst the company of several good citizens one night, Plummer became frustrated with the intrusion of his old crony Jack Cleveland and impetuously shot him. One of Plummer's objectives was to silence Jack. This he surely did, but the shooting aroused suspicion. Plummer was tried for Cleveland's killing, but was acquitted on a plea of self defense. As time passed, however, he again pursued a life of crime and violence and led another aggressive outlaw band, even while serving as a sheriff for a period of time! But one day a determined vigilante committee walked in on him as he stood grooming himself in his cabin. Abbreviated justice being their usual method, the vigilantes denied his impassioned pleas for mercy and hanged him on a gallows Plummer himself had constructed as sheriff the previous season. The gambler, dandy, gunslinger, sheriff and outlaw was twenty-seven.

Plummer and his gang were surely the most notorious of the outlaws, even today in the still told lore of Clearwater Country. However, perhaps the most heinous of crimes perpetrated against men in the area, followed by an astounding tracking of the outlaws who committed it, involved the murder of another sojourner between Idaho and Montana, an honest man named Lloyd Magruder.

Magruder was a well-liked, Lewiston-based merchant who traveled regularly to the boom town of Elk City which sat in a mountain-ringed meadow in the upper reaches of the South Fork of the Clearwater. His business was to provide the miners with sundry supplies. Having heard about the gold rush to the Bannack mines in southwestern Montana, he elected in August of 1863 to trek the rugged five hundred miles from Lewiston to Bannack with a pack train full of supplies to sell. He hoped to profit well in gold dust.

Strangely, however, and unknown to Magruder, a close friend of his who ran the Luna House Hotel in Lewiston had a most discomfiting dream the night before Magruder left. This friend, Hill Beachy, dreamt with excruciating clarity of the murder of Magruder. Beachy dismissed the dream for the time being, but remained noticeably anxious until he heard of Magruder's safe arrival at Bannack. There Magruder found that the gold rush had moved to the Alder Gulch mines at Virginia City, seventy-five miles further, so he continued on to that area.

In booming Virginia City, Magruder quickly sold his goods for a satisfying quantity of gold dust. He then secured the assistance of a few men who had left Lewiston on the

Hill Beachy

same day of his departure and who had kept him company during his eastward journey. Doc Howard, William Page, Chris Lowry, and Jim Romaine had even worked for Magruder during his time in Virginia City. Thus they knew well the amount of his earnings, and Magruder had come to trust them. Now for two hundred dollars apiece they would serve as pack train guards on the homeward trek. Little did Magruder know that Howard, Lowry, and Romaine had formerly led violent lives of crime. Even had they tried, such villains as they were, they could not resist coveting Magruder's new found wealth — twenty-four thousand dollars in gold dust and seventy-five healthy mules.

Shortly before they left Virginia City, Magruder accepted the requests of a miner named Charley Allen, two brothers named Horace and Robert Chalmers, and an older man named William Phillips to join Magruder and his crew on the trip to Lewiston. And in October the group of nine left Virginia City. Magruder felt well protected. He had no suspicion of Doc Howard's increasing awareness that the time was growing ripe for a robbery.

On a cold evening under a threatening wintry sky well into the mountains about forty-three miles east of Elk City, the party camped. After supper Page built a fire near the mule herd where Magruder and Lowry would stand guard until 10 p.m. As the two walked to the herd, Lowry picked up his ax in order, he said, to cut firewood. The others went to their beds. Magruder and Lowry wiled away the hours in warm conversation until Magruder leaned towards the fire to light his pipe. Lowry rose on the ruse that he would chop a little wood. Chop he did ...Magruder's skull! Howard suddenly appeared, grabbed the ax and administered several additional blows. The two then returned to the main camp and slew the Chalmers brothers with the ax while Romaine knifed Phillips. Allen awoke at the noise, but had no time to assess the situation before Howard shot him in the back of the head with a double-barrelled shotgun.

As a snowstorm descended, hoping that wolves or other creatures would devour the corpses, the three murderers and Page removed the bodies from the scene by throwing them over a cliff. They burned most of the personal effects, including the saddles and guns of the dead men. Next day, realizing that they could not effect an escape if followed by Magruder's seventy-five mules, the villains drove the herd into a steep draw and shot most of them. Then they circumvented Elk City and rode on toward Lewiston. Once there they attempted to steal a boat and make their way downriver, but the boat stalled on an island. So, disguised as much as possible by hats and mufflers about their faces, they went back to Lewiston and the hotel of Hill Beachy to book passage on a coach to Walla Walla.

When the four outlaws boarded the coach next day, Beachy got a quick look at their faces and recognized the ruffians who had left Lewiston the same day as Magruder. He also noticed that each clutched closely a canteen. The coach joggled out of town, and Beachy pondered the contents of those canteens. He felt intuitively sure, despite the slightness of the evidence, that his dream had been tragically realized, that these men concealed gold dust in their canteens, and that the dust belonged to a murdered man — his friend Lloyd Magruder.

He tried to convince locals to form a posse to follow and arrest the escaping foursome, but no one would give credence to Beachy's dream. He searched the town for days to find the horses the roughs had been riding when they arrived. Finally Beachy located a man with whom the four had stabled their horses till spring and with the help of a stable boy identified one of Magruder's saddles among their gear — the first lead! Then when a pack train arrived from Bannack, a man among them identified one of the stabled horses as a horse that had been ridden by one of the men in the Magruder party. Beachy was then thoroughly convinced the four suspicious men had murdered Magruder and perhaps others as well.

Then began an extraordinary pursuit. Beachy gained the assistance of a gutsy fellow named Tom Farrell, and together they hurriedly drove a wagon to Walla Walla where they discovered that the four bandits had left for Portland four days earlier. Beachy and Farrell boarded a boat in the charge of Captain Ankey, an old and skilled river pilot, who felt sure he could steer them safely through the perilous Umatilla Rapids. From Umatilla they took a steamboat to Celilo, where they rented horses and rode sixteen miles to

A Hanging

The Dalles to learn that Romaine, Lowry, Page and Howard had left two days before. Farrell and Beachy again boarded a steamer. They arrived at Portland twenty-four hours behind the fugitives. There Beachy tricked a confidant of the criminals into telling him that they had taken a steamer to San Francisco, where they would have their gold dust made into coins before leaving for New York. Knowing another ocean steamer would not leave for ten more days, Beachy prepared to ride overland seven hundred miles to San Francisco. He went by horse and buggy to Salem, Oregon, then by horseback and coach to Yureka, California. At Yureka he telegraphed the San Francisco chief of police, who, thanks to Beachy's forewarning, nabbed and arrested the murderers as they stepped off the steamer. Beachy, of course, was most gratified.

Four week's effort in San Francisco won extradition of the four men back to Lewiston, where they were incarcerated in a room on the top floor of the Luna House. Eventually, through a turn of legal deception, Beachy drew the heinous story out of Page and offered to let him turn state's evidence if he would testify against the others. And, thus, the case was won. On March 4, 1864, in view of an estimated ten thousand onlookers, Lowry, Howard and Romaine were hanged.

Page later led Beachy and a small party of others to the crime scene to recover the remains, which were returned to Lewiston for burial. About a year later Page himself was killed in a drunken row.

Thus time and morality won out over the Magruder murderers, as it had over numerous other outlaws who roamed and sometimes ruled the mining towns and trailways scattered throughout Clearwater Country. It is doubtful that anyone in the region in the old days ever fully felt a sense of safety, for many potential attackers lurked round the corners of everyday life — incurable illness, high water drownings, Indian skirmishes, accidents enroute from place to place throughout the rugged country. But it is likely that the most malevolent nightmares of the ordinary folk of the region bore witness to their major fright — that of the outlaws. Vermin indeed they were, who sniffed out and followed the many trails of greed and vice to prey upon good folk, even upon each other, and most often upon miners and packers bringing out Clearwater Country gold.

A Fight and Flight For Freedom

The Nez Perce War

As the first missionaries arrived in Clearwater Country, some among the Nez Perces had begun to foresee not just the many *wondrous things* they might learn from the white man, but also his encroachment upon Indian lands. However, until 1855, the Nez Perces' span of ancestral motherland remained a vast, plentiful, wilderness domain. It stretched from the Bitterroots on the east to beyond the Blue Mountains on the west and roughly from the Salmon River on the south to the prairies and mountains north of the Clearwater River.

The People, the Nee Mee Poo, owned this land. No one among them claimed any piece — all was for all. They had been born from their mother, the earth. She gave them sustenance throughout their lifetimes, and they returned to her when they died.

During the second quarter of the nineteenth century, white settlers began migrating to Indian land bordering Clearwater Country. As was their way, the white men and their wives and children, in ever increasing numbers, claimed plots of land in order to gain exclusive rights of ownership. The Indian was not free, as before, to roam throughout the region wherever he pleased. Soon he began to realize that his ancestral land was being consumed and that he was being squeezed out of his own country. Resentment, frustration, foreboding, and hostility grew among the Indians and whites alike.

At the same time the United States government was in the process of planning a railroad route across the Northwest and needed land clearances and assurances of non-harassment from the Indians. In May 1855, Governor Isaac Stevens of the recently created Washington Territory was sent to confer with the Indians. He and members of several tribes entered into lengthy negotiations in the Walla Walla Valley. The resulting treaty established the boundaries of Indian reservations, including one for the Nez Perces. Not all Nez Perce leaders, however, had favored giving up portions of their lands. Generally, these anti-treaty, or non-treaty leaders were also non-Christians. Yes, the earlier created fracture — Christians *versus* non-Christians — lent itself now to disagreement regarding the terms of the treaty and to a further split among the Nez Perces. But the proposed Nez Perce reservation was nearly as vast as their ancestral territory, so most Nez Perces found the treaty acceptable as a means to protect their homeland and to maintain peace. They were promised remuneration for those portions of land they ceded to the U.S. Government through the treaty, though little of this compensation ever reached them. Much of the country they did retain was rich in natural resources important to the white man's economy — timber, agricultural lands, and unknown at that time to the signers of the treaty — gold.

White inroads into the established reservations were reasonably held in abeyance by enforcement of the treaty for the first few years. Before long, however, whites began moving onto Indian land to the west and north of Clearwater Country. There farmers and cattlemen came in growing numbers. Tensions among whites and Indians erupted into warfare which waged until September of 1858, when government troops crushed a combined force of warriors from four major tribes, the Spokans, Coeur d'Alenes, Palouses and Yakimas. The Nez Perces had managed to safeguard their own territory by at times assisting the white soldiers, but were agitated by the final submission of the other tribes and shocked by the hangings of several Indian leaders that took place after the Indians' surrender. Also, the Nez Perces realized they were now isolated from other tribes and, of course, still disunified themselves.

In 1860, gold was discovered in tributaries of the Clearwater River, and by 1861, a rush was on. The center of activity developed into a settlement which the miners named Pierce City, at Canal Gulch, a headwater of the stream now called Orofino Creek. Within months the invisible fences of the Treaty of 1855 were being torn asunder as hundreds of gold seekers scrambled for dust and nuggets and claims. The white men went wherever they wanted, and the enforcers of the treaty, United States troops, were ineffectual in stopping them.

As a result, the United States Government felt increasing pressure to renegotiate the Treaty of 1855 in order to allow access by whites to the mining districts of Clearwater Country. Thus in April of 1861, the Superintendent of Indian Affairs for Oregon and Washington, Edward Geary, met with one of the Nez Perce chiefs called *Lawyer* due to his intellect and abilities in debate, and with a large gathering of his followers. Lawyer had been highly influential among the Christian and pro-white factions during the 1855 negotiations. Because of his conciliatory position with the whites, the remunerations he accepted from them, and his presumptive role of importance in conferences with government officials, Lawyer was much resented by the non-Christian anti-white Nez Perces. While some of the latter had at times attempted to keep the white miners out of Clearwater Country, little could they actually accomplish. Some of Lawyer's people had profited from selling cattle, food and services to the miners and were not eager to lose that opportunity. Also, since the principle settlement of miners was not the village site of any of the Nez Perce bands, the immediacy of the miners' threat to land ownership was not strongly nor universally felt. On April 10th, Lawyer and forty-nine others among his group signed an agreement to allow miners to enter the reservation north of the Clearwater River and the Nez Perce Trail. No where else were whites to be allowed. Ignored at this signing was the Nez Perces' ancient tradition of egalitarian independence which gave no tribesman ultimate leadership status – in this case, no right to sign away rights and lands for all Nez Perces.

The agreement was destined to quickly fail anyway. A month later a large contingent of whites toting loads of goods and gear stepped off a sternwheeler on the southeastern shore of the confluence of the Snake and Clearwater Rivers. Little did the Nez Perces realize that the first tent stake driven into the ground by these new arrivals would root forever an American city on Nez Perce land. The town was named Lewiston after one of the forerunners of all the whites who'd come since 1805, Meriwether Lewis.

Within days of the creation of this fledgling city, new strikes along the Clearwater's South Fork sent reverberations of excitement throughout the Northwest. The now fragile net of the Treaty of 1855 fully burst from the resulting onrush of whites onto the reservation. *Civilization* pounded to dust the straggling strings of that net as towns laid themselves out with roadways, shops, saloons, inns, ferries, and the rustic but permanent houses of the whites.

The Nez Perces made what protest they could, but were largely overrun. Many became absorbed to an extent into the ways and endeavors of the whites – trading, selling, guiding, dispatching for the miners and other settlers, and gaining material goods and money in return. Nevertheless, hostilities simmered throughout the reservation and frequently heated into altercations so that by mid-1862, when the white population had substantially grown, mutual intolerance had become pervasive. Quarrels among the Nez Perces themselves also increased as the anti-whites disgustingly pointed fingers of blame at Lawyer.

Eventually it became apparent to government officials in the Northwest that the white settlers and miners needed governance. To apply such, however, meant that the government had to own the land upon which the whites lived. Thus, in 1863, the government decided it must officially buy more land from the Nez Perces...thus, decreasing the size of the reservation. Lawyer and his fellow headmen were summoned to a council at Fort Lapwai, and additional troops were moved in and stationed there.

Shock, dismay, fright — the Nez Perces remembered what had happened to the Indian tribes to the west of them in 1858. Had the Nez Perces' turn now come? Lawyer's key participation in these new negotiations stimulated even greater divisiveness between the treaty and non-treaty Indians, so that the anti-white bands did not at first appear. Lawyer, himself begrudging this new design upon Nez Perce land, debated eloquently with the officials and refused to sell more land. A recess was called. Six days later the council reconvened, this time with the participation of several bands who were antagonistic towards Lawyer. Their headmen — Thunder Eyes, Red Owl, White Bird, Eagle From The Light, and Old Joseph of the Wallowa country would have a voice in the negotiations.

The headmen resisted, offering only to sell the land at Lewiston and in the gold districts. American negotiator Calvin Hale, then resorted to more manipulative tactics by privately pressuring and persuading the headmen one-by-

Nez Perce Treaty Negotiations, 1863
Seated: Tamootssu, Lawyer, Jason
Standing in center: Robert Newell, Perrin Whitman

one. Jealousies and bitterness stirred them until at one
point Thunder Eyes declared that the Nez Perces were no
longer one, but two eternally separate Indian groups.
Refusing to negotiate, White Bird led his people away to
return home, as did Joseph after symbolically ripping apart
copies of the Treaty of 1855 and the Gospel of Matthew
which had been given to him by Rev. Spalding at Joseph's
baptism years before. These two leaders would themselves
sell no more land. In leaving the conference, they did not
once imagine that any other headman would or could take
it upon himself to sell their land for them. But in their
absence Lawyer was convinced, and he and fifty-one of his
followers signed the Treaty of 1863, which included the
selling of much land, portions of which were the ancestral
grounds of White Bird's and Joseph's bands.

The new treaty reduced the reservation by close to
ninety percent and required the crowding of all of the
Indians of both factions onto the remaining much smaller
area of land. In the spring of 1867, the treaty was finally
ratified by the U.S. Senate. Until then the Indians had
remained free and for the most part had carried on with

their lives as before, although ever increasing numbers of whites settled on the ceded lands prior to treaty ratification. Among those lands was the Wallowa Mountain region, beloved motherland of Joseph.

Moving those bands, such as Joseph's, whose village sites sat outside the reservation boundaries, would prove to be a lengthy process fraught with friction. In 1871 old Joseph died in the Wallowas and was returned to his mother earth. As he lay dying, he told his son, Thunder In The Mountains, known later as Young Chief or Chief Joseph, "My son ...always remember that your father never sold this country ...This country holds your father's body. Never sell the bones of your father and mother." Thunder In The Mountains would not forget his father's words.

Young Joseph began a peaceful campaign to demonstrate to the whites that neither his father, nor any of his people, had ever sold the Wallowas. He and other Nez Perce leaders convened councils with the whites in continual attempts to explain what had happened in 1863 — that only Lawyer and his followers had sold any land. Understanding the misperception that had occurred among the whites in

Gen. Oliver Otis Howard

1863, Indian Agent John B. Monteith wrote the United States' Commissioner of Indian Affairs imploring him to leave the Wallowas to the Indians. Department of the Interior personnel concurred in part, and in June of 1873 decided to divide the Wallowa region into a white section for the settlers and a Nez Perce section for Joseph's people.

Chief Joseph had been widely recognized among the whites as a peace-loving, dignified, eloquent and wise man. However, suddenly the whites, sensing the Interior Department had forced the whites to kowtow to the Indians, turned against him. Rumors and newspaper reports now depicted Joseph as an unreasonable hostile. Thus in June of 1875, the 1873 decision was revoked and Joseph's band, as well as all other off-reservation, non-treaty bands, were told they must now move onto the reservation. Chief Joseph still said *no*. He continued to meet with groups of whites and also with groups of other non-treaties, some of whom considered war as a means of resistance. Joseph, however, foresaw the destruction of his people were they to fight the whites and, therefore, helped dissuade the Indians from warfare.

Several other white leaders in the Northwest, including General Oliver Otis Howard, commander of the Department of the Columbia at Fort Vancouver, saw the truth in Joseph's plea and addressed the issue with the United States Government. In 1876 the Secretary of the Interior designated Howard and four others to meet with Joseph, his brother Ollicut and other members of his band. In November of that year, Howard and the other commissioners attempted to officially buy Joseph's Wallowa country to settle the issue. Again, Joseph said *no*, and stated that his people would never sell their land.

Frustrated in their efforts, the commissioners then recommended to the U.S. Government that an order be given to the off-reservation Indians to move onto the reservation within a reasonable time or be forced to move. Thus Agent Monteith sent four treaty Nez Perces to tell Joseph that he and his band must move onto the reservation by April 1st or Gen. Howard and his men would move them. Knowing that Gen. Howard had earlier sympathized with the Indians, Chief Joseph arranged

The Great Spirit Chief made the world as it is and as He wanted it, and He made a part of it for us to live upon. I do not see where you [General Howard] get authority to say that we shall not live where He placed us... Who are you, that you ask us to talk and then tell me I shan't talk? Are you the Great Spirit? Did you make the world? Did you make the sun? did you make the rivers to run for us to drink? Did you make the grass to grow? Did you make all these things that you talk to us as though we were boys? If you did, then you have a right to talk as you do.

Toohool-hool-zote,
May 7, 1877

213

to meet with him to determine the true impact of this latest declaration. When they met at Fort Lapwai in early May, already past the April 1st deadline, the attending non-treaties elected as their negotiator headman Toohool-hool-zote, known for his ability to argue well and persistently. But Howard had his orders; he knew he must make the Indians recognize the firmness of the government's mandate. He informed them he would use troops to enforce that mandate, argued angrily with Toohool-hool-zote, then had him seized and thrown into the guardhouse. The Indians realized the stunning truth – they must become reservation Indians or fight.

Again they remembered the costly battles of the tribes to the west and north in 1858. The non-treaty Nez Perces finally informed Howard they would peacefully move onto the reservation. Despite their request for more time due to the spring run-off conditions of the rivers they must cross, Howard gave them thirty days.

The chiefs jointly canvassed the available village sites on the reservation, agreed upon sites for each band, then dejectedly rode their horses home to begin the move. Despite raging spring waters, Joseph's band forged their way across the Snake and the Salmon, losing many livestock and goods in the crossings. They reached Tolo Lake on the Camas Prairie by June 2nd with a few days remaining. There they visited with the other non-treaty bands who had assembled with them just beyond the reservation boundaries. The bands of Chief White Bird from the Salmon River, Chief Toohool-hool-zote from the wild country between the Salmon and the Snake, and a few other smaller bands increased the total group to about five hundred. Fewer than two hundred were warriors.

The intention of the chiefs was to enjoy these last few days of freedom, despite grumblings about the forced move and deep sadness over the loss of their ancestral homes. With two days left, the young men raced horses, played games, gambled, paraded in battle finery, and told of their brave war deeds. Remembering a white man who had killed the father of one of the young Nez Perce warriors in order to settle on a select piece of land, an older Nez Perce watching the parade taunted the dead man's son — "If you're so brave, why don't you kill the man who killed your father?" Revenge had been a time-honored privilege of the

Indians, and these words shamed young Wahlitits. He brooded throughout the night. He had not wanted to bring his people trouble by seeking revenge, but now... In the morning he gathered two of his friends and rode haughtily off towards the Salmon River. During their fateful pursuit they slew four settlers, and the next day, joined by fourteen more warriors, swept along the river killing a dozen more white men, two women and a child, and wounding several others. When they returned that evening, the Tolo Lake campsite flared into a blaze of war talk.

Looking Glass had earlier moved his band to Clear Creek, within the reservation boundaries. Joseph and his brother Ollicut were across the Salmon River at the time of the murders. Upon hearing the news, they hastily returned to the main camp, where Joseph and White Bird decided to move their bands closer to the camps of Looking Glass and Red Owl. Looking Glass learned of their intent and sent his brother to meet the non-treaties on the Camas Prairie to advise them they were not welcome in his camp, for he wished to live in peace with the whites. Thus Joseph and Ollicut, White Bird, and TooHool-hool-zote moved their people south to the Salmon River and set up a defensive position a mile up White Bird Creek.

At dawn on June 17th they were ready when Captain David Perry with two companies of cavalry and eleven settler volunteers breached the brow of White Bird Hill. Perry's orders from Gen. Howard at Fort Lapwai had been to proceed to the prairie and protect the white settlers, but urged by residents of Grangeville to attack the Indians before the latter could cross the Salmon River, he and his men had spent a second night in the saddle.

The cavalry descended the hill. Lieutenant Edward Theller's patrol formed an advance guard, and halted as six Nez Perces approached from behind a nearby knoll — under a white flag of truce. Theller deployed the patrol as the truce party advanced. Suddenly a rifle *crrraaaackkk* burst from the cavalry line. In abrupt reaction, a Nez Perce dismounted, dropped to one knee, and fired a four hundred-yard shot that killed the Company F bugler. The Nez Perces were at war with the United States!

Having lost their communications — their bugler — and being startled by this unplanned turn of events, the cavalry had little time to effectively position themselves for

> *The men on the left, seeing the citizens in full retreat and the Indians occupying their places and the right falling back in obedience to orders, were seized with a panic which was uncontrollable, and then the whole right of the line, seeing the mad rush for horses on the left, also gave way and the panic became general. I have never seen anything to equal it... To stem the onrush was simply impossible. I did everything in human power to halt and reform my line, but no sooner would one squad halt and face about than the other, just placed in position, would be gone.*
>
> Captain David Perry,
> U.S.Cavalry Commander
> White Bird Hill Battle

the battle that ensued. Perry hastily ordered his men into fighting lines, with Company F at the center behind a low ridge, Company H to the west, and the volunteers to the east. This eastern flank was hit first by Two Moons and fifteen whooping warriors who shortly sent the panicked volunteers fleeing toward Grangeville, leaving two dead on the field. Two Moons turned his party to the west to attack Company F. Shooting wildly from horseback, a second and larger group of warriors charged directly into the center of the cavalry line.

At that point Perry ordered one of his flanks to move back for better positioning, but the center line perceived this movement as a retreat. Under heavy fire from the Indians, this misperception panicked the line, and a disorderly rout began. Lt. Theller and eighteen men launched a rear guard action, but all were slain.

After a series of efforts to hold their positions failed, Perry and two other officers scrambled to regain enough control to organize a retreat, but with limited success. The remaining soldiers were finally able to regroup at the summit and then rode hard to Grangeville. After chasing the cavalry most of the way, the Nez Perce warriors returned to the river and to their waiting women and children. They had not lost a single warrior. The U.S Army had lost thirty-four soldiers and two volunteers. The battle gave a decisive victory to the Nez Perces, as well as an important supply of guns and ammunition.

Back at Fort Lapwai Gen. Howard, who had originally dispatched Perry, had days earlier sent orders to Fort Walla

Walla for two more cavalry companies and one of infantry. On June 22nd, five days after the Battle of White Bird Canyon, Howard set out in pursuit of the Indians. With him traveled the 4th Artillery, the 21st Infantry, two hundred twenty-seven cavalry troops, twenty volunteers, packers and guides. He had not underestimated the Nez Perce force nor the intelligence of the chief he surmised led the warriors — Chief Joseph, headman of the largest band.

When the troops reached the Salmon near the mouth of White Bird Creek, they found that the Nez Perces had crossed to the other side. Later Gen. Howard noted, "No general could have chosen a safer position [for the Nez Perces] or one that would be more likely to puzzle and obstruct a pursuing foe." Of their several options from that position, the Indians chose to head northwest through the mountains on the west side of the river.

It was July 1st when Gen. Howard and the troops with their two howitzers and two gatling guns began crossing the Salmon in pursuit. The crossing was completed the next day; however, the Indians would that same day recross the Salmon at Craig Billy crossing downstream. Howard's troops scrambled and stumbled across the mountainous terrain only to reach this crossing three days behind the Indians. Howard, however, found it impossible to cross the roiling river at that point, and so laboriously returned to the White Bird crossing. He and his troops finally reached Grangeville on July 8th. There they came under verbal attack by the townspeople and several newspaper reporters, who criticized Howard's falderal in light of the events that had meantime taken place on the Camas Prairie.

Howard had earlier begun to worry that Looking Glass and his warriors might join the warring Nez Perces. In response to this fear, he had dispatched Capt. Stephen Whipple with two companies of cavalry and a group of volunteers to arrest Looking Glass and his band at their campsite on Clear Creek, about a mile east of present-day Kooskia. The troops descended the slopes on the west side of Clear Creek near the creek's mouth at dawn on July 1st. Astonished, Looking Glass attempted through intermediaries to reason with Whipple, but a misunderstanding led to an attack in which a woman and her child died, the camp was destroyed, and over seven hundred Nez Perce horses were seized.

The non-treaties had meanwhile appeared once again on the Camas Prairie. On July 3rd the chiefs sent out an advance party of men in case soldiers waited for them near the present town of Cottonwood. On their route the party was spotted by two volunteers, one of whom was killed. The other hurried back to his unit, which was under Capt. Whipple's command. Whipple then dispatched Lt. Sevier Rains, ten of the cavalry, and two volunteers to scout the Indian line. While watching Rains and his men, Nez Perce scouts also observed a band of Indians, mostly on foot, slowly crossing the prairie to the east of their position. It was the Looking Glass and Red Owl bands, now ready for war! Upon joining the larger group, Looking Glass assumed the position of war chief. He immediately ordered an attack on the Rains scouting party, all of whom were killed.

The next day Whipple's forces in Cottonwood were surrounded by Nez Perce warriors. A battle of several hours ensued without casualties on either side, and the Indians eventually returned to their main group. The next day the Nez Perces began crossing the prairie, heading north and east toward the South Fork of the Clearwater River. Seventeen Mount Idaho volunteers on their way to assist Perry inadvertently rode into the Indians' range, and they attacked, killing three and losing one of their own. they also attacked a group of civilians fleeing across the Prairie towards Mt. Idaho, killing one and mortally wounding two others.

By July 8th, Howard reached Grangeville. The non-treaties were already camped at the mouth of Cottonwood Creek on the South Fork. The non-treaties now totaled about five hundred children, women, and elders and

Chief Looking Glass

approximately two hundred forty warriors. Since no one appeared to be pursuing them, the Indians took time to visit friends and relatives in Kamiah, but upon returning to their camp found a line of citizen volunteers scouting their position. The volunteers retreated, but the Nez Perces drove away their horses and then held the volunteers on the crest of a hill for more than twenty-four hours – an altercation which later earned the hill the name "Mount Misery." On July 11th a second volunteer party came to the rescue of the first. The Nez Perces returned to their camp, and the volunteers retreated to the safety of Mount Idaho.

Now the chiefs debated their position. They presumed Howard was not too close, or he would surely, they thought, have joined in the rescue of the volunteers. The chiefs suspected that when Howard arrived with his four hundred or so soldiers and one hundred volunteers, they would come from the west, down Cottonwood Creek. In fact, however, as the volunteers were retreating on the west side of the South Fork, Howard was drawing near in a long column atop the bluffs that formed the east side of the river canyon. In the early afternoon of July 11th, the first howitzer blast from the eastern bluffs, a thousand feet above the Indian camp and across the river, riveted the Nez Perces with alarm. The warriors scrambled for their rifles and horses and quickly swept into lines riding across the river and up the wooded draws that would take them alongside and above the soldiers. Those cavalry still proceeding towards the battle site were stopped where they were, and the military pack train lost two men at the outset and was nearly given up entirely to the Indians. The two forces fought at a mutual stand-off throughout the day, lobbied a few shots at one another during the night, and awoke the next morning to continued combat.

During the night, however, the Nez Perce chiefs had begun to consider withdrawal. The warriors feared for the lives of their families, so that some individually did withdraw. By mid-afternoon Howard had organized a charge, which was delayed when a supply train with troop escort appeared from the south. The artillery battalion set to lead the charge was instead detailed to bring in the supply train. Once the train was safely within the army lines, the trailing troops under Capt. Marcus P. Miller attacked the Nez Perces at an angle in a military maneuver called *rolling up the line.* The Indians quickly withdrew. Somewhat taken aback by the warriors' quick disappearance, the soldiers vollied shots down the bluffs and across the river where the Nez Perces had hastily organized a mass retreat up Cottonwood Creek.

The cavalry descended the bluffs and ransacked what was left of the abandoned Nez Perce camp. The Battle of the Clearwater, as this engagement later became known, was claimed by Howard as a major victory for the army. But despite the army's advantage of superior numbers, surprise and a favorable physical position, fifteen of Howard's men were killed and twenty-five wounded. The Indians suffered four warriors dead and six wounded. Resting from the battle and on their presumed laurels, the troops postponed further pursuit of the fleeing Nez Perces until the next day. By then, however, the Nez Perces and all their livestock, which included about two thousand horses, had reached the Kamiah Valley and crossed the main Clearwater River. When two advance cavalry units arrived at the crossing site, they were greeted by a rear guard's bullets and caught only glimpses of the main body ascending the hills to safety. Once again a river had effectively halted the U.S. Army.

Reaching the Weippe Prairie on July 15th, the non-treaty chiefs convened a council. Some wanted to retreat to the Seven Devils on the eastern fringe of the Snake River Canyon, others to the Salmon, and still others to surrender. Looking Glass favored a retreat across the Bitterroots along the Nez Perce Trail to the country of the Crow Indians, who he felt sure would be of assistance to the Nez Perces. He also noted that the whites on the other side of the mountains were not at war with the Nez Perces. His argument won out, and he became the designated leader for the journey. On July 16th the Nez Perces gathered their horses, along with the goods and supplies they had managed to take with them in their hasty retreat from Cottonwood Creek, and headed east.

Realizing the Nez Perces' chosen route, Gen. Howard telegraphed the news to the U.S. Department of War and received orders in return to pursue the Indians. Howard also telegraphed military officers stationed in Montana, so they could ready themselves for the Nez Perces. He then arranged for the defense of the whites along the Clearwater, Salmon, and Snake Rivers in case the treaty Indians should become hostile. On July 30th, Howard left the Kamiah Valley and led his seven hundred men toward the Nez Perce Trail.

The non-treaties were, of course, traveling a familiar route, one that had many times taken them to the buffalo grounds. Wearily, but nevertheless steadily, they traversed canyons, hillsides, forests and meadows to reach an unknown fate on the other side of the Bitterroots. Their hearts were heavy with the realization that they might never again see their homeland.

For the soldiers, traveling the rugged Nez Perce Trail was a miserable physical travail. Encumbered by equipment and artillery, they found the tangled creek bottoms and steep ascents exceedingly difficult. At one point Howard wrote in his diary,

> It does not appear far to the next peak, and it is not so in a straight course, but such a course is impossible. ...Conceive this climbing ridge after ridge in the wildest kind of wilderness, with the only possible pathway filled with timbers small and large, criss-crossed; and now while the horses and mules are feeding on innutritious wire grass you will not wonder at our advancing only 16 miles a day."

Howard and his men would spend nine days on the trail.

When the Nez Perces neared the mouth of Montana's Lolo Creek on the eastern side of the mountains, they found a barrier blocking the route — thirty-five soldiers, several dozen volunteers from the Bitterroot Valley, a few Flathead Indians, and a barricade of logs across the trail. For three days the Nez Perces negotiated unsuccessfully to be allowed passage and then avoided violence by simply moving to higher ground to circumnavigate the barrier. This wise move later tagged the barrier's location with the name *Fort Fizzle*.

The Nez Perces moved south up the Bitterroot, keeping their promise to harm no one and even purchasing food and supplies along the way, frequently with gold dust. Feeling secure in their belief that they were not at war with the whites of Montana and that Howard was far behind them, on August 7th the non-treaty Nez Perces settled in for a rest at the confluence of Ruby Creek and Trail Creek in the Big Hole Valley. During the late hours of August 8th, their dancing and singing resonated throughout the surrounding countryside. Thus it was from the depths of sleep that they heard at dawn the crack of a gunshot as one hundred sixty-three Montana infantry troops and thirty-four volunteers charged the camp. The shocked reaction of the Nez Perces at first was to flee. Women, children, elders and even warriors ran every which way to escape the melee. But also within minutes, many warriors had found their weapons and begun to fight back — so fiercely that the whites were forced to form a defensive line on a wooded knoll. The Indians quickly ran a line around them and thereby kept the army pinned down until nightfall.

In the Nez Perce camp, meanwhile, the many dead — women, children, elders and warriors, sixty to ninety in all — were accounted for and hastily buried. The survivors gathered what goods they could, constructed travois for the transportation of the seriously wounded, including Joseph's wife, and at midday they moved southward. At day's end several of the warriors encircling the soldiers slipped away into the darkness to join their families. Joseph's brother, Ollicut, formed a rear guard to keep the whites in place until daybreak when the last few warriors left to join the others.

When Gen. Howard reached the battle site two days later, he found thirty-one of the whites killed and forty others wounded, including the commanding officer, General Gibbon. The Nez Perces now realized that they were at war with all whites. Thus the young warriors began harassing civilians as the Nez Perces made their way across Horse Prairie and Bannock Pass, reentered Idaho to the south, and then traveled east into Yellowstone National Park.

Howard followed. On August 20th, at Camas Meadows west of Yellowstone in southern Idaho, however, a group of warriors stampeded his mule herd during the night. Howard had no choice but to halt in order to retrieve the mules, since without them the soldiers had no way to transport supplies and ammunition. Howard was more than chagrined. Newspaper reporters from all over the United States plied him with questions, demanding to know why the U.S. troops were still unable to capture this small band of Indians.

Led by Lean Elk, who had some knowledge of the region, the Nez Perces wound their way northeastward through the park. Several companies of troops organized to block their passage along possible routes, but the Indians outwitted them all and reached the Yellowstone River the second week in September, well beyond the park and fifty miles ahead of Howard.

Anticipating the Indians' movement northward and hoping for an interception, Howard sent messengers to alert Col. Nelson Miles at Fort Keogh, which was about one hundred fifty miles northeast of the Indians' position. In the meantime Col. Samuel Sturgis with six companies overtook the Nez Perces at Canyon Creek, near Billings, on September 13th. A party of warriors quickly established a rear guard as the rest of the group hustled northward into a protective canyon. The troops dismounted and attempted to follow the Indians on foot, all the while being shot at from the canyon cliffs. At dusk Sturgis called in his troops to rest for the night. The next day, now aided by Bannock and Crow scouts, they caught up with the Nez Perces' column and began a series of skirmishes at the tail of the line.

The Nez Perces managed to turn away Sturgis' soldiers, but were growing more and more weary and disillusioned. They saw now that the Crows, from whom they had expected assistance, had instead become their enemy. Their thoughts turned to Sitting Bull across the Canadian border. The Sioux would surely befriend them, and the border crossing would offer them sanctuary from U.S. troops.

On September 29th, in the chill of autumn under a threatening sky, the Nez Perces stopped — just north of the Bear Paw Mountain range and only forty miles south of the Canadian border. They knew they were well ahead of Gen. Howard's force. Confident that they would make their way to safety the next day, Looking Glass convinced the other chiefs to rest for the night.

Before dawn the next morning their camp was spotted by army scouts under the command of Col. Nelson Miles. At first light Col. Miles' troops approached. Catching the Indians off guard, this army, new to the war, swiftly launched an attack. The Indians opened fire as the troops neared the camp, creating surprise and disarray among the soldiers, fifty-three of whom died as a result of this initial ambush. The battle raged throughout the day, with heavy losses on both sides, until Miles reconnoitered and then dispatched his troops to dig rifle pits and surround the camp. As night fell the Nez Perces lit no fires but huddled together

Chief Joseph

for what little warmth they could garner. Twenty-two were dead. The blackened sky turned white as snow began to fall. A few of the Indians snuck through soldier lines and fled to Canada. Those who stayed hoped the escapees would return with a force of Sitting Bull's warriors. But that was not to happen.

For four more days the remaining Nez Perces withstood skirmishes with Miles' troops. At times Miles tried to negotiate with the Nez Perce chiefs, telling them they could return to Idaho if they surrendered. Joseph counseled surrender, but Looking Glass and White Bird were convinced that the whites would never keep the promise of the Nez Perces' returning to Idaho.

On the evening of October 4th, his troops but one day away, Gen. Howard arrived in Miles' camp. The following day, Capt. John and George, two treaty Nez Perces traveling with the army, were sent into the Nez Perce camp under a flag of truce. Earlier in the day, Joseph had advised White Bird and Looking Glass of his intention to cease fighting. In light of Joseph's decision, the two latter chiefs concluded that they would leave that night for Canada. However, later that morning, Looking Glass was hit by a bullet to the forehead and, thereby, became the last of the casualties of the Bear Paw Battlefield.

That afternoon, Joseph accepted what he interpreted as a cease fire offer from Col. Miles. That night, White Bird and his followers escaped through the military pickets. the escapees included one hundred three warriors, sixty women and eight children.

In the history books since, much has been made of Joseph's Bear Paw Battlefield surrender speech. Historical records suggest that the general contents of his message was given to Capt. John and George, who then reported it to Col. Miles and Gen. Howard through the interpreter Arthur Chapman. Some eyewitness accounts, however, make no mention of a Joseph speech. Others mention only a brief statement delivered from Joseph to the effect that he would never again fight the white man, that his people were tired, and that they had always desired peace. The much longer and well known oration printed in various newspapers at the time and in other publications since appears to have been prepared by C.E.S. Woods, Howard's Aide-de-Camp, and written by him into Howard's military report at a later date.

The Nez Perce War had ended. It left strewn along its fifteen hundred mile route one hundred twenty dead Nez Perce men, women, and children; one hundred eighty dead whites, and one hundred fifty whites wounded. Across the United States, people had followed the progress of the 3 1/2-month war through news reports. They had read of the Nez Perces' determination, cleverness and courage with increasing admiration and sympathy for the Indians. Unbeknownst to the military and reporters alike, among the Indian prisoners taken at the Bear Paws was a seventy-one year old man named Tsa-ya-hah and his daughter and granddaughter — the son and granddaughters of the first white man welcomed to Clearwater Country by the Nez Perce people, Captain William Clark.

According to Commanding General of the U.S. Army, William Tecumseh Sherman, the war had been,

> ...one of the most extraordinary Indian wars of which there is any record. The Indians throughout displayed a courage and skill that elicited universal praise. They abstained from scalping; let captive women go free; did not commit indiscriminate murder of peaceful families ...and fought with almost scientific skill, using advance and rear guards, skirmish lines, and field fortifications.

However, Gen. Sherman went on to say that the Nez Perce leaders "should be executed" and the rest of the Nez Perces "never allowed to return" to their homeland.

Thus despite the promises of Col. Miles that the Nez Perces could return home, they were taken as prisoners of war to Fort Leavenworth, Kansas, where twenty-one died of malaria. In 1878, they were moved to Baxter Springs, Kansas, then later to northeastern Oklahoma. Chief Joseph continually appealed to government officials to let the captives go home. He was even granted a visit with President Rutherford Hays in January of 1879 in Washington, D.C., and also addressed an assembly of officials there. Despite an impassioned speech which aroused widespread empathy, Joseph's attempt to convince them failed. Settlers in Idaho, still angry and fearful, had persuasively lobbied for the non-treaties' continued exile.

Newspaper reporters, however, kept alive Joseph's plea and the plight of the Nez Perces in Oklahoma. During the 1879 trip to Washington, D.C., for example, Joseph granted a lengthy interview during which he reviewed his life and the history of his people and the war. The following is an excerpt from the words he spoke that day, as translated and reported by the media:

> If we ever owned the land we own it still, for we never sold it. In the treaty councils the commissioners have claimed that our country had been sold to the Government. Suppose a white man should come to me and say, 'Joseph, I like your horses, and I want to buy them.' I say to him, 'No, my horses suit me. I will not sell them.' Then he goes to my neighbor and says to him, 'Joseph has some good horses. I want to buy them, but he refuses to sell.' My neighbor answers, 'Pay me the money and I will sell you Joseph's horses.' The white man returns to me and says, 'Joseph, I have bought your horses, and you must let me have them' If we sold our lands to the Government, this is the way they were bought.

In 1883, James Reuben, a Nez Perce who had earlier been sent to minister to the exiles, was allowed to take two elderly men and twenty-seven women and children back to Lapwai. In 1884, the U.S. Congress finally authorized the return of the remaining exiles to the Northwest. A trainload of 268 Nez Perces arrived at Wallula, Washington, in late May of 1885. Chief Joseph was to be banished to the Colville Reservation in eastern Washington. As reported by Yellow Wolf, the others were asked a simple question:

Where do you want to go? Lapwai and be Christian or Colville and be yourself?

One hundred forty-nine survivors of the eight years of exile joined Joseph for the trip north. The remaining Indians returned to their families and relatives in Lapwai.

Notwithstanding persistent further efforts to gain the right to return to his beloved Wallowas, including a second trip to Washington, D.C., Joseph was never allowed to return to the land of his ancestors. On September 21, 1904, on the Colville Reservation and with no known living descendants, Joseph died, as reported by the agency doctor, of a broken heart.

Suggested Readings

Alt, David D. and Donald W. Hyndman, ROADSIDE GEOLOGY OF IDAHO. (Mountain Press Publishing, 1989)

Ambrose, Stephen E., UNDAUNTED COURAGE. (Simon and Schuster, 1996)

Brady, Cyrus Townsend, NORTHWESTERN FIGHTS AND FIGHTERS. (University of Nebraska Press, 1979)

Brink, Carol Ryrie, BUFFALO COAT. (Washington State University Press, 1993)

Brown, Mark H., THE FLIGHT OF THE NEZ PERCE. (University of Nebraska Press, 1967)

DeVoto, Bernard, Ed., THE JOURNALS OF LEWIS AND CLARK. (Houghton Mifflin, 1953)

Drury, Clifford M., HENRY HARMAN SPALDING. (Caxton, 1936)

Drury, Clifford M., THE DIARIES AND LETTERS OF HENRY H. SPALDING AND ASA BOWEN SMITH RELATING TO THE NEZ PERCE MISSION, 1838-1842. (Arthur H. Clark Company, 1958)

Elsonsohn, M. Alfreda, PIONEER DAYS IN IDAHO COUNTY, Vols. 1 and 2, 1947. (Caxton, 1951)

Gay, Jane, WITH THE NEZ PERCES: ALICE FLETCHER IN THE FIELD 1889-1892.

Haines, Aubrey L., AN ILLUSIVE VICTORY: THE BATTLE OF THE BIG HOLE. Glacier Natural History Association, 1991)

Hamilton, Ladd, THIS BLOODY DEED. (Washington State University Press, 1994)

Himmelwright, Abraham Lincoln Artman, IN THE HEART OF THE BITTERROOT MOUNTAINS; THE STORY OF THE CARLIN HUNTING PARTY, SEPTEMBER-DECEMBER, 1893. (Mountain Meadow Press, 1993)

Joseph, Chief, THAT ALL PEOPLE MAY BE ONE PEOPLE, SEND RAIN TO WASH THE FACE OF THE EARTH, 1879. (Mountain Meadow Press, 1995)

Josephy, Alvin M., Jr., THE NEZ PERCE INDIANS AND THE OPENING OF THE NORTHWEST. (University of Nebraska Press , 1979)

Langford, Thomas, VIGILANTE DAYS AND WAYS. (University Press, 1957)

Laughy, Linwood, compiler; IN PURSUIT OF THE NEZ PERCES; THE NEZ PERCE WAR OF 1877, AS RECORDED BY GEN. O.O. HOWARD, DUNCAN MCDONALD AND CHIEF JOSEPH.. (Mountain Meadow Press, 1993)

McBeth, Sue, THE NEZ PERCES SINCE LEWIS AND CLARK. (University of Idaho Press, 1993)

McWhorter, Lucullus Virgil, HERE ME, MY CHIEFS. (Caxton, 1984)

McWhorter, Lucullus Virgil., YELLOW WOLF: HIS OWN STORY. (Caxton, 1984)

Moore, Bud, THE LOCHSA STORY: LAND ETHICS IN THE BITTERROOT MOUNTAINS. (Mountain Press, 1996)

Moulton, Gary E., Editor, THE JOURNALS OF THE LEWIS AND CLARK EXPEDITION, Volumes 1-12.

Schultz, James Willard, BIRD WOMAN; SAGACAWEA'S OWN STORY. (Mountain Meadow Press, 1999)

Seton, Alfred, JOURNAL OF A VOYAGE TO COLUMBIA RIVER ON THE NORTH WEST COAST OF AMERICA. (date unknown)

Space, Ralph, THE LOLO TRAIL. (1970)

Spinden, Herbert Joseph, THE NEZ PERCE INDIANS. (Kraus Reprint Company, 1974)

Stuart, Granville, MONTANA FRONTIER, 1852-1864 and PIONEERING IN MONTANA, 1864-188, a two-volume set. (University of Nebraska Press, 1989)

To inquire about Clearwater Collection books published by Mountain Meadow Press and noted above, write to Mountain Meadow Press, P.O. Box 447, Kooskia ID 83539.